Nature and Causes of Apostasy from the Gospel

By John Owen
Edited by Anthony Uyl

Devoted Publishing
Woodstock, Ontario, Canada 2018

Nature and Causes of Apostasy from the Gospel
By John Owen (1616-1683)
Edited by Anthony Uyl

The nature of apostasy from the profession of the gospel and the punishment of apostates declared, in an exposition of Hebrews vi. 4-6; with an inquiry into the causes and reasons of the decay of the power of religion in the world, or the present general defection from the truth, holiness, and worship of the gospel; also, of the proneness of churches and persons of all sorts unto apostasy.

　　With remedies and means of prevention.

Search the scriptures - John v. 39.

Originally Published in:
London: 1676.

What kind of philosophies do you have?
Let us know!

Contact us at: devotedpub@hotmail.com
Visit our shop on Facebook: Devoted Publishing

Published in Woodstock, Ontario, Canada 2018.

For bulk educational rates, please contact us at the above email address.

ISBN: 978-1-77356-231-5

Table of Contents

Prefatory note

It is not uncommon for Christians, in a desponding mood, to ascribe unusual degeneracy in morals and religion to their own age. The sudden change, however, from the strict decorum of the Commonwealth to the license which marked the reign of Charles II has often been the subject of speculation and inquiry. Mr Macaulay thus confirms our author's estimate of the rapid decline of morality at this time:-- "A change still more important took place in the morals and manners of the community. Those passions and tastes which, under the rule of the Puritans, had been sternly repressed, and, if gratified at all, had been gratified by stealth, broke forth with ungovernable violence as soon as the cheek was withdrawn." -- Hist. of Eng., vol. i. p. 179. The historian, dealing with the surface of affairs rather than with the springs of conduct, may account the vulgar theory of a reaction against enforced strictness sufficient to explain this sudden lowering of the moral tone of a community; and in regard to a portion of society the theory may be admitted to be correct. The causes of the change, however, must have lain deeper; the blighting influence extended even into Puritan circles, where the contamination of courtly vices could hardly reach, and where early training would countervail any cessation of restraint, and beyond Britain, into other countries, where a similar decline can be traced, for which it is impossible to account simply on the principle of a reaction. Puritan decorum might as well be said to have been a mere reaction against such irreligious frivolity as bore the stamp of royal sanction in the "Book of Sports." Besides, the austerity ascribed to the Puritans is absurdly exaggerated; many a glimpse we possess into their domestic life shows that in reality it was the chosen scene of every genial influence, and household affections never appeared to more advantage than in the families of the Henrys. Owen, with his usual wisdom, avoids the extreme generalization that would resolve the complex apostasy of his age into any one predominant cause, and reviews in succession various influences which conspired to produce the result deplored. His treatise will be found to be a successful treatment of a deeply interesting question; and it closes in a strain of solemn appeal, appropriate to a work written, according to its author, "amid prayers and tears."

It is in substance an expansion of his commentary on Heb. vi. 4-6; and his Exposition on this passage is accordingly brief and meagre, having been forestalled by the publication of this treatise. Doddridge seems to regard it as most replete with the characteristic excellencies of Owen. "Owen's style," he remarks, "resembles St Paul's. There is great zeal and much knowledge of human life discovered in all his works, especially in his book on Apostasy. The Means of Understanding the Mind of God' is one of his best."

Ana*lysis*

The basis of the discourse is Heb. vi. 4-6; and inquiry is made, -- 1. Into the connection of the words; 2. The persons spoken of; 3. The supposition implied respecting them; and, 4. The truth affirmed on that supposition, chap. i. A charge of partial, as distinguished from final and complete apostasy, is adduced against all the churches and nations of Christendom; the claim of the Church of Rome to be indefectible is refuted, ii. I. Apostasy from the doctrines of the gospel is illustrated by facts in the history of the ancient church, and by the predictions of the a apostles, who foretold, -- 1. That the teachers of the gospel would soon corrupt its simplicity, by an admixture of vain philosophy; 2. That heresies would arise, consisting of unintelligible vagaries, as Gnosticism, and affecting the person of Christ, as Arianism, or the grace of Christ, as Pelagianism; 3. That men would be impatient of sound doctrine; and, 4. That the mystery of iniquity would continue to be developed till it reached its consummation in the Papacy. Apostasy is traced in the decline of the zealous orthodoxy of the Reformation, the rise of Arminianism and Socinianism, and kindred errors, iii. The causes of this declension from orthodoxy in Britain are enumerated:-- 1. Rooted enmity to spiritual things; 2. Spiritual ignorance on the part of men who possess some knowledge, and make a profession of the truth; 3. Pride of heart; 4. Careless security; 5. Love of the world. 6. The influence of Satan; and lastly, Judicial blindness, iv.-vi. Particular reasons are assigned for such defection from the truth:-- ignorance of the necessity for the mediation of Christ, want of spiritual views of the excellency of Christ in his person and offices, inexperience of the efficacy of the Spirit, ignorance of the righteousness of God, reluctance to admit the sovereignty of God, and an incapacity to discern the self-evidencing power of the Word, vii. II. Apostasy from the holiness of the gospel is next considered theoretically, in reference, -- 1. To the morals of Romanism, defective because inconsistent with spiritual freedom: founded on human rules and systems, capable of being observed without faith in Christ, and pervaded by the vitiating principle of merit and supererogation; 2. To those who confine the whole of obedience to morality; and 3. To those who pretend to perfection in this life. The causes of this kind of apostasy are mentioned, viii. Practical apostasy into open profanity and vice is traced to defects in the public teachers of religion; the false appropriation of names and titles, as when men living in sin claim to be "The Church;" evil example in high places; the influence of persecution; want of due watchfulness against national vices; ignorance of the spiritual beauty of religion; the operations of Satan; and the scandal created by the strictest professors of religion through their divisions and inactivity in good works and offices, ix., x. III. Apostasy from purity of worship is exhibited, in the neglect of what God has appointed, and by additions which he has not appointed, in the ordinances of the gospel, xi. The danger arising from the prevailing apostasy is declared, and directions are given in order to escape being involved in it, xii., xiii. -- Ed.

To the Reader

Some brief account of the occasion and design of the ensuing discourse I judge due unto the reader, that, upon a prospect of them, he may either proceed in its perusal or desist, as he shall see cause.

That the state of religion is at this day deplorable in most parts of the Christian world is acknowledged by all who concern themselves in any thing that is so called; yea, the enormities of some are come to that excess that others publicly complain of them, who, without the countenance of their more bold provocations, would themselves be judged no small part or cause of the evils to be complained of. However, this, on all hands, will, as I suppose, be agreed unto, that among the generality of professed Christians, the glory and power of Christianity are faded and almost utterly lost, though the reasons and causes thereof are not agreed upon; for however some few may please themselves in supposing nothing to be wanting unto a good state of things in religion, but only security in what they are and enjoy, yet the whole world is so evidently filled with the dreadful effects of the lusts of men, and sad tokens of divine displeasure, that all things from above and here below proclaim the degeneracy of our religion, in its profession, from its pristine beauty and glory. Religion is the same that ever it was, only it suffers by them that make profession of it. Whatever disadvantage it falls under in the world, they must at length answer for in whose misbelief and practice it is corrupted. And no man can express a greater enmity unto or malice against the gospel, than he that should assert or maintain that the faith, profession, lives, ways, and walkings of the generality of Christians are a just representation of its truth and holiness. The description which the apostle gives of men in their principles, dispositions, and actings, before there hath been any effectual influence on their minds and lives from the light, power, and grace of the gospel, is much more applicable unto them than any thing that is spoken of the disciples of Christ in the whole book of God: "Foolish are they, and disobedient, deceived, serving divers lusts and pleasures, living in malice and envy, hateful, and hating one another." The way, paths, and footsteps of gospel faith, love, meekness, temperance, self-denial, benignity, humility, zeal, and contempt of the world, in the honours, profits, and pleasures of it, with readiness for the cross, are all [so] overgrown, and almost worn out amongst men, that they can hardly be discerned where they have been. But in their stead the "works of the flesh" have made a broad and open road, that the multitude travel in, which, though it may be right for a season in their own eyes, yet is the way to hell, and goeth down to the chambers of death; for these "works of the flesh are manifest" in the world, not only in their nature, what they are, but in their open perpetration and dismal effects: such are "adultery, fornication, uncleanness, lasciviousness, idolatry, witchcraft, hatred, variance, emulations, wrath, strife, seditions, heresies, envyings, murders, drunkenness, revellings, and such like," as they are reckoned up by the apostle. How these things have spread themselves over the face of the Christian world, among all sorts of persons, is manifest beyond all contradiction or pretence to the contrary. And that so it should come to pass in the latter times is both expressly and frequently foretold in the Scripture, as in the ensuing discourse will be more fully declared.

Many, indeed, there are who are not given up in the course of their lives unto the open practice of such abominations; and therefore, in that grand defection from the truth and holiness of the gospel which is so prevalent in the world, the grace of God is greatly to be admired, even in the small remainders of piety, sobriety, and modesty, and common usefulness that are yet left among us. But those openly flagitious courses are not the only way whereby men may fall off from, and even renounce, the power, grace, and wisdom of our Lord Jesus Christ. For even of those who will not "run out to the same excess of riot" with other men, the most are so ignorant of the mysteries of the gospel, so negligent or formal in divine worship, so infected with pride, vanity, and love of the world, so regardless of the glory of Christ and honour of the gospel, that it is no easy thing to find Christian religion in the midst of professed Christians, or the power of godliness among them who openly avow the form thereof.

By this means is Christianity brought into so great neglect in the world, that its great and subtle adversary seems encouraged to attempt the ruining of its very foundations, that the name of it should no more be had in remembrance; for wherever religion is taken off from a solid consistency by its power in the lives and minds of men, when it hath no other tenure but an outward, unenlivened profession, and the secular interest of its professors, it will not long abide the shock of that opposition which it is continually exposed unto. And whilst things are in this state, those who seem to have any concernment therein are so engaged in mutual charging one another with being occasions thereof, mostly on such principles of difference in judgment as have no considerable influence thereinto, as that a joint endeavour after proper remedies is utterly neglected.

And there is yet another consideration rendering the present state of Christian religion in the world yet more deplorable. The only principle of evangelical obedience is sacred truth, and our faith therein. That alone is "the doctrine which is according to godliness;" and all acceptable obedience unto God is "the obedience of faith." Whatever men do or pretend unto in a way of duty unto him, whereof the truth of the gospel is not the spring and measure, which is not guided and animated thereby, it is not what God at present requireth, nor what he will eternally reward. Wherefore, although men may, and multitudes do, under a profession of that truth, live in open rebellion against its power, yet the wounds of religion are not incurable nor its stains indelible, whilst the proper remedy is owned and wants only due application. But if this truth itself be corrupted or deserted, if its most glorious mysteries be abused or despised, if its most important doctrines be impeached of error and falsehood, and if the vain imaginations and carnal reasonings of the serpentine wits of men be substituted in their room or exalted above them, what hope is there of a recovery? the breach will grow like the sea, until there be none to heal it. If the fountains of the waters of the sanctuary be poisoned in their first rising, they will not heal the nations unto whom they come. Where the doctrine of truth is corrupted, the hearts of men will not be changed by it nor their lives reformed.

How all this hath come to pass in the apostasy of the Roman church, and what multitudes of professed Christians are carried down the stream of that defection, is acknowledged among us who are called Protestants. How, therein, by various degrees, the corruption of the doctrine of the gospel gave occasion unto the depravation of men's manners on the one hand, and the wickedness of men's lives on the other hand, led the way unto, and served to make necessary, a farther perverting of the doctrine itself, until at length it is hard to determine whether the multiplied errors of that church have made the reintroduction of true holiness and evangelical obedience, or the corrupt, worldly conversation of the generality of the members of its communion has rendered the restoration of truth, more difficult and unpracticable in their present station, is in part declared in the ensuing discourses, and deserves yet a more particular and distinct inquiry into. In general, certain it is that as error, with superstition, on the one hand, in the minds of the teachers or guides of the church, and sin, with conformity unto the ways, manners, and course of the present evil world in the body of the people, were mutually assistant unto their joint introduction into the profession and lives of Christians; so having possessed themselves of the visible church-state of many nations, they are so interwoven in their interests as to be mutually assistant to the exclusion of that truth and holiness which they have dispossessed. And whereas, moreover, they have found out the pretence of infallibility, stretched wide enough, in their own apprehensions, to cover, patronize, and justify the most enormous errors and highest inconformity of life unto the gospel, all hopes of their recovery are utterly defeated, but what are placed on the sovereign grace and almighty power of God.

That there is also another endeavour of the same kind, and for the same general end, -- namely, to corrupt the doctrine of the gospel, -- though in another way, and unto another extreme, vigorously carried on in the world by the Socinians, and those who either absolutely or for the most part comply with them in their pernicious ways, is no less known, nor ought to be much less bewailed; for this endeavour also is attended with many advantages to give it success. The corruption of the doctrine of the gospel in the Roman church, as it sprang out of the ignorance, darkness, superstition, and carnal affections of the minds of men, so it is by the same means preserved. But although those things, in those ages and places where they abounded, gave sufficient and effectual advantage to its gradual introduction, and although the principles of it be now so inlaid with the secular interests of the generality of mankind in most of the nations in Europe as to secure its station and possessions; yet, in that emancipation of reason from under the bond of superstition and tradition, in that liberty of rational inquiry into the true nature and causes of all things, in that refusal to captivate their understandings in religion to the bare authority of men no wiser than themselves, which all pretend unto at present who dare venture on an ordinary converse in the world, it may seem marvellous how it should get ground and enlarge its territories, unless it be among them who are evidently bought off from themselves and from under the conduct of their own minds by some outward advantages, which they look upon as a valuable consideration. The true reasons hereof are inquired into in the ensuing discourse. But this new attempt, despising the baffled aids of superstition and carnal affections, which were in former ages predominant and effectual, takes shelter under a pretence of reason, and the suitableness of what is proposed in it unto the natural light and understandings of men. Whatever there is or is not in this matter of the relation that is between religion and reason, yet this being grown, through the increase of learning and converse, with a decay of the true fear of God, the very idol of this age, whoever will prepare a sacrifice unto it, though it be of the most holy mysteries of the gospel, he shall not fail of good entertainment and applause; and whoever shall refuse to cast incense on its altar shall be sure to be exploded, as one that professeth himself to be a fool, and even a common enemy unto mankind. Tell men that there are some things in religion that are above reason as it is finite and limited, and some things contrary unto it as it is depraved and corrupted, and they will reply (what is true in itself, but woefully abused) that yet their reason is the best, yea, only means which they have to judge of what is true or false. The liberty of men's own rational faculties having got the great vogue in the world (as indeed it is that which is most excellent therein of what is merely in and of it), it is fond to expect that it should not meet with a pernicious abuse, as every thing that hath any worth in it hath always done, when advanced unto such a reputation as might render it liable thereunto; for no man will ever adventure to prevail himself [1] of that which others have no respect unto or do despise.

Herein, then, lies the advantage of this sort of men, -- the Socinians I mean, and their adherents, -- in attempting to corrupt the doctrine of the gospel, and hereon depends all their success therein: First, they get the advantage of the ground in general, by pretending to reduce all men unto right reason, as the just measure and standard of truth. Put in any exceptions unto this proposal, endeavour to affix its bounds and proper measure, offer the consideration of divine revelation in its proper use and place, and you give away the cause among the many, who design at least to come in as common sharers in the reputation that reason hath got above all things in the world. By the confident use of this artifice, and the most absurd application of this principle unto things infinite and the most holy mysteries of divine revelation, have this sort of men, otherwise, for the most part, as weak and insufficient in their reasonings as their predecessors in the like attempts, got the reputation of the most rational handlers of sacred things! And when, being harnessed with this advantage, they proceed to the proposal of their opinions in particular, they have such an interest beforehand in the minds of men by nature, and have things so disposed and prepared for their reception, that it is no wonder if ofttimes they obtain success. For they are all of them designed unto one of these two heads:-- first, "That there is no reason why we should believe any thing that reason cannot comprehend; so that we may safely conclude that whatever is above our reason is contrary unto it; and for what is so, it is destructive to the very natural constitution of our souls not to reject:" and, secondly, "That the mind of man is, in its present condition, every way sufficient unto the whole of its duties, both intellectual and moral, with respect unto God, and to answer whatever is required of us." Upon the matter, they pretend only to undertake the patronage of human nature, and the common reason and honesty of mankind, against those imputations of weakness, depravation, and corruption, in things spiritual, wherewith by some it is charged and defamed. And although it be contrary unto the universal experience of the whole world, yet might this design be allowed what commendation men please, so that the defence of nature were not undertaken expressly against the grace of our Lord Jesus Christ, the redemption that is in his blood, and the whole mystery of the gospel. But whereas it is a part of the depravation of our nature not to discover its own depravations, and all those opinions are suited to give it countenance against what it is not sensible of, and whereof it is not willing to own the charge, it is no wonder if with very many they receive a ready entertainment. And whereas they seem to interest men in that reputation which reason in the things of God hath obtained in the world, and thereby to countenance them in the contempt of others as weak and irrational, -- things pleasing to the depraved minds of men, -- it is more than probable that they will make a pernicious progress in one degree or another. So doth the subtle enemy of our salvation make his advantage of the disposition, inclination, and state of every age and season. Without his interposition, devotion of old might have been carried on without superstition, and in this age the use of reason might be vindicated without a rejection of the necessity of supernatural illumination and the great truths of the gospel. But the better any thing is, the more noisome it will be when once he hath mixed his poison with it.

It were to be wished that the defection from the truth of the gospel complained of were confined unto the instances already mentioned, though in them the event be deplorable among multitudes of professed Christians. But the same, in some measure and degree, is come to pass among Protestants also. Men grow weary of the truths which have been professed ever since the Reformation, yea, of those in particular which gave occasion thereunto, and without which it had never been attempted; for besides that many fall off unto those extremes of error before insisted on, some on the one hand, and some on the other, the reformed religion is by not a few so taken off from its old foundations, so unhinged from those pillars of important truths which it did depend upon, and so sullied by a confused medley of noisome opinions, as that its loss in reputation of stability and usefulness seems almost irreparable. Hence are divisions, debates, and animosities multiplied about the principal articles of our religion, whereby those tongues are divided and hands engaged in mutual intestine conflicts, which all united were few enough to preserve the remainders of the protestant profession from the artifices and power of him who doth not despair once more to impose his yoke on the neck of the whole Christian world; for nothing can more prepare the way of his success than the shaking of the doctrine of the reformed churches from that consistency wherein for so long a time it stood firm and stable against all opposition.

But there is in this matter nothing absolutely new under the sun. No instance can be given of any church or nation in the world, which ever received the profession of the gospel, that did not, sooner or later, either totally or in some considerable degrees, fall off from the doctrine which it reveals and the obedience which it requireth. Men do but deceive themselves who suppose that the purity of religion will be preserved in confessions and canons, whilst some make it their business to corrupt its truth, and few or none make it their business to preserve its power. And, therefore, at this day, on one account or other, the defection is almost catholic; for it is in vain for any to pretend that the present general visible profession of Christianity doth in any tolerable measure answer the original pattern of it in the Scripture, or the first transcript thereof in the primitive believers. And that which, in this degenerate state of things, doth principally exercise the minds of considerate men is, whether there ought to be an immediate endeavour to reduce as many as will or can comply therewith unto the original standard in profession, obedience, and worship, or whether the present posture of things be not so far to be complied withal as to preserve therein the small remainders of religion among the community of Christians, who are not capable of such a reduction. The difference that is in the judgments of men herein is the ground of all those lesser controversies and opinions, which will be composed and have an end put unto them when God shall graciously afford unto us all a fresh revival of evangelical faith, love, and holiness, and, I fear, not before.

Upon some considerations of this state of things in the world, and under fears, perhaps not altogether groundless, that a farther progress will yet be made in this woeful declension from the power and purity of evangelical truth, I set myself unto a general inquiry what might be the secret causes and reasons whence it is that all sorts of persons, in all ages, have been so prone to apostatize from the sincere profession of the gospel in faith and obedience, as experience in the success of things manifests them to have been. And, moreover, an occasion was administered unto thoughts of that nature from my engagement in the exposition of the sixth chapter of the Epistle to the Hebrews, wherein the apostle so eminently describes the nature of total apostasy, with the end of apostates in the righteous judgment of God; for considering the greatness of that sin, and the terror of the Lord with respect thereunto, and not knowing whereunto the daily advance of impiety, profaneness, and abominable lusts, with ignorance, error, and superstition, might at length arrive, thoughtfulness of what might Be required at the last day of myself, though cast in a men and obscure condition in the world, did not a little exercise my mind. The glory of God, the honour of Christ and the gospel, and the eternal welfare of the souls of men, being eminently concerned, I knew not how he could have the least satisfaction in the truth and reality of his own Christianity who was not greatly affected with, and did not really mourn for, their suffering in this woful apostasy. What I have attained unto in that kind I have no reason to declare, but hope I may say, without the offence of any, that as I verily believe neither my prayers nor tears have been proportionable unto the causes of them in this matter, so I can and will say that they have been real and sincere.

I was not ignorant of the weakness and impertinency of all thoughts that a person of my mean condition in the world, disadvantaged by all imaginable circumstances that might prejudice the most sincere endeavours, should attempt any thing with respect unto the relief of nations or national churches, which yet are not without the verge of this fatal evil. To mourn for them in secret, to labour in prayers and supplications for a more plentiful effusion of the Spirit of Christ upon them for their good, are things which, although they may despise, yet God will accept in and from the meanest of them that call on his name in sincerity. Unto whom other opportunities and advantages are granted, from them other things will be required; and it is, no doubt, a great account they have to give who are admitted and esteemed as those whose place and duty it is to stem the current of overflowing impiety and profaneness, and effectually to apply the sovereign remedies of all those evils unto the souls and consciences of men. Sad will it be for them under whose hand this breach shall be, if they endeavour not to prevent it with their utmost diligence, and the open hazard of all their earthly concerns. A learned writer of the church of England affirms, "That there were two no small sins of noisome hypocrisy that he had espied among others; -- the one, an opinion that there can be no fit matter of martyrdom in a state authorizing the true profession of that religion which among many we like best, and, left unto ourselves, would make choice of; the other, which in part feeds this, a persuasion that mere errors in doctrine or opinion are more pernicious than affected indulgence to lewd practices, or continuance in sinful courses, or open breaches of God's commandments." And after he had declared that "ministers of the gospel may deny Christ, or manifest their being ashamed of the gospel, by not opposing his word at they ought unto the sins of men," he adds, "That any age, since Christian religion was first propagated, hath wanted store of martyrs, is more to be attributed unto the negligence, ignorance, and hypocrisy, or want of courage in Christ's ambassadors, or appointed pastors, than unto the sincerity, mildness, or fidelity of the flock, especially of the bell-weathers or chief ringleaders," Jac. tom. i. b. 4. c. 4; with much more to the same purpose, which well deserve some men's consideration before all things of this nature be too late.

But there is a duty of trading with a single talent; and if there be a ready mind, it is accepted according to what a man hath, and not according to what he hath not.

And this alone hath made me adventure the proposal of my thoughts about the nature, causes, and occasions of the present defection from the gospel and decay of holiness, with the means of preservation from its infection, and prevention of its prevalency in private persons; for it is to no purpose to shut up all endeavours under fruitless complaints, nor yet to attempt an opposition unto effects whose causes are not well known and considered. Wherefore the investigation and declaration of the causes of this evil are the principal subject of the ensuing discourses. And if I have attained but thus much, that persons of more understanding and abilities to find out the hidden springs of the inundation of sin and errors in the Christian world, and who have more advantages to improve their discoveries unto public good, shall be hereby excited to undertake so necessary a work and duty, I shall esteem myself to have received a full reward.

There is one thing yet whereof I must advise those readers which are pleased to concern themselves in any writings of mine. The publishing of this exposition of some verses of the sixth chapter of the Epistle unto the Hebrews may have an appearance of my deserting that continued exposition of the whole epistle which I had designed. But as I know not what I may attain unto in the very near approach of that season wherein I must lay down this tabernacle, and the daily warning which, through many infirmities, I have thereof, so I am resolved whilst I live to proceed in that work as God shall enable, and other present necessary duties will allow. And the sole reason, added unto the seasonableness, as I supposed, of this discourse, why this part of the Exposition is singly proposed unto public view, was because the thoughts which arose thereon were drawn forth into such a length as would have been too great a digression from the context and design of the apostle.

Footnote:

1. In the sense of the French "se prévaloir," -- "to take advantage of." -- Ed.

Chapter I – The nature of apostasy from the gospel declared, in an exposition of Hebrews vi. 4-6

Intending an inquiry into the nature, causes, and occasions of the present defection that is in the world from the truth, holiness, and worship of the gospel, I shall lay the foundation of my whole discourse in an exposition of that passage in the Epistle of Paul the apostle unto the Hebrews, wherein he gives an account both of the nature of apostasy and of the punishment due unto apostates; for as this will lead us naturally unto what is designed, so an endeavour to free the context from the difficulties wherewith it is generally supposed to be attended, and to explain the mind of the Holy Ghost therein, may be neither unacceptable nor unuseful. And this is chap. vi. 4-6, whose words are these that follow:--

Adunaton gar tous hapax photisthentas, geusamenous te tes doreas tes epouraniou, kai metochous genethentas Pneumatos hagiou, kai kalon geusamenous Theou rhema, dunameis te mellontos aionos, kai parapesontas, palin anakainizein eis metanoian, anastaurountas heautois ton Huion tou Theou kai paradeigmatizontas.

Adunaton gar. "Impossibile enim," that is, "est;" -- "It is impossible." Syr., ל ל מסכטשין?, -- "But they cannot." This respects the power of the persons themselves, and not the event of things; it may be not improperly as to the sense. Beza and Erasmus, "Fieri non potest," -- "It cannot be;" the same with "impossible." But the use of the word adunaton in the New Testament, which signifies sometimes only what is very difficult, not what is absolutely denied, makes it useful to retain the same word, as in our translation, "For it is impossible."

Tous hapax photisthentas. הנווך דטשד זווך למודיט נטשטוו?; -- "Those who one time," or "once descended unto baptism;" of which intepretation we must speak afterward. All others, "Qui semel fuerint illuminati;" -- "Who were once enlightened." Only the Ethiopic follows the Syriac. Some read "illustrati" to the same purpose.

Geusamenous te tes doreas tes epouraniou. Vulg. Lat., "Gustaverant etiam donum coeleste;" "etiam," for "et." Others express the article by the pronoun, by reason of its reduplication: "Et gustaverint donum illud coeleste;" -- "And have tasted of that heavenly gift." Syr., "The gift that is from heaven." And this the emphasis in the original seems to require: "And have tasted of that heavenly gift."

Kai metochous genethentas Pneumatos hagiou. "Et participes facti sunt Spiritus Sancti," Vulg. Lat.; -- "And are made partakers of the Holy Ghost." All others, "facti fuerint," "have been" made partakers of the Holy Ghost. Syr., רווך דקוודס?, -- The Spirit of holiness."

Kai kalon geusamenous Theou rhema. Vulg. Lat., "Et gustaverunt nihilominus bonum Dei verbum." Rhem., "Have moreover tasted the good word of God." But "moreover" doth not express "nihilominus." [It must be rendered,] "And have notwithstanding," etc., which hath no place here. Kalon rhema, -- "verbum pulchrum."

Dunameis te mellontos aionos. "Virtutesque seculi futuri." Syr., טשיל?, -- "virtutem," the "power." Vulg., "seculi venturi." We cannot in our language distinguish between "futurum" and "venturum," and so render it "the world to come."

Kai parapesontas. Vulg., "Et prolapsi sunt." Rhem., "And are fallen." Others, "Si prolabantur," which the sense requires; "If they fall," that is, "away," as our translation, properly. Syr., דטטוו יטשטווו?, "That sin again," -- somewhat dangerously, for it is one kind of sinning only that is included and expressed.

Palin anakainizein eis metanoian. Vulg., "Rursus renovari ad poenitentiam," -- "To be renewed again to repentance," rendering the active verb passively. So Beza also, "Ut denuo renoventur ad resipiscentiam;" -- "That they should again be renewed to repentance." The word is active as rendered by ours, "To renew them again to repentance."

Anastaurountas heautois ton Huion tou Theou. "Rursum crucifigentes sibimetipsis Filium Dei." Kai paradeigmatizontas. Vulg., "Et ostentui habentes." Rhem., "And making him a mockery." Erasmus, "Ludibrio habentes" Beza, "Ignominiæ exponentes." One of late, "Ad exemplum Judæorum excruciant;" -- "Torment him as did the Jews."

"For it is impossible for those who were once enlightened, and have tasted of the heavenly gift, and were made partakers of the Holy Ghost, and have tasted the good word of God, and the powers of the world to come, if they shall fall away," (for any) "to renew them again to repentance; seeing they crucify again to themselves the Son of God, and put him to open shame" (or treat him ignominiously.)

That this passage in our apostle's discourse hath been looked upon as accompanied with great difficulties is known to all, and many have the differences been about its interpretation; for both doctrinally and practically, sundry have here stumbled and miscarried. It is almost generally agreed upon that from these words, and the colourable but indeed perverse interpretation and application made of them by some in the primitive times, occasioned by the then present circumstances of things, to be mentioned afterwards, the Latin church was so backward in receiving the epistle itself, that it had not absolutely prevailed therein in the days of Jerome, as we have elsewhere declared. Wherefore it is necessary that we should a little inquire into the occasion of the great contests which have been in the church, almost in all ages, about the sense of this place.

It is known that the primitive church, according to its duty, was carefully watchful about the holiness and upright walking of all that were admitted into the society and fellowship of it. Hence, upon every known and visible failing, they required an open repentance from the offenders before they would admit them unto a participation of the sacred mysteries. But upon flagitious and scandalous crimes, such as murder, adultery, or idolatry, in many churches they would never admit those who had been guilty of them into their communion any more. Their greatest and most signal trial was with respect unto them who, through fear of death, complied with the Gentiles in their idolatrous worship in the time of persecution; for they had fixed no certain general rule whereby they should unanimously proceed, but every church exercised severity or lenity according as they saw cause, upon the circumstances of particular instances. Hence Cyprian, in his banishment, would not positively determine concerning those of the church in Carthage who

had so sinned and fallen, but deferred his thoughts until his return, when he
resolved to advise with the whole church, and settle all things according to the
counsel that should be agreed on amongst them. Yea, many of his epistles are on
this subject peculiarly: and in them all, if compared together, it is evident that there
was no rule agreed upon herein; nor was he himself well resolved in his own mind,
though strictly on all occasions opposing Novatianus; wherein it had been well if
his arguments had answered his zeal. Before this, the church of Rome was
esteemed in particular more remiss in their discipline, and more free than other
churches in their re-admission unto communion of notorious offenders. Hence
Tertullian, in his book de Poenitentia, reflects on Zephyrinus, the bishop of Rome,
that he had "admitted adulterers unto repentance, and thereby unto the communion
of the church." But that church proceeding in her lenity, and every day enlarging
her charity, Novatus and Novatianus, taking offence thereat, advanced an opinion
in the contrary extreme: for they denied all hope of church pardon or of a return
unto ecclesiastical communion unto them who had fallen into open sin after
baptism; and, in especial, peremptorily excluded all persons whatsoever who had
outwardly complied with idolatrous worship in time of persecution, without respect
unto any distinguishing circumstances; yea, they seem to have excluded them from
all expectation of forgiveness from God himself. But their followers, terrified with
the uncharitableness and horror of this persuasion, tempered it so far as that,
leaving all persons absolutely to the mercy of God upon their repentance, they only
denied such as we mentioned before a re-admission unto church communion, as
Acesius speaks expressly in Socrates, lib. i. cap. 7. Now, this opinion they
endeavoured to confirm, as from the nature and use of baptism, which was not to
be reiterated, -- whereon they judged that no pardon was to be granted unto them
who fell into those sins which they lived in before, and were cleansed from at their
baptism, -- so principally from this place of our apostle, wherein they thought their
whole opinion was taught and confirmed. And so usually doth it fall out, very
unhappily, with men who think they clearly see some peculiar opinion or
persuasion in some singular text of Scripture, [2] and will not bring their
interpretation of it unto the analogy of faith, whereby they might see how contrary
it is to the whole design and current of the word in other places. But the church of
Rome, on the other side, though judging rightly, from other directions given in the
Scripture, that the Novatians transgressed the rule of charity and gospel discipline
in their severities, yet, as it should seem, and is very probable, knew not how to
answer the objection from this place of our apostle. Therefore did they rather
choose for a season to suspend their assent unto the authority of the whole epistle
than to prejudice the church by its admission. And well was it that some learned
men afterward, by their sober interpretations of the words, plainly evinced that no
countenance was given in them unto the errors of the Novatians; for without this it
is much to be feared that some would have preferred their interest in their present
controversy before the authority of it: which would, in the issue, have proved
ruinous to the truth itself; for the epistle, being designed of God unto the common
edification of the church, would have at length prevailed, whatever sense men,
through their prejudices and ignorance, should put upon any passages of it. But this
controversy is long since buried, the generality of the churches in the world being
sufficiently remote from that which was truly the mistake of the Novatians; yea,
the most of them do bear peaceably in their communion, without the least exercise
of gospel discipline towards them, such persons as concerning whom the dispute
was of old, whether they should ever in this world be admitted into the communion

of the church, although upon their open and professed repentance. We shall not therefore at present need to labour in this controversy.

But the sense of these words hath been the subject of great contests on other occasions also; for some do suppose and contend that they are real and true believers who are deciphered by the apostle, and that their character is given us in and by sundry inseparable adjuncts and properties of such persona Hence they conclude that such believers may totally and finally fall from grace, and perish eternally; yea, it is evident that this hypothesis of the final apostasy of true believers is that which influenceth their minds and judgments to suppose that such are here intended. Wherefore others who will not admit that, according to the tenor of the covenant of grace in Christ Jesus, true believers can perish everlastingly, do say that either they are not here intended, or if they are, that the words are only comminatory, wherein, although the consequence in them in a way of arguing be true, namely, that on the supposition laid down the inference is certain, yet the supposition is not asserted in order unto a certain consequent, whence it should follow that true believers might so really fall away and absolutely perish. And these things have been the matter of many contests among learned men.

Again; there have been sundry mistakes in the practical application of the intention of these words unto the consciences of men, mostly made by themselves who are concerned; for whereas, by reason of sin, they have been surprised with terrors and troubles of conscience, they have withal, in their darkness and distress, supposed themselves to be fallen into the condition here described by our apostle, and consequently to be irrecoverably lost. And these apprehensions usually befall men on two occasions; for some having been overtaken with some great actual sin against the second table, after they have made a profession of the gospel, and having their consciences harassed with a sense of their guilt (as it will fall out where men are not greatly hardened through the deceitfulness of sin), they judge that they are fallen under the sentence denounced in this Scripture against such sinners, as they suppose themselves to be, whereby their state is irrecoverable. Others do make the same judgment of themselves, because they have fallen from that constant compliance with their convictions which formerly led them unto a strict performance of duties, and this in some course of long continuance.

Now, whereas it is certain that the apostle in this discourse gives no countenance unto that severity of the Novatians whereby they excluded offenders everlastingly from the peace and communion of the church; nor to the final apostasy of true believers, which he testifieth against in this very chapter, in compliance with innumerable other testimonies of Scripture to the same purpose; nor doth he teach any thing whereby the conscience of any sinner who desires to return to God and to find acceptance with him should be discouraged or disheartened; we must attend unto the exposition of the words in the first place, so as not to break in upon the boundaries of other truths, nor transgress against the analogy of faith. And we shall find that this whole discourse, compared with other scriptures, and freed from the prejudices that men have brought unto it, is both remote from administering any just occasion to the mistakes before mentioned, and is a needful, wholesome commination, duly to be considered by all professors of the gospel.

In the words we consider, -- 1. The connection of them unto those foregoing, intimating the occasion of the introduction of this whole discourse. 2. The subject described in them, or the persons spoken of, under sundry qualifications, which may be inquired into jointly and severally. 3. What is supposed concerning them. 4.

What is affirmed of them on that supposition.

1. The connection of the words is included in the causal conjunction, gar, "for." It respects the introduction of a reason for what had been before discoursed, as also of the limitation which the apostle added expressly unto his purpose of making a progress in their farther instruction, "If God permit." And he doth not herein express his judgment that they to whom he wrote were such as he describes, for he afterward declares that he "hoped better things" concerning them; only, it was necessary to give them this caution, that they might take due care not to be such. And whereas he had manifested that they were slow as to the making of a progress in knowledge and a suitable practice, he lets them here know the danger that there was in continuing in that slothful condition; for not to proceed in the ways of the gospel and obedience thereunto is an untoward entrance into a total relinquishment of the one and the other. That therefore they might be acquainted with the danger hereof, and be stirred up to avoid that danger, he gives them an account of the miserable condition of those who, after a profession of the gospel, beginning at a non-proficiency under it, do end in apostasy from it. And we may see that the severest comminations are not only useful in the preaching of the gospel, but exceeding necessary, towards persons that are observed to be slothful in their profession.

2. The description of the persons that are the subject spoken of is given in five instances of the evangelical privileges whereof they were made partakers; notwithstanding all which, and against their obliging efficacy to the contrary, it is supposed that they may wholly desert the gospel itself. And some things we may observe concerning this description of them in general; as, -- (1.) The apostle, designing to express the fearful state and judgment of these persons, describes them by such things as may fully evidence it to be, as unavoidable, so righteous and equal. Those things must be some eminent privileges and advantages, whereof they were made partakers by the gospel. These, being despised in their apostasy, do proclaim their destruction from God to be rightly deserved. (2.) That all these privileges do consist in certain especial operations of the Holy Ghost, which were peculiar unto the dispensation of the gospel, such as they neither were nor could be made partakers of in their Judaism; for the Spirit in this sense was not received by "the works of the law, but by the hearing of faith," Gal. iii. 2. And this was a testimony unto them that they were delivered from the bondage of the law, namely, by a participation of that Spirit which was the great privilege of the gospel. (3.) Here is no express mention of any covenant grace or mercy in them or towards them, nor of any duty of faith or obedience which they had performed. Nothing of justification, sanctification, or adoption, is expressly assigned unto them.

Afterwards, when he comes to declare his hope and persuasion concerning these Hebrews, that they were not such as those whom he had before described, nor such as would so fall away unto perdition, he doth it upon three grounds, whereon they were differenced from them; as, -- [1.] That they had such things as did accompany salvation, -- that is, such as salvation is inseparable from. None of these things, therefore, had he ascribed unto those whom he describeth in this place; for if he had so done, they would not have been unto him an argument and evidence of a contrary end, that these should not fall away and perish as well as those. Wherefore he ascribes nothing to these here in the text that doth peculiarly "accompany salvation," verse 9. [2.] He describes them by their duties of obedience and fruits of faith. This was their "work and labour of love" towards the name of God, verse 10. And hereby also doth he difference them from these in the text, concerning whom he supposeth that they may perish eternally, which these fruits of saving faith and sincere love cannot do. [3.] He adds, that in the preservation of those there mentioned the faithfulness of God was concerned: "God is not unrighteous to forget." For they were such he intended as were interested in the covenant of grace, with respect whereunto alone there is any engagement on the faithfulness or righteousness of God to preserve men from apostasy and ruin; and there is so with an equal respect unto all who are so taken into that covenant. But of these in the text he supposeth no such thing, and thereupon doth not intimate that either the righteousness or faithfulness of God was any way engaged for their preservation, but rather the contrary. This whole description, therefore, refers unto some especial gospel privileges, which professors in those days were promiscuously made partakers of; and what they were in particular we must in the next place inquire.

The first thing in the description is, that they were hapax photisthentes, "once enlightened." Saith the Syriac translation, as we observed, "once baptized." It is very certain that, early in the church, baptism was called photismos, "illumination;" and photizein, to "enlighten," was used for to "baptize." And the set times wherein they solemnly administered that ordinance were called hemerai ton photon, "the days of light." Hereunto the Syriac interpreter seems to have had respect; and the word hapax, "once," may give countenance hereunto. Baptism was once only to be celebrated, according to the constant faith of the church in all ages. And they called baptism "illumination," because it being one ordinance of the initiation of persons into a participation of all the mysteries of the church, they were thereby translated out of the kingdom of darkness into that of light and grace. And it seems to give farther countenance hereunto in that baptism really was the beginning and foundation of a participation of all the other spiritual privileges that are mentioned afterwards; for it was usual in those times, that, upon the baptizing of persons, the Holy Ghost came upon them, and endowed them with extraordinary gifts, peculiar to the days of the gospel, [3] as we have showed in our consideration of the order between baptism and imposition of hands. And this opinion hath so much of probability in it, that, having nothing therewithal unsuited unto the analogy of faith or design of the place, I should embrace it, if the word itself, as here used, did not require another interpretation; for it was good while aider the writing of this epistle and all other parts of the New Testament, at least an age or two, if not more, before this word was used mystically to express baptism. In the whole Scripture it hath another sense, denoting an inward operation of the Spirit, and not the outward administration of an ordinance. And it is too much boldness to take a word in a peculiar sense in one single place, diverse from its proper signification and constant use, if there be no circumstances in the text forcing us thereunto, as here are not. And for the word hapax, "once," it is not to be restrained unto this particular, but refers equally unto all the instances that follow, signifying no more but that those mentioned were really and truly partakers of them.

Photizomai is to give light or knowledge by teaching, the same with הורה?, which is therefore so translated ofttimes by the Greeks; as by Aquila, Exod. iv. 12, Ps. cxix. 33, Prov. iv. 4, Isa. xxvii. 11, as Drusius observes. And it is so by the LXX., Judges xiii. 8, 2 Kings xii. 2, xvii. 27. Our apostle useth it for to "make manifest," -- that is, to "bring to light," 1 Cor. iv. 5; 2 Tim. i. 10. And the meaning of it, John i. 9, where we render it "lighteth," is to teach. And photismos is knowledge upon instruction: 2 Cor. iv. 4, Eis to me augasai autois ton photismon tou euangeliou· -- "That the light of the gospel should not shine into them," -- that is, the knowledge of it. So verse 6, Pros photismon tes gnoseos· -- "The light of the knowledge." Wherefore, to be "enlightened" in this place is to be instructed in the doctrine of the gospel, so as to have a spiritual apprehension thereof; and this is so termed on a double account:--

1. Of the objects, or the things known or apprehended; for "life and immortality are brought to light through the gospel," 2 Tim. i. 10. Hence it is called "light," -- "The inheritance of the saints in light." And the state which men are thereby brought into is so called in opposition to the darkness that is in the world without it, 1 Pet. ii. 9. The world without the gospel is the kingdom of Satan: Ho kosmos holos en to ponero keitai, 1 John v. 19. The whole of the world, and all that belongs unto it, in distinction from and opposition unto the new creation, is under the power of the wicked one, the prince of the power of darkness, and so is full of darkness. It is topos auchmeros, 2 Pet. i. 19, -- "a dark place," wherein ignorance, folly, errors, and superstition do dwell and reign. By the power and efficacy of this darkness are men kept at a distance from God, and know not whither they go. This is called "walking in darkness," 1 John i. 6, whereunto "walking in the light," -- that is, the knowledge of God in Christ by the gospel, -- is opposed, verse 7. On this account is our instruction in the knowledge of the gospel called "illumination," because itself is light.

2. On the account of the subject, or the mind itself, whereby the gospel is apprehended; for the knowledge which is received thereby expels that darkness, ignorance, and confusion which the mind before was filled and possessed withal. The knowledge, I say, of the doctrines of the gospel concerning the person of Christ, of God's being in him reconciling the world to himself, of his offices, work, and mediation, and the like heads of divine revelation, doth set up a spiritual light in the minds of men, enabling them to discern what before was utterly hid from them, whilst alienated from the life of God through their ignorance. Of this light and knowledge there are several degrees, according to the means of instruction which men do enjoy, the capacity they have to receive it, and the diligence they use to that purpose; but a competent measure of the knowledge of the fundamental and most material principles or doctrines of the gospel is required unto all that may thence be said to be illuminated, -- that is, freed from the darkness and ignorance they once lived in, 2 Pet. i. 19-21.

This is the first property whereby the persons intended are described: they are such as were illuminated by the instruction they had received in the doctrines of the gospel, and the impression made thereby on their minds by the Holy Ghost; for this is a common work of his, and is here so reckoned. And the apostle would have us know that, --

I. It is a great mercy, a great privilege, to be enlightened with the doctrine of the gospel by the effectual working of the Holy Ghost. But, --

II. It is such a privilege as may be lost, and end in the aggravation of the sin, and condemnation of those who were made partakers of it. And, --

III. Where there is a total neglect of the due improvement of this privilege and mercy, the condition of such persons is hazardous, as inclining towards apostasy.

Thus much lies open and manifest in the text. But that we may more particularly discover the nature of this first part of the character of apostates, for their sakes who may look after their own concernment therein, we may yet a little more distinctly express the nature of that illumination and knowledge which is here ascribed unto them; and how it is lost in apostasy will afterward appear. And, --

1. There is a knowledge of spiritual things that is purely natural and disciplinary, attainable and attained without any especial aid or assistance of the

Holy Ghost As this is evident in common experience, so especially among such as, casting themselves on the study of spiritual things, are yet utter strangers unto all spiritual gifts. Some knowledge of the Scripture and the things contained in it is attainable at the same rate of pains and study with that of any other art or science.

2. The illumination intended, being a gift of the Holy Ghost, differs from and is exalted above this knowledge that is purely natural; for it makes nearer approaches unto the light of spiritual things in their own nature than the other doth. Notwithstanding the utmost improvement of scientifical notions that are purely natural, the things of the gospel, in their own nature, are not only unsuited unto the wills and affections of persons endued with them, but are really foolishness unto their minds. And as unto that goodness and excellency which give desirableness unto spiritual things, this knowledge discovers so little of them that most men hate the things which they profess to believe. But this spiritual illumination gives the mind some satisfaction, with delight and joy in the things that are known. By that beam whereby it shines into darkness, although it be not fully comprehended, yet it represents the way of the gospel as a "way of righteousness," 2 Pet. ii. 21, which reflects a peculiar regard of it on the mind.

Moreover, the knowledge that is merely natural hath little or no power upon the soul, either to keep it from sin or to constrain it to obedience. There is not a more secure and profligate generation of sinners in the world than those who are under the sole conduct of it. But the illumination here intended is attended with efficacy, so as that it doth effectually press in the conscience and whole soul unto an abstinence from sin and the performance of all known duties. Hence persons under the power of it and its convictions do ofttimes walk blamelessly and uprightly in the world, so as not with the other to contribute unto the contempt of Christianity. Besides, there is such an alliance between spiritual gifts, that where any one of them doth reside, it hath assuredly others accompanying of it, or one way or other belonging unto its train; as is manifest in this place. Even a single talent is made up of many pounds. But the light and knowledge which is of a mere natural acquirement is solitary, destitute of the society and countenance of any spiritual gift whatever. And these things are exemplified unto common observation every day.

3. There is a saving, sanctifying light and knowledge which this spiritual illumination riseth not up unto; for though it transiently affect the mind with some glances of the beauty, glory, and excellency of spiritual things, yet it doth not give that direct, steady, intuitive insight into them which is obtained by grace. See 2 Cor. iii. 18, iv. 6. Neither doth it renew, change, or transform the soul into a conformity unto the things known, by planting of them in the will and affections, as a gracious, saving light doth, 2 Cor. iii. 18; Rom. vi. 17, xii. 2.

These things I judged necessary to be added, to clear the nature of the first character of apostates.

The second thing asserted in the description of them is, that they have "tasted of the heavenly gift," -- geusamenous te tes doreas tes epouraniou. The doubling of the article gives emphasis to the expression. And we must inquire, -- 1. What is meant by the "heavenly gift;" and, 2. What by "tasting" of it.

1. The gift of God, dorea, is either dosis, "donatio," or dorema, "donum." Sometimes it is taken for the grant or giving itself, and sometimes for the thing given. In the first sense it is used, 2 Cor. ix. 15, "Thanks be unto God epi te anekdiegeto autou dorea," -- for his gift that cannot be declared;" that is, fully or sufficiently. Now this gift was his grant of a free, charitable, and bountiful spirit to

the Corinthians in ministering unto the poor saints. The grant hereof is called "God's gift." So is the gift of Christ used also: Eph. iv. 7, "According to the measure of the gift of Christ;" that is, "According as he is pleased to give and grant of the fruits of the Spirit unto men." See Rom. v. 15-17; Eph. iii. 7. Sometimes it is taken for the thing given, properly doron or dorema, as James i. 17. So it is used John iv. 10, "If thou knewest the gift of God," ten dorean tou Theou, "The gift of God," -- that is, the thing given by him, or to be given by him. It is, as many judge, the person of Christ himself which in that place is intended; but the context makes it plain that it is the Holy Ghost, for he is that "living water" which the Lord Jesus in that place promiseth to bestow. And, so far as I can observe, dorea, the "gift," with respect unto God, as denoting the thing given, is nowhere used but only to signify the Holy Ghost; and if it be so, the sense of this place is determined, Acts ii. 38, "Ye shall receive ten dorean tou hagiou Pneumatos, -- the gift of the Holy Ghost;" not that which he gives, but that which he is. Chap. viii. 20, "Thou hast thought dorean tou Theou, -- that the gift of God may be purchased with money;" that is, the power of the Holy Ghost in miraculous operations. So expressly chap. x. 45, 11, 17. Elsewhere dorea, so far as I can observe, when respecting God, doth not signify the thing given, but the grant itself. The Holy Spirit is signally the gift of God under the new testament.

And epouranios, "heavenly," or from heaven. This may have respect unto his work and effect, -- they are heavenly, as opposed to carnal and earthly; but principally it regards his mission by Christ, after his ascension into heaven: Acts ii. 33, being exalted, and having received the promise of the Father, he sent the Spirit. The promise of him was, that he should be sent from heaven, or מל?, "from above," as God is said to be above, which is the same with "heavenly," Deut. iv. 39; 2 Chron. vi. 23; Job xxxi. 28; Isa. xxxii. 15, מרום?, and chap. xxiv. 18. When he came upon the Lord Christ to anoint him for his work, "the heavens were opened," and he came from above, Matt. iii. 16. So Acts ii. 2, at his first coming on the apostles, there came "a sound from heaven." Hence he is said to be apostaleis ap' ouranou, -- that is, to be he dorea tou Theou, e epouranios, "sent from heaven," 1 Pet. i. 12. Wherefore, although he may be said to be "heavenly" upon other accounts also, which therefore are not absolutely to be excluded, yet his being sent from heaven by Christ, after his ascension thither and exaltation there, is principally here regarded. He therefore is this he dorea he epouranios, the "heavenly gift" here intended, though not absolutely, but with respect unto an especial work.

That which riseth up against this interpretation is, that the Holy Ghost is expressly mentioned in the next clause: "And were made partakers of the Holy Ghost." It is not therefore probable that he should be here also intended.

Ans. (1.) It is ordinary to have the same thing twice expressed, in various words, to quicken the sense of them; and it is necessary it should be so, when there are divers respects unto the same thing, as there are in this place.

(2.) The following clause may be exegetical of this, declaring more fully and plainly what is here intended; which is usual also in the Scripture: so that nothing is cogent from this consideration to disprove an interpretation so suited to the sense of the place, and which the constant use of the word makes necessary to be embraced. But, --

(3.) The Holy Ghost is here mentioned as the great gift of the gospel times, as coming down from heaven, not absolutely, not as unto his person, but with respect unto an especial work, -- namely, the change of the whole state of religious worship in the church of God, -- whereas we shall see in the next words, he is spoken of only with respect unto external actual operations. But he was the great, the promised heavenly gift, to be bestowed under the new testament, by whom God would institute and ordain a new way and new rites of worship, upon the revelation of himself and his will in Christ. Unto him was committed the reformation of all things in the church, whose time was now come, chap. ix. 10. The Lord Christ, when he ascended into heaven, left all things standing and continuing in religious worship as they had done from the days of Moses, though he hod virtually put an end unto it [the Mosaic dispensation]; and he commanded his disciples that they should attempt no alteration therein until the Holy Ghost were sent from heaven to enable them thereunto, Acts i. 4, 5. But when he came as the great gift of God, promised under the new testament, he removes all the carnal worship and ordinances of Moses, and that by the full revelation of the accomplishment of all that was signified by them, and appoints the new, holy, spiritual worship of the gospel, that was to succeed in their room. The Spirit of God, therefore, as bestowed for the introduction of the new gospel state in truth and worship, is the "heavenly gift" here intended. Thus our apostle warneth these Hebrews that they "turn not away from him who speaketh from heaven," chap. xii. 25, -- that is, from Jesus Christ speaking in the dispensation of the gospel by the "Holy Ghost sent down from heaven." And there is an antithesis included herein between the law and the gospel, the former being given on earth, the latter being immediately from heaven. God, in giving of the law, made use of the ministry of angels, and that on the earth; but he gave the gospel church-state by that Spirit which, although he worketh in men on earth, and is said in every act or work to be sent from heaven, yet is he still in heaven, and always speaketh from thence, as our Saviour said of himself with respect unto his divine nature, John iii. 13.

2. We may inquire what it is to "taste" of this heavenly gift, The expression of "tasting" is metaphorical, and signifies no more but to make a trial or experiment; for so we do by tasting naturally and properly of that which is tendered unto us to eat. We taste such things by the sense given us to discern our food, and then either receive or refuse them, as we find occasion. It doth not therefore include eating, much less digestion and turning into nourishment of what is so tasted; for its nature being only thereby discerned, it may be refused, yea, though we like its relish and savour, upon some other consideration. Some have observed, that "to taste is as much as to eat; as 2 Sam. iii. 35, I will not taste bread, or ought else.' "But the meaning is, "I will not so much as taste it," whence it was impossible he should eat it. And when Jonathan says that he only tasted a little of the honey, 1 Sam. xiv. 29, it was an excuse and extenuation of what he had done. But it is unquestionably used for some kind of experience of the nature of things: Prov. xxxi. 18, טמה קי טוו סכרה? -- "She tasteth that her merchandise is good," or hath experience of it, from its increase. Ps. xxxiv. 8, "O taste and see that the Lord is good;" which Peter respects, 1 Pet. ii. 3, "If so be that ye have tasted that the Lord is gracious," or found it so by experience. It is therefore properly to make an experiment or trial of any thing, whether it be received or refused, and is sometimes opposed to eating and digestion, as Matt. xxvii. 34. That, therefore, which is ascribed unto these persons is, that they had had an experience of the power of the Holy Ghost, that gift of God, in the dispensation of the gospel, the revelation of the truth, and institution of the spiritual worship of it, Of this state, and of the excellency of it, they had made some trial and had some experience; a privilege that all men were not made partakers of. And by this taste they were convinced that it was far more

excellent than what they had been before accustomed unto, although now they had a mind to leave the finest wheat for their old acorns Wherefore, although tasting contains a diminution in it, if compared with that spiritual eating and drinking, with that digestion of gospel truths, turning them into nourishment, which are in true believers, yet, absolutely considered, it denotes that apprehension and experience of the excellency of the gospel as administered by the Spirit, which is a great privilege and spiritual advantage, the contempt whereof will prove an unspeakable aggravation of the sin, and the remediless ruin of apostates The meaning, then, of this character given concerning these apostates is, that they had some experience of the power and efficacy of the Holy Spirit from heaven, in gospel administrations and worship. For what some say of faith, it hath here no place; and what others affirm of Christ, and his being the gift of God, comes in the issue unto what we have proposed. And we may observe, farther to clear the design of the apostle in this commination, --

I. That all the gifts of God under the gospel are peculiarly heavenly, John iii. 12; Eph. i. 3; -- and that in opposition, 1. To earthly things, Col. iii. 1, 2, ii.. To carnal ordinances, Heb. ix. 23. Let them beware by whom they are despised.

II. The Holy Ghost, for the remission of the mysteries of the gospel, and the institution of the ordinances of spiritual worship, is the great gift of God under the new testament.

III. There is a goodness and excellency in this heavenly gift which may be tasted or experienced in some measure by such as never receive them in their life, power, and efficacy. They may taste, -- 1. Of the word in its truth, not its power; 2. Of the worship of the church in its outward order, not in its inward beauty; 3. Of the gifts of the church, not its graces.

IV. A rejection of the gospel, its truth and worship, after some experience had of their worth and excellency, is a high aggravation of sin, and a certain presage of destruction.

The third property whereby these persons are described is added in these words, Kai metochous genethentas Pneumatos hagiou, -- "And were made partakers of the Holy Ghost," This is placed in the middle or centre of the privileges enumerated, two preceding it and two following after, as that which is the root and animating principle of them all. They all are effects of the Holy Ghost, in his gifts or his graces, and so do depend on the participation of him. Now, men do so partake of the Holy Ghost as they do receive him; and he may be received either as unto personal inhabitation or as unto spiritual operations. In the first way, "the world cannot receive him," John xiv. 17, -- where the world is opposed unto true believers; and therefore those here intended were not in that sense partakers of him. His operations respect his gifts. So to partake of him is to have a part, share, or portion in what he distributes by way of spiritual gifts; in answer unto that expression, "All these worketh that one and the selfsame Spirit, dividing to every man severally as he will," 1 Cor. xii. 11. So Peter told Simon the magician that he had no part in spiritual gifts; he was not partaker of the Holy Ghost, Acts viii. 21. Wherefore, to be partaker of the Holy Ghost is to have a share in and benefit of his spiritual operations.

But whereas the other things mentioned are also gifts or operations of the Holy Ghost, on what ground or for what reason is this mentioned here in particular, that they were "made partakers of him," which, if his operations only be intended, seems to be expressed in the other instances?

Ans. 1. It is, as we observed before, no unusual thing in the Scripture to express the same thing under various notions, the more effectually to impress a consideration and sense of it on our mind, especially where an expression hath a singular emphasis in it, as this hath here used; for it is an exceeding aggravation of the sins of those apostates, that in these things they were "partakers of the Holy Ghost."

2. As was before intimated also, this participation of the Holy Ghost is placed, it may be, in the midst of the several parts of this description, as that whereon they do all depend, and that they are all but instances of it. They were "partakers of the Holy Ghost" in that they were "once enlightened;" and so of the rest.

3. It expresseth their own personal interest in these things. They had an interest in the things mentioned not only objectively, as they were proposed and presented to them in the church, but subjectively, as they themselves in their own persons were made partakers of them. It is one thing for a man to have a share in and benefit by the gifts of the church, another to be personally himself endowed with them.

4. To mind them in an especial manner of the privilege, they enjoyed under the gospel, above what they had in their Judaism: for whereas they had not then so much as heard that there was a Holy Ghost, -- that is, a blessed dispensation of him in spiritual gifts, Acts xix. 2, -- now they themselves in their own persons were made partakers of him; than which there could be no greater aggravation of their apostasy. And we may observe, in our way, that the Holy Ghost is present with many as unto powerful operations with whom he is not present as to gracious inhabitation; or, many are made partakers of him in his spiritual gifts who are never made partakers of him in his saving graces, Matt. vii. 22, 23.

Fourthly, It is added in the description, that they had tasted kalon Theou rhema, "the good word of God." And we must inquire, -- 1. What is meant by the "word of God;" 2. How it is said to be "good;" and, 3. In what sense they "taste" of it.

1. Rhema is properly "verbum dictum," a word spoken; and although it be sometimes used in another sense by our apostle, and by him alone, -- Heb. i. 3, xi. 3, where it denotes the effectual active power of God, -- yet both the signification of the word and its principal use elsewhere denote words spoken, and, when applied unto God, his word as preached and declared. See Rom. x. 17; John vi. 68. The word of God, -- that is, the word of the gospel as preached, -- is that which they thus tasted of. But it may be said, that they enjoyed the word of God in their state of Judaism. They did so as to the written word, for "unto them were committed the oracles of God," Rom. iii. 2; but it is the word of God as preached in the dispensation of the gospel that is eminently thus called, and concerning which such excellent things are spoken, Rom. i. 16; Acts xx. 32; James i. 21.

2. This word is said to be kalon, "good," desirable, amiable, as the word here used signifieth. Wherein it is so we shall see immediately. But whereas the word of God preached under the dispensation of the gospel may be considered two ways, -- (1.) In general, as to the whole system of truths contained therein; and, (2.) In especial, for the declaration made of the accomplishment of the promise in sending Jesus Christ for the redemption of the church, -- it is here especially intended in this latter sense. This is emphatically called rhema Kuriou, 1 Pet. i. 25. So the promise of God in particular is called his "good word:" Jer. xxix. 10, "After seventy years be accomplished I will visit you, and perform my good word toward you;" as he calls it the "good thing that he had promised," chap. xxxiii. 14. The gospel is the "good tidings" of peace and salvation by Jesus Christ, Isa. lii. 7.

3. Hereof they are said to "taste," as they were before of the heavenly gift. The apostle, as it were, studiously keeps himself to this expression, on purpose to manifest that he intendeth not those who by faith do really receive, feed, and live on Jesus Christ as tendered in the word of the gospel, John vi. 35, 49-51, 54-56. It is as if he had said, "I speak not of those who have received and digested the spiritual food of their souls, and turned it into spiritual nourishment, but of such as have so far tasted of it as that they ought to have desired it as sincere milk, to have grown thereby; but they had received such an experiment of its divine truth and power as that it had various effects upon them." And for the farther explication of these words, and therein of the description of the state of these supposed apostates, we may consider the ensuing observations, which declare the sense of the words, or what is contained in them.

I. There is a goodness and excellency in the word of God able to attract and affect the minds of men who yet never arrive at sincere obedience unto it.

II. There is an especial goodness in the word of the promise concerning Jesus Christ and the declaration of its accomplishment.

For the first of these propositions, we may inquire what is that goodness, and wherein it doth consist; as also, how apostatizing backsliders may taste thereof: which things tend to the explanation of the words, and what is designed by the apostle in them.

1. (1.) This goodness and excellency of the word of God consists in its spiritual, heavenly truth. All truth is beautiful and desirable; the perfection of the minds of men consists in the reception of it and conformity unto it; and although "true" be one consideration of any thing, and "good" another, yet they are inseparable properties of the same subject. Whatever is true is also good. So are these things put together by the apostle, Phil. iv. 8. And as truth is good in itself, so is it in its effects on the minds of men; it gives them peace, satisfaction, and contentment. Darkness, errors, falsehood, are evils in themselves, and fill the minds of men with vanity, uncertainty, superstition, dread, and bondage. It is truth that makes the soul free in any kind, John viii. 32. Now, the word of God is the only pure, unmixed, and solid truth: "Thy word is truth," John xvii. 17. In most other things, as to the best evidence attainable, men wander in the wilderness of endless conjectures. The truth of the word of God alone is stable, firm, infallible; which gives rest to the soul. As God is a "God of truth," Deut. xxxii. 4, the "only true God," John xvii. 3, so he is, and he alone is, essentially truth, and the eternal spring of it unto all other things. Hereof is this word the only revelation. How excellent, how desirable, therefore, must it needs be! and what a goodness, to be preferred above all other things, must it be accompanied withal! As it is infallible truth, giving light to the eyes and rest to the soul, it is the "good word of God."

(2.) It is so in the matter of it, or the doctrines contained in it; as, -- [1.] The nature and properties of God are declared therein. God being the only good, the only fountain and cause of all goodness, and in whose enjoyment all rest and blessedness do consist, the revelation made of him, his nature and attributes, reflects a singular goodness on it, John xvii. 3. If it be incomparably better to know God than to enjoy the whole world and all that is in it, that word must be good whereby he is revealed unto us, Jer. ix. 23, 24. [2.] It is exceeding good in the revelation of the glorious mystery of the Trinity, therein alone contained. This is that mystery the knowledge whereof is the only means to have a right apprehension of all other sacred truths; and without it no one of them can be understood in a due manner, nor improved unto a due end. This is that alone which will give true rest and peace to the soul. And there is not the meanest true believer in the world, who is exercised in faith and obedience, but he hath the power of this truth in and upon his mind, though he be not able to speak much of the notions of it. All grace and truth are built hereon and do centre herein, and thence derive their first power and efficacy. Not one saving apprehension can we have of any gracious dispensation of God towards us, but it is resolved into the existence of God in a trinity of persons, and the economy of their operations with respect unto us. It is a "good word" whereby that mystery is revealed. [3.] It is so in the revelation of the whole mystery of the incarnation of the Son of God, with all the effects of infinite wisdom and grace thereunto belonging. What a satisfactory goodness this is accompanied withal, it is the most part of my business in this world to inquire and declare. [4.] It is so in the declaration of all the benefits of the mediation of Christ, in mercy, grace, pardon, justification, adoption, etc.

(3.) It is a good word with respect unto its blessed effects, Ps. xix. 7-9; Acts xx. 32; James i. 21. On this account the psalmist assures us that it is "more to be desired than gold, yea, than much fine gold;" that it is "sweeter than honey and the honey-comb," Ps. xix. 10; -- that is, there is an incomparable excellency, worth, and goodness in it. And he who discerns not this goodness in the word of God is a stranger unto all real benefits by it.

2. How apostatizing persons do taste of this good word of God may be briefly declared. And their so doing hath respect unto the threefold property of it mentioned, whence it is denominated "good:" (1.) Its truth; (2.) Its subject-matter; (3.) Its effects.

And, -- (1.) They taste of it as it is true, in the convictions they have thereof, in their knowledge in it, and acknowledgment of it. This gives (as it is the nature of truth to do) some serenity and satisfaction unto their minds, although they are not renewed thereby. They that heard John preach the truth rejoiced in his light, as finding much present satisfaction therein, John v. 35. So was it with them, Luke iv. 22, John vii. 46, and others innumerable, on the like occasion of hearing our Saviour preach.

When men, through the knowledge of our Lord and Saviour Jesus Christ, do escape the pollutions that are in the world through lust, and them that live in error, they taste a goodness, a sweetness, in the rest and satisfaction of their minds, so as that they suppose they are really possessed of the things themselves.

(2.) With respect unto the matter of the word, they have a taste of its goodness in the hopes which they have of their future enjoyment. Mercy, pardon, life, immortality, and glory, are all proposed in the "good word of God." These, upon those grounds which will fail them at last, they have such hopes to be made partakers of as that they find a great relish and satisfaction therein, especially when they have relief thereby against their fears and convictions; for, even in those ways wherein they deceive themselves, they have a taste of what sweetness and goodness there is in these things unto them by whom they are enjoyed. And as those who really believe and receive Jesus Christ in the word do thereon "rejoice with joy unspeakable and full of glory," 1 Pet. i. 8, so those who only taste of the word do feel in themselves a great complacency in their affections, Matt. xiii. 20; for, --

(3.) By this taste they may receive many effects of the word on their minds and consciences, and therein have an experience of the word as unto its power and efficacy. It belongs unto the exposition of the place to speak a little hereunto, and withal to declare what the difference is between them, and wherein this tasting comes short of that receiving and feeding on the word by faith which is peculiar unto true believers.

[1.] This taste is accompanied, or it may be so, with delight, pleasure, and satisfaction in hearing of the word preached, especially when it is dispensed by any skillful "master of assemblies," who finds out "acceptable words," or "words of delight," which yet are "upright, and words of truth," Eccles. xii. 10, 11. So was it with those naughty Jews, Ezek. xxxiii. 31, 32; and with Herod, who heard John the Baptist gladly, finding delight and pleasure in his preaching. So was it with multitudes that pressed after Christ to hear the word; and so it is to be feared that it is with many in the days wherein we live.

[2.] It gives not only delight in hearing, but some joy in the things heard. Such are the hearers of the word whom our Saviour compared to the stony ground; they receive it with joy, Matt. xiii. 20, as it was with the hearers of John the Baptist, John v. 35. The word, as tasted only, hath this effect on their minds, that they shall rejoice in the things they hear, not with abiding solid joy, not with joy unspeakable and full of glory, but with that which is temporary and evanid. And this ariseth from that satisfaction which they find in hearing of the good things declared; such are mercy, pardon, grace, immortality, and glory. They cannot but rejoice sometimes at the hearing of them, though they will not be at the pains of getting an interest in them.

[3.] The word only thus tasted of will work on men a change and reformation of their lives, with a readiness unto the performance of many duties, 2 Pet. ii. 18, 20; Mark vi. 20. And, --

[4.] What inward effects it may have on the minds and affections of men, in illumination, conviction, and humiliation, I have declared at large elsewhere. But, all this while, this is but tasting. The word of the gospel, and Christ preached therein, is the food of our souls; and true faith cloth not only taste it, but feed upon it, whereby it is turned into grace and spiritual nourishment in the heart. And hereunto is required:-- 1st. The laying it up, or treasuring of it in the heart, Luke i. 66, ii. 19. No nourishment will ever be obtained by food unless it be received into the stomach, where the means and causes of digestion and communication are placed; and if the word be not placed in the heart by fixed meditation and delight, it may please for a season, but it will not nourish the soul. 2dly. Food must be mixed and incorporated with the digestive humour, power, and faculty of the stomach, whereinsoever it consists, or it will not nourish. Give a man never so much food, if there be any noxious humour in the stomach hindering it from mixing itself with the means of digestion, it will no way profit him; and until the word in the heart be mixed and incorporated with faith, it will not advantage us, Heb. iv. 2; -- and there is nothing hereof where there is a taste of the word only. 3dly. When men feed on the word, it is turned into a principle of life, spiritual strength, and growth within; which a taste of it only will not give. As food, when it is digested, turns into flesh and blood and spirits, so doth the word, and Christ therein, unto the souls of men spiritually. Hence Christ becometh "our life," and "liveth in us," as the efficient cause of our spiritual life, Gal. ii. 20; Col. iii. 3; and we grow and increase by the word, 1 Pet. ii. 2. A mere taste, though it may yield present refreshment, yet it communicates no abiding strength. Hence multitudes relish the word when it is preached, but never attain life, or strength, or growth by it. 4thly. The word received as it ought will transform the soul into the likeness of God, who sends us this food to change our whole spiritual constitution, and to render our nature like unto his, in "righteousness and true holiness," Eph. iv. 21-24; 2 Cor. iii. 18. This a taste only will effect nothing towards; nor, to conclude, will it give us such a love of the truth as to abide by it in trials or temptations, 2 Thess. ii. 10, nor bring forth the fruits of it in universal obedience. And I might farther discourse from hence of the deplorable condition of them who satisfy their minds in mere notions of the truth, and empty speculations about it, without once attaining so much as a taste of the goodness of the word, -- of which sort there are many in the world; as also show the necessity, which all the hearers of the word lie under, of a severe scrutiny into their own souls, whether they do not rest in a taste only of the word, but come short of feeding upon it and of Christ therein, but that I must not divert from the text. What hath been here spoken was needful to declare the true state and condition of the persons spoken of. The second proposition mentioned hath been treated of elsewhere.

Lastly, It is added, Dunameis te mellontos aionos, -- "And the powers of the world to come." Dunameis are הגוורוט? or נפל ווט?, the mighty, great, miraculous operations and works of the Holy Ghost. What they were, and how they were wrought among these Hebrews, hath been declared in our Exposition on chap. ii. 4, whither I refer the reader; and they are known from the Acts of the Apostles, where sundry instances of them are recorded. I have also proved on that chapter, that by "The world to come," our apostle in this epistle intends the days of the Messiah, that being the usual name of it in the church at that time, as the new world which God had promised to create. Wherefore these "powers of the world to come" were the gifts whereby those signs, wonders, and mighty works, were then wrought by the Holy Ghost, according as it was foretold by the prophets that they should be so. See Joel ii. 28-32 compared with Acts ii. 16-21. These the persons spoken of are supposed to have tasted, for the particle te refers to geusamenous foregoing. Either they had been wrought in and by themselves, or by others in their sight, whereby they had had an experience of the glorious and powerful working of the Holy Ghost in the confirmation of the gospel. Yea, I do judge that themselves in their own persons were partakers of these powers, in the gift of tongues and other miraculous operations; which was the highest aggravation possible of their apostasy, and that which peculiarly rendered their recovery, impossible: for there is not in the Scripture an impossibility put upon the recovery of any but such as peculiarly sin against the Holy Ghost; -- and although that guilt may be otherwise contracted, yet in none so signally as by this of rejecting that truth which was confirmed by his mighty operations in them that rejected it; which could not be done without an ascription of his divine power unto the devil. Yet would I not fix on extraordinary gifts exclusively unto those that are ordinary. They also are of the "powers of the world to come;" so is every thing that belongs to the erection or preservation of the new world, or the kingdom of Christ. To the first setting up of a kingdom great and mighty power is required; but being set up, the ordinary dispensation of power will preserve it. So it is in this matter. The extraordinary miraculous gifts of the Spirit were used in the erection of Christ's kingdom, but it is continued by ordinary gifts; which therefore also belong unto the "powers of the world to come."

From the consideration of this description in all the parts of it, we may understand what sort of persons it is that is here intended by the apostle. And it appears, yea, is evident, --

1. That the persons here intended are not true and sincere believers in the strict and proper sense of that name, at least they are not described here as such; so that from hence nothing can be concluded concerning them that are so, as to the

possibility of their total and final apostasy: for, -- (1.) There is in their full and large description no mention of faith or believing, either expressly or in terms equivalent. And in no other place of the Scripture are such intended, but [except where] they are mentioned by what belongs essentially to their state. And, (2.) There is not any thing ascribed to these persons that is peculiar to them as such, or discriminative of them, as taken either from their especial relation unto God in Christ, or any such property of their own as is not communicable unto others. For instance, they are not said to be called according to God's purpose; to be born again, not of the will of man, nor of the will of the flesh, but of God; not to be justified, or sanctified, or united unto Christ, or to be the sons of God by adoption; nor have they any other characteristical note of true believers ascribed to them. (3.) They are in the following verses compared to the ground on which the rain often falls, and beareth nothing but thorns and briers. But this is not so with true believers; for faith itself is an herb peculiar to the enclosed garden of Christ, and meet for him by whom we are dressed. (4.) The apostle, discoursing afterwards of true believers, doth in many particulars distinguish them from such as might be apostates, which is supposed of the persons here intended, as was in part before declared; for, -- [1.] He ascribes unto them in general "better things," and such as "accompany salvation," as we observed, verse 9. [2.] He ascribes unto them a "work and labour of love," as it is true faith alone which worketh by love, verse 10, whereof he speaks not one word concerning these. [3.] He asserts their preservation, on the account, -- 1st. Of the righteousness and faithfulness of God, verse 10; 2dly. Of the immutability of his counsel concerning them, verses 17, 18. In all these and sundry other instances doth he put a difference between these apostates and true believers. And whereas the apostle intends to declare the aggravation of their sin in falling away by the principal privileges whereof they were made partakers, here is not one word, in name or thing, of those which he expressly assigns to be the chief privileges of true believers, Rom. viii. 27-30.

2. Our next inquiry is more particularly whom he doth intend; and, -- (1.) They were such as not long before were converted from Judaism unto Christianity, upon the evidence of the truth of its doctrine, and the miraculous operations wherewith its dispensation was accompanied. (2.) He intends not the common sort of them, but such as had obtained especial privileges among them; for they had received extraordinary gifts of the Holy Ghost, as speaking with tongues or working of miracles. And, (3.) They had found in themselves and others convincing evidences that the kingdom of God and the Messiah, which they called "The world to come," was come unto them, and had satisfaction in the glories of it. (4.) Such persons as these, as they have a work of light on their minds, so, according unto the efficacy of their convictions, they may have such a change wrought upon their affections and in their conversation, as that they may be of great esteem among professors; and such these here intended might be. Now, it must needs be some horrible frame of spirit, some malicious enmity against the truth and holiness of Christ and the gospel, some violent love of sin and the world, that could turn off such persons as these from the faith, and blot out all that light and conviction of truth which they had received. But the least grace is a better security for heaven than the greatest or privileges whatever.

These are the persons concerning whom our apostle discourseth; and of them it is supposed by him that they may "fall away," kai parapesontas. The especial nature of the sin here intended is afterward declared in two instances or aggravating circumstances. This word expresseth the respect it had to the state and condition of the sinners themselves; they "fall away," -- do that whereby they do so. I think we have well expressed the word, "If they shall fall away." Our old translations rendered it only, "If they shall fall," which expressed not the sense of the word, and was liable unto a sense not at all intended; for he doth not say, "If they shall fall into sin," this or that, or any sin whatever that can be named, suppose the greatest sin imaginable, -- namely, the denial of Christ in the time of danger and persecution. This was that sin (as we intimated before) about which so many contests were raised of old, and so many canons were multiplied about the ordering of them who had contracted the guilt thereof. But one example, well considered, had been a better guide for them than all their own arbitrary rules and imaginations.

But Peter fell into this sin, and yet was renewed again to repentance, and that speedily. Wherefore we may lay down this, in the first place, as to the sense of the words: There is no particular sin that any man may fall into occasionally, through the power of temptation, that can cast the sinner under this commination, so that it should be impossible to renew him to repentance. It must, therefore, secondly, be a course of sin or sinning that is intended. But there are various degrees herein also, yea, there are divers kinds of such courses in sin. A man may so fall into a way of sin as still to retain in his mind such a principle of light and conviction as may be suitable to his recovery. To exclude such from all hopes of repentance is expressly contrary to Ezek. xviii. 21, Isa. lv. 7, yea, and to the whole sense of the Scripture. Wherefore, men, after some conviction and reformation of life, may fall into corrupt and wicked courses, and make a long abode or continuance in them. Examples hereof we have every day amongst us, although, it may be, none to parallel that of Manasseh. Consider the nature of his education under his father Hezekiah, the greatness of his sins, the length of his continuance in them, with his following recovery, and he is a great instance in this case. Whilst there is in such persons any seed of light, or conviction of truth which is capable of an excitation or revival, so as to put forth its power and efficacy in their souls, they cannot be looked on to be in the condition intended, though their case be dangerous.

3. Our apostle makes a distinction between ptaio and pipto, Rom. xi. 11, between "stumbling" and "falling," and would not allow that the unbelieving Jews of those days were come so far as piptein, -- that is, to fall absolutely: Lego oun, Me eptaisan hina pesosi; me genoito· -- "I say then, Have they stumbled that they should fall? God forbid!" that is, absolutely and irrecoverably. So, therefore, doth that word signify in this place. And parapipto increaseth the signification, either as to perverseness in the manner of the fall, or as to violence in the fall itself.

From what hath been discoursed, it will appear what falling away it is that the apostle here intendeth. And, --

(1.) It is not a falling into this or that actual sin, be it of what nature it will; which may be, and yet not be a "falling away."

(2.) It is not a falling upon temptation or surprisal, for concerning such fallings we have rules of another kind given us in sundry places, and those exemplified in especial instances; but it is that which is premeditated, of deliberation and choice.

(3.) It is not a falling by relinquishment or renunciation of some, though very material, principles of Christian religion, by error or seduction, as the Corinthians fell in denying the resurrection of the dead, and the Galatians by denying justification by faith in Christ alone. Wherefore, --

(4.) It must consist in a total renunciation of all the constituent principles and doctrines of Christianity, whence it is denominated. Such was the sin of them who relinquished the gospel to return unto Judaism, as it was then stated, in opposition unto it and hatred of it. This it was, and not any kind of actual sins, that the apostle manifestly discourseth concerning.

(5.) For the completing of this falling away, according to the intention of the apostle, it is required that this renunciation be avowed and professed, as when a man forsaketh the profession of the gospel and falls into Judaism, or Mohammedanism, or Gentilism, in persuasion and practice; for the apostle discourseth concerning faith and obedience as professed, and so, therefore, also of their contraries. And this avowment of a relinquishment of the gospel hath many provoking aggravations attending it. And yet whereas some men may in their hearts and minds utterly renounce the gospel, but, upon some outward, secular considerations, either dare not or will not profess that inward renunciation, their falling away is complete and total in the sight of God; and all they do to cover their apostasy, in an external compliance with Christian religion, is in the sight of God but a mocking of him, and the highest aggravation of their sin.

This is the "falling away" intended by the apostle, -- a voluntary, resolved relinquishment of, and apostasy from, the gospel, the faith, rule, and obedience thereof; which cannot be without casting the highest reproach and contumely imaginable upon the person of Christ himself, as it is afterward expressed.

Concerning these persons, and their thus "falling away," two things are to be considered in the text:-- 1. What is affirmed of them; 2. The reason of that affirmation.

1. The first is, That it is impossible to renew them again unto repentance. The thing intended is negative; to "renew them again unto repentance," this is denied of them. But the modification of that negation turns the proposition into an affirmation, "It is impossible so to do."

Adunaton gar. The importance [import] of this word is dubious; some think an absolute, and others only a moral impossibility is intended thereby. This latter most fix upon, so that it is a matter rare, difficult, and seldom to be expected, that is intended, and not that which is absolutely impossible. Considerable reasons and instances are produced for either interpretation. But we must look farther into the meaning of it.

(1.) All future events depend on God, who alone doth necessarily exist. Other things may be or may not be, as they respect him or his will; and so things that are future may be said to be impossible, to be so either with respect unto the nature of God, or his decrees, or his moral rule, order, and law. Things are impossible with respect unto the nature of God, either absolutely, as being inconsistent with his being and essential properties; so it is impossible that God should lie; -- or on some supposition; so it is impossible that God should forgive sin without satisfaction, on the supposition of his law and the sanction of it. In this sense, the repentance of these apostates, it may be, is not impossible. I say it may be. It may be there is nothing in it contrary to any essential properties of the nature of God, either directly or reductively, but I will not be positive herein; for the things ascribed unto these apostates are such, -- namely, their "crucifying the Son of God afresh, and putting him to an open shame," -- as that I know not but that it may be contrary to the holiness, and righteousness, and glory of God, as the supreme ruler of the world, to have any more mercy on them than on the devils themselves or those that are in hell But I will not assert this to be the meaning of the place.

(2.) Again; things possible in themselves and with respect unto the nature of God are rendered impossible by God's decree and purpose; he hath absolutely determined that they shall never be. So it was impossible that Saul and his posterity should be preserved in the kingdom of Israel It was not contrary to the nature of God, but God had decreed that it should not be, 1 Sam. xv. 28, 29. But the decrees of God respecting persons in particular, and not qualifications in the first place, they cannot be here intended; because they are free acts of his win, not revealed, neither in particular nor by virtue of any general rule, as they are sovereign acts, making differences between persons in the same condition, Rom. ix. 11, 12. What is possible or impossible with respect unto the nature of God we may know in some good measure, from the certain knowledge we may have of his being and essential properties; but what is so, one way or other, with respect unto his decrees or purposes, which are sovereign, free acts of his will, knoweth no man, no, not the angels in heaven, Isa. xl. 13, 14; Rom. xi. 34.

(3.) Things are possible or impossible with respect unto the rule and order of all things that God hath appointed. When in things of duty God hath neither expressly commanded them, nor appointed means for the performance of them, then are we to look upon them as impossible; and then, with respect unto us, they are so absolutely, and so to be esteemed. And this is the impossibility here principally intended. It is a thing that God hath neither commanded us to endeavour, nor appointed means to attain it, nor promised to assist us in it. It is therefore that which we have no reason to look after, attempt, or expect, as being not possible by any law, rule, or constitution of God.

The apostle instructs us no farther in the nature of future events but as our own duty is concerned in them. It is not for us either to look, or hope, or pray for, or endeavour the renewal of such persons unto repentance. God gives law unto us in these things, not unto himself. It may be possible with God, for ought we know, if there be not a contradiction in it unto any holy properties of his nature; only he will not have us to expect any such things from him, nor hath he appointed any means for us to endeavour it. What he shall do we ought thankfully to accept; but our own duty towards such persons is absolutely at an end, -- and indeed they put themselves wholly out of our reach.

That which is said to be thus impossible with respect unto these persons is, palin anakainizein eis metanoian, "to renew them again unto repentance." Metanoia in the New Testament, with respect unto God, signifies a "gracious change of mind" on gospel principles and promises, leading the whole soul into conversion unto God. צווה?, this is the beginning and entrance of our turning to God, without which neither the will nor the affections will be engaged unto him, nor is it possible for sinners to find acceptance with him.

It is impossible anakainizein, "to renew." The construction of the words is defective, and must be supplied. Se may be added, to renew "themselves," -- it is not possible they should do so: or tinas, that "some" should, that any should renew them; and this I judge to be intended, for the impossibility mentioned respects the duty and endeavours of others. In vain shall any attempt their recovery, by the use of any means whatever. And we must inquire what it is to be "renewed," and what it is to be "renewed again."

Now, our anakainismos is the renovation of the image of God in our nature, whereby we are dedicated again unto him; for as we had lost the image of God by sin, and were separated from him as things profane, this anakainismos respects both the restoration of our nature and the dedication of our persons to God. And it is twofold:--

(1.) Real and internal, in regeneration and effectual sanctification: "The washing of regeneration and renewing of the Holy Ghost," Tit. iii. 5; 1 Thess. v.

23. But this is not that which is here intended; for this these apostates never had, and so cannot be said to be renewed again unto it, for no man can be renewed again unto that which he never had.

(2.) It is outward in the profession and pledge of it. Wherefore renovation in this sense consists in the solemn confession of faith and repentance by Jesus Christ, with the seal of baptism received thereon; for thus it was with all those who were converted unto the gospel. Upon their profession of repentance toward God and faith in our Lord Jesus Christ, they received the baptismal pledge of an inward renovation, though really they were not partakers thereof. But this estate was their anakainismos, their renovation. From this state they fell totally, renouncing Him who is the author of it, his grace which is the cause of it, and the ordinance which is the pledge thereof.

Hence it appears what it is palin anakainizein, "to renew them again." It is to bring them again into this state of profession by a second renovation, and a second baptism as a pledge thereof. This is determined impossible, and so unwarrantable for any to attempt; and, for the most part, such persons do openly fall into such blasphemies against, and engage (if they have power) into such persecution of the truth, as that they give themselves sufficient direction how others should behave themselves towards them. So the ancient church was satisfied in the case of Julian. This is the sum of what is affirmed concerning these apostates -- namely, that "it is impossible to renew them again unto repentance;" that is, so to act towards them as to bring them to that repentance whereby they may be instated in their former condition.

Hence sundry things may be observed for the clearing of the apostle's design in this discourse; as, --

(1.) Here is nothing said concerning the acceptance or refusal of any upon repentance, or the profession thereof after any sin, to be made by the church; whose judgment is to be determined by other rules and circumstances. And this perfectly excludes the pretence of the Novatians from any countenance in these words; for whereas they would have drawn their warranty from hence for the utter exclusion from church communion of all those who had denied the faith in times of persecution, although they expressed a repentance whose sincerity they could not evince, those only are intended who neither do nor can come to repentance itself, nor make a profession of it; with whom the church had no more to do. It is not said that men who ever thus fell away shall not, upon their repentance, be admitted again into their former state in the church, but that such is the severity of God against them that he will not again give them repentance unto life.

(2.) Here is nothing that may be brought in bar against such as, having fallen by any great sin, or any course in sinning, and that after light, convictions, and gifts received and exercised, desire to repent of their sins and endeavour after sincerity therein; yea, such a desire and endeavour exempt any one from the judgment here threatened.

There is therefore in it that which tends greatly to the encouragement of such sinners; for whereas it is here declared, concerning those who are thus rejected of God, that "it is impossible to renew them," or to do any thing towards them that shall have a tendency unto repentance, those who are not satisfied that they do yet savingly repent, but only are sincerely exercised how they may attain thereunto, have no concernment in this commination, but evidently have the door of mercy still open unto them, for it is shut only against those who shall never endeavour to turn by repentance. And although persons so rejected of God may fall under convictions of their sin, attended with despair (which is unto them a foresight of their future condition), yet as unto the least attempt after repentance, on the terms of the gospel, they do never rise up unto it. Wherefore, the impossibility intended, of what sort soever it be, respects the severity of God, not in refusing or rejecting the greatest sinners which seek after and would be renewed unto repentance (which is contrary unto innumerable of his promises); but in the giving up such sinners as these are, here mentioned, unto such obdurateness and obstinacy in sinning, that blindness of mind and hardness of heart, as that they neither will nor shall ever sincerely seek after repentance, nor may any means, according to the mind of God, be used to bring them thereunto. And the righteousness of the exercise of this severity is taken from the nature of this sin, or what is contained in it, which the apostle declares in the ensuing instances. And we may in our passage observe, that, --

In the preaching of the gospel, it is necessary to propose unto men, and to insist on, the severity of God in dealing with provoking sinners against it. And indeed the severity of God is principally, though not solely, exercised with respect unto sins against the gospel. This our apostle calls us to the consideration of in the case of the unbelieving Jews: Rom. xi. 22, Ide oun chrestoteta kai apotomian tou Theou· epi men tous pesontas apotomian· -- "Behold the goodness and severity of God: on them which fell" (those in the text), "severity." Apotomia is a sharp direction or cutting off. I do not, therefore, understand by it an essential property of the nature of God. It is not the same with his holiness, righteousness, or vindictive justice. These are essential properties of the divine nature, whence it is that he neither will nor can absolutely suffer men to sin and let them go for ever unpunished, without any satisfaction or atonement made for their sins; whereof we have treated elsewhere. But by God's "severity" is intended the free act of his will, acting according unto these properties of his nature in an eminent manner, when and how he pleaseth; and therefore into them it is resolved. So our apostle, when he would intimate this severity unto us, to ingenerate in us a holy fear and reverence of God in his worship, adds as his motive, "For our God is a consuming fire," Heb. xii. 29; that is, of an infinitely pure, holy, righteous nature, according to which he will deal with us, and so may unexpectedly break forth upon us in severity if we labour not for "grace to serve him acceptably with reverence and godly fear." Wherefore, this severity of God is his exemplary dealing with provoking sinners, according to the exigence of his holiness and wisdom, without an interposition of longer patience or forbearance. There are some sins, or degrees in sinning, that neither the holiness, nor majesty, nor wisdom of God can so bear withal as to suffer them to pass unpunished or unremarked on in this world. In such cases is God said to exercise his severity; and he doth so, --

(1.) In extraordinary, outward judgments upon open, profligate sinners, especially the enemies of his church and glory. Hence on such an occasion doth God give that description of himself, Nahum i. 2, "God is jealous, and the Lord revengeth; the Lord revengeth, and is furious; the Lord will take vengeance on his adversaries, and he reserveth wrath for his enemies. When God acteth towards his adversaries according to the description here given of himself, he deals with them in severity. And two things are required to make these judgments of God against his adversaries in this world to be instances thereof:-- [1.] That they be unusual, such as do not commonly and frequently fall out in the ordinary dispensation of divine providence, Num. xvi. 29, 30. God doth not, in the government of the world, suffer any thing to fall out or come to pass that in the issue shall be contrary to his justice or inconsistent with his righteousness; but yet he beareth with things so, for the most part, as that he will manifest himself to be exceedingly full of patience and long-suffering, as also to exercise the faith of them that believe in the expectation of a future judgment. Wherefore there must be somewhat extraordinary in those judgments wherein God will exercise and manifest severity. So it is expressed, Isa. xxviii. 21, "The Lord shall rise up as in mount Perazim, he shall be wroth as in the valley of Gibeon, that he may do his work, his strange work; and bring to pass his act, his strange act." The work he will do is his work, but it is his "strange work;" -- that is, not strange from or opposite unto his nature, for so he will do nothing; but that which is unusual, which he doth but seldom, and is therefore marvellous. Thus, in sudden destructions of persecutors or persons of a flagitious wickedness, in great desolations of provoking families, cities, and nations, in fire from heaven, in inundations, plagues, earthquakes, and such sudden, extraordinary, consuming judgments, God giveth instances of his severity in the world, Rom. i. 18. [2.] In this case it is required that such judgments be open, visible, and manifest, both unto those who are punished and to others who wisely consider them. So God speaketh of himself, Deut. vii. 10, "God that re-payeth them that hate him to their face, to destroy them: he will not be slack to him that hateth him, he will repay him to his face;" -- that is, he will do it openly and manifestly, so that themselves and all others shall take notice of his severity therein. This, I say, is one way whereby God acts his severity in this world. And hereby he poureth everlasting contempt upon the security of his proudest and haughtiest adversaries; for when they think they have sufficiently provided for their own safety, and stopped all avenues of evil, according to the rules of their policy and wisdom, with the best observations they are able to make of the ordinary effects of his providence, and so give up themselves to take satisfaction in their lusts and pleasures, he breaks in upon them with an instance and example of his severity to their utter destruction. So, "when they say, Peace and safety; then sudden destruction cometh upon them, as travail upon a woman With child; and they shall not escape," 1 Thess. v. 3. This will be the state one day of the whole Babylonish interest in the world, Rev. xviii. 7-10. But this is not directly intended in this place, although even this effect of God's severity overtook these apostates afterward.

(2.) In spiritual judgments. By these God in his severity leaveth unprofitable, provoking, and apostate professors under the impossibility here intended of being renewed unto repentance. And this is the sorest of all God's judgments. There is in it a sentence of eternal damnation denounced on men aforehand in this world. So our apostle tells us, "Some men's sins are open beforehand, going before to judgment," 1 Tim. v. 24. God so passeth judgment concerning them in this world as that there shall be no alteration in their state and condition to eternity. And this severity of God towards sinners under the gospel, shutting them up under final impenitency, consists in these four things:--

[1.] God puts an end unto all his expectation concerning them; he looks for no more from them, and so exerciseth no more care about them. Whilst God is pleased to afford the use of means for conversion and repentance unto any, he is said to look for and expect answerable fruits: "I did," saith he, "so and so to my vineyard; and I looked that it should bring forth grapes," Isa. v. 2, 4. Wherefore, when God takes away all means of grace and repentance from any, then he puts an end unto his own expectation of any fruits; for if a man can have no fruit from his vineyard whilst he dresseth it, or from his field whilst he tilleth it, he will never look for any after he hath given them up and laid them waste. And, on the other side, when he utterly ceaseth to look for any fruit from them, he will till them no more; for why should he put himself to charge or trouble to no purpose? Woe unto the souls of men when God in this sense looks for no more at their hands! -- that is, when he puts an end unto that patience or long-suffering towards them from whence all supplies of the means of conversion and repentance do arise and spring. This God doth by some, and that in such ways as we shall afterward declare.

[2.] God will actually punish them with, or inflict on them, hardness of heart and blindness of mind, that they never shall repent or believe: John xii. 39, 40, "Therefore they could not believe, because that Esaias said again, He hath blinded their eyes, and hardened their heart; that they should not see with their eyes, nor understand with their heart, and be converted, and I should heal them." God will now judicially blind them and harden them, and, by one means or other, every thing that befalls them shall promote their induration. So it was with these Jews; the doctrine of Christ filled them with envy, his holiness with malice, and his miracles with rage and madness. Their table was a snare to them, and that which should have been for their good turned to their hurt. So is it with all them whom God in his severity hardeneth. Whether the outward means be continued unto them or no, all is one; every thing shall drive them farther from God, and increase their obstinacy against him. From hence they become scoffers and persecutors, avowedly scorning and hating the truth; and herein, it may be, they shall please themselves until they are swallowed up in despair or the grave.

[3.] God usually in his severity gives them up unto sensual lusts. So he dealt with the idolaters of old: he "gave them up unto vile affections," Rom. i. 26, such as those there described by the apostle; and in the pursuit of them "gave them over to a reprobate mind, to do those things which are not convenient," verse 28; whence they were "filled with all unrighteousness," verse 29. So doth God frequently deal with apostates from the gospel, or from the principal truths of it, unto idolatry and superstition. And when they are engaged in the pursuit of these lusts, especially when they are judicially given up unto them, they are held assuredly, as under cords and chains, unto final impenitency.

[4.] God gave such persons up unto Satan, to be blinded, and led by him into pernicious delusions: "Because they received not the love of the truth, that they might be saved, God shall send them strong delusion, that they should believe a lie: that they all might be damned who believed not the truth, but had pleasure in unrighteousness," 2 Thess. ii. 10-12. This was the state and condition of the persons here prophesied of. The truth of the gospel was preached unto them, and for some time professed by them. They received the truth; but they received not the love of it, so as to comply with it and improve it unto its proper end. This kept them barren and unfruitful under their profession; for where the truth is not loved, as well as believed or assented unto, it will bring forth no fruit. But this was not all; they had pleasure in their sins, lusts, and unrighteousnesses, resolving not to part with them on any terms. Whereas, therefore, these are all of them absolutely and without limitation judged and condemned by the truth of the gospel, they began to dislike and secretly to hate the truth itself. But whereas, together with their lusts and unrighteousnesses, wherein they had pleasure, they found a necessity of a religion, one or other, or the pretence of some religion or other, to give them countenance against the truth which they rejected, they were in a readiness to any thing that should offer itself unto them. In this condition, in the way of punishment, and as a revenge of their horrible ingratitude and contempt of his gospel, God gives them up to the power of Satan, who blinds, deludes, and deceives them with such efficacy as that they shall not only readily embrace, but obstinately believe and adhere to, the lies, errors, and falsehoods that he shall suggest unto them. And this is the way and course whereby so many carnal gospellers are turned off unto Romish idolatry every day.

Other instances of the severity of God on this occasion might be given, but these are fully sufficient to declare the manner of his dealing with such as those described in the text: whence it follows that their renovation unto repentance is impossible; for what hopes or expectations should we have concerning such as God hath utterly forsaken, whom he hath judicially smitten with blindness and hardness of heart, whom he hath given up not only to the power and efficacy of their own lusts and vile affections, but also immediately unto Satan, to be deluded and led captive at his pleasure? In vain shall the repentance of such persons be either expected or endeavoured.

And this severity of God ought to be preached and insisted on in the declaration of the gospel Let the reader consult what hath been already offered concerning the use of gospel threatenings and comminations on the third and fourth chapters. There is a proneness in corrupted nature to "despise the riches of the goodness, forbearance, and long-suffering of God, not knowing that the goodness of God leadeth them to repentance;" and thereon, "after their hardness and impenitent heart, they treasure up to themselves wrath against the day of wrath," as our apostle speaks, Rom. ii. 4, 5. Considering nothing in God but mercy and long-suffering, and nothing in the gospel but grace and pardon, they are ready to despise and turn them into lasciviousness, or from them both to countenance themselves in their sins. By this means, on such mistaken apprehensions, suited to their lusts and corrupt inclinations, heightened by the craft of Satan, do multitudes under the preaching of the gospel harden themselves daily to destruction. And others there are who, although they will not on such wicked pretences give up themselves to their lusts and carnal affections, yet, for want of constant vigilancy and watchfulness, are apt to have sloth and negligence, with many ill frames of spirit, to increase and grow upon them. Both sorts are to be stirred up by being put in mind of this severity of God. They are to be taught that there are secret powers, accompanying the dispensation of the gospel, continually "in a readiness to revenge all disobedience," 2 Cor. x. 6; -- that "God is not mocked, for whatsoever a man soweth, that shall he also reap: for he that soweth to his flesh, shall of the flesh reap corruption; but he that soweth to the Spirit shall of the Spirit reap life everlasting," Gal. vi. 7, 8. But I have elsewhere already showed the necessity there was of arming the gospel with threatenings, as well as confirming of it with promises, so as that it may not be here again at large insisted on.

From what hath been discoursed, it is evident how necessary and wholesome a warning or threatening is here expressed by the apostle. It is the open mistakes of men that have drawn undue entanglements out of it; in itself it is both plain and necessary. Shall we be afraid to say that God will not renew such sinners as those before described unto repentance? or to declare unto sinners that without repentance they cannot be saved? or shall we preach to men, that whatever light they have had, whatever gifts they have received, whatever privileges they have been made partakers of, whatever profession they have made, or for how long a season soever, if they fall totally and despitefully from the gospel into that which is most opposite both to its truth and holiness, yet there is no doubt but they may again repent and be saved? God forbid so great a wickedness should fall from our mouths! Nay, we are to warn all persons in danger of such apostasies that "if any one so draw back, God's soul shall have no pleasure in him;" that "it is a fearful thing to fall into the hands of the living God;" that he will harden such sinners, and "give them up to strong delusions, that they may be damned;" that he is not under the engagement of any promise to give them repentance, but hath rather given many severe threatenings to the contrary. He hath told us that such persons are as "trees twice dead, plucked up by the roots," of which there is no hope; that "denying the Lord that bought them, they bring on themselves, swift destruction, -- whose damnation slumbereth not;" with the like declarations of severity against them innumerable.

But what shall be said unto them who, having through great temptations, and it may be fears and surprises, for a season renounced the gospel, or such as, by reason of great sins against light and backsliding in profession, do apprehend themselves to be fallen into this condition, and yet are greatly desirous of a recovery, and do cry to God for repentance and acceptance? I answer as before, they are not at all concerned in this text. Here is nothing excluding them from acceptance with God and eternal salvation, be they who or what they will that seek it by repentance; only there are some who are excluded by God, and do obstinately shut up themselves from all endeavours after repentance itself, with whom we have not any thing to do.

It is true, those alone are here firstly and directly intended who in those days had received extraordinary or miraculous gifts of the Holy Ghost. But this, by just analogy, may be extended unto others, now those gifts are ceased in the church; for those gifts and privileges which are yet continued unto men do lay (in present circumstances) the same obligation upon them unto perseverance in profession, and give the same aggravation unto their apostasy, as did those extraordinary gifts formerly conferred upon profession. "Let us not, then, be high-minded, but fear." It is not good approaching too near a precipice. Let unprofitable hearers and backsliders in heart and ways be awaked, lest they may be nearer falling under God's severity than they are aware of. But we must return unto our apostle, giving an account of the nature of this sin, which is attended with so sore a judgment. And this he doth in a double instance.

2. Anastaurountas heautois ton Huion tou Theou. Beza affirms that heautois, "to themselves," is absent from some copies, and then the words may admit of a sense diverse from that which is commonly received; for anastaurountas, "crucifying again;" may refer unto tinas included and supposed in anakinizein, that some or any should renew them. It is impossible that any should renew them to repentance; for this cannot be done without crucifying the Son of God again, since these apostates have utterly rejected all interest in and benefit by his death, as once undergone for sinners. This none can do. We ought not, we cannot, crucify Christ again, that they may be renewed and saved. Who can entertain a thought tending towards a desire that so it might be? And this sense, in the same or an alike case, the apostle plainly expresseth, chap. x. 26, 27, "If we sin wilfully after that we have received the knowledge of the truth, there remaineth no more sacrifice for sins." Christ cannot be offered again, and so crucified again, without which the sins of such persons cannot be expiated; for the unbloody sacrificing of Christ every day in the mass was not as yet invented, and it is a relief fit only for them to trust unto who have no interest in that sacrifice which he offered once for all. But there is in that other place an allusion to the sacrifices under the law. Because they could legally expiate no sins but what were past before their offering, they were to be frequently repeated, upon reiterated sinning. So from time to time they sinned (as

no man liveth and sinneth not), and had sacrifices renewed for their sins, applied unto the particular sins they had committed. This could now be so no more. Christ being once offered for sin, whoever loseth his interest in that one offering, and forfeiteth the benefit of it, there is no more sacrifice for him: "Christ henceforth dieth no more." It cannot be hence imagined that the grace of the gospel is restrained, as being all confined unto that one sacrifice, from what was represented in the multiplied sacrifices of the law; for, --

(1.) The one sacrifice of Christ extended farther, as to sins and persons, than all those of the law with all their repetitions put together: "By him all that believe are justified from all things, from which they could not be justified by the law of Moses," Acts xiii. 39. There were some sins under the law for which no sacrifice was provided, seeing he who was guilty of them was to die without mercy, as in the cases of murder and adultery, with respect whereunto David saith, "Thou desirest not sacrifice; else would I give it: thou delightest not in burnt-offering," Ps. li. 16, -- namely, in such cases as his then was. But, --

(2.) In case of apostasy from the one and the other, the event was the same. There was under the law no sacrifice appointed for him who had totally apostatized from its fundamental principles, or sinned vyd chzqh?, "presumptuously," with a hand high and stubborn. This was that "despising of Moses' law," for which those that were guilty thereof were to "die without mercy," Heb. x. 28. And so it is under the gospel. Willful apostates forfeiting all their interest in the sacrifice of Christ, there is no relief appointed for them, but God will cut them off and destroy them; as shall, God willing, be declared on that place. And this may be the sense of the words, supposing heautois not to belong originally unto this place. God hath confined all hopes of mercy, grace, and salvation, unto the one single offering and sacrifice of Jesus Christ. This our apostle insisteth on and presseth, chap. ix. 25-28, x. 12, 14. Infinite wisdom and sovereign pleasure have centered all grace, mercy, and blessedness in him alone, John i. 14, 16, 17; Acts iv. 12; Col. i. 19. And this "one offering" of his is so sufficient and effectually powerful unto all that by faith seek an interest therein, that this restraint is no restraint, nor hath any sinner the least cause to complain of it. If they reject and despise it, it is their own fault, and at their own peril; nor is it the reiterated sacrifice of the mass, or whatever else they may betake themselves unto, that will afford them any relief.

But the word is constant enough in ancient copies to maintain its own station, and the context requires its continuance; and this makes the work of "crucifying again" to be the act of the apostates themselves, and to be asserted as that which belongs unto their sin, and not denied as belonging to a relief from their sin: "They crucify him again to themselves." They do it not really, they cannot do so; but they do it to themselves morally. This is in their sin of falling away, part of it comprised in it, which renders it unpardonable; they again crucify the Son of God, not absolutely, but in and to themselves.

And we must inquire how they did it, or in what sense it is by the apostle charged on them. Now, this (to omit all other things that may be thought to concur herein) was --

(1.) Principally by an accession in suffrage unto them who had crucified him once before. Hereby they went over the same work with them, and did that for their own parts which the others had done before for theirs. They approved of and justified the fact of the Jews in crucifying him as a malefactor; for there is no medium between these things. The Lord Christ must be esteemed to be the Son of God, and consequently his gospel to be indispensably obeyed, or be supposed to be justly crucified as a seducer, a blasphemer, and a malefactor; for professing himself to be the Son of God, and witnessing that confession unto his death, he must be so received or rejected as an evil-doer. And this was done by these apostates; for, going over to the Jews, they approved of what they had done in crucifying of him as such an one.

(2.) They did it by declaring, that having made trial of him, his gospel and ways, they found nothing of substance, truth, or goodness in them, for which they should continue their profession. Thus that famous or infamous apostate, Julian the emperor, gave this as the motto of his apostasy, Anegnon, egnon, kategnon, -- "I have read, known, and condemned" your Gospel. And this hath been the way of apostates in all ages. In the primitive times they were the Gentiles' intelligencers, and, like the spies of old, brought up a false report upon the land; for they were not satisfied, for the most part, to declare their disapprobation of what was really taught, believed, and practised among the Christians, but, the more to countenance their apostasy, not only invidiously represented and odiously traduced what was really professed, but withal invented lies and calumnies about conspiracies, seditions, and inconsistencies with public peace among them, so [as], if it were possible, to ruin the whole interest and all that belonged unto it. This is to "crucify Christ afresh, and to put him to an open shame." And such is the manner of them unto this day. If any have made an accession to the more intimate duties of religion, as prayer and preaching, by virtue of spiritual gifts, with other acts of mutual spiritual communion, which the generality of men concern not themselves in, when, in compliance with their occasions and temptations, they fall from them and renounce them, they aim at nothing more than, by malicious, scurrilous representations of them, and false additions unto them of things perverse or ridiculous, to expose them to open shame and ignominy. Their language is, Anegnomen, egnomen, kategnomen, -- "We have known and tried these things, and declare their folly;" so hoping to be believed, because of their pretended experience, which alone is sufficient to render them suspected with all persons of wisdom and sobriety. Now, no man living can attempt a higher dishonour against Jesus Christ, in his person or in any of his ways, than openly to profess that upon trial of them they find nothing in them for which they should be desired. But "it had been better for such persons not to have known the way of righteousness, than, after they have known it, to turn from the holy commandment delivered unto them."

And this is the first aggravation of the sin mentioned, taken from the act ascribed unto the sinners, "they crucify him again;" they do it as much as in them lieth, and declare that they would actually do it if it were in their power. He adds another from the consideration of the person who was thus treated by them. It was the "Son of God" whom they dealt thus withal. This they did, not when he had "emptied himself, and made himself of no reputation," so that it was not an easy matter to look through all the veils of his outward weakness and condition in this world, to "behold his glory, as the glory of the only-begotten of the Father" (in which state he was crucified by the Jews); but now when he had been "declared to be the Son of God with power, according to the Spirit of holiness, by the resurrection from the dead," and when his divinity was variously attested unto in the world and among themselves. And this is the great aggravation of sin against the gospel, namely, of unbelief, that it is immediately against the "Son of God." His person is despised in it, both absolutely and in the discharge of all his offices; and therefore is God himself so, because he hath nothing to do with us but by his Son.

Thirdly, The apostle adds, as another aggravation of their sin, kai paradeigmatizontas, "exposing him again to public ignominy," or "shame." Paradeigmatizo is to bring any supposed offenders unto such open punishment as is shameful in the eyes of men, and renders them vile who are so traduced and punished. The word is but once more used in the New Testament, namely, Matt. i. 19, where it is spoken of Joseph in reference unto his espoused wife, the holy Virgin: Me thelon auten paradeigmatisai, -- "Not willing to make her a public example;" that is, by bringing of her forth unto a shameful punishment, for the terror of others.

According unto this sense, our apostle, expressing the death of Christ as inflicted by men, reduces the evils that accompanied it unto two heads, -- (1.) The pain of it; and, (2.) The shame: Heb. xii. 2, "He endured the cross and despised the shame;" for as the death of the cross was penal, or painful and dolorous, so in the manner of it, in all its circumstances of time, place, person, it was most highly shameful. He was in it paradeigmatistheis, "ignominiously traduced," or "put to an open shame;" yes, the death of the cross amongst all people was peculiarly shameful. Thus in calling over his death in this place, he refers it unto the same heads of suffering and shame, -- "crucifying him," and "putting him to an open shame." And in this latter he was not spared by these apostates more than in the former, so far as it lay in their power.

And hence we may raise a sufficient answer unto an objection of no small importance that ariseth against our exposition of this place: for it may be said, "That if those, or many of them, or any of them, who actually and really crucified the Son of God in his own person, and put him to open shame, did yet obtain mercy and pardon of that and all other sins, as it is confessed they did, whence is it that those who renounce him, and do so crucify him and put him to shame only metaphorically and to themselves, should be excluded from all hopes of repentance and pardon?"

I answer, That the sin of those who forsake Christ and the gospel, after their conviction of its truth and profession of it, is on many accounts far greater than that of those who crucified him in the days of his flesh. And there are sundry reasons whereon God will exercise more severity towards this latter sort of sinners than towards the former:--

1. The sin is greater, because no way to be extenuated by ignorance. This is everywhere allowed as that which made the sin of crucifying of Christ pardonable upon their repentance, and their repentance possible. So Peter, in his sermon to them, lays down this as the foundation of his exhortation unto repentance: "And now, brethren, I wot that through ignorance ye did it, as did also your rulers," Acts iii. 17. "Had they known it, they would not have crucified the Lord of glory," 1 Cor. ii. 8; which our apostle pleads also in his own case, 1 Tim. i. 13. This put their sin among the number of those which sacrifices were allowed for of old, and which fell under the care of Him who knows how to have "compassion on the ignorant, and on them that are out of the way."

But it may be inquired, "How they could be excused by ignorance who had so many means and evidences of conviction as to the truth of his person, that he was the Messiah, and of his doctrine, that it was from heaven? for besides the concurrent testimony of Moses and the prophets given unto him, the holiness of his person and life, the efficacy of his doctrine, and the evidence of his miracles, did abundantly prove and confirm the truth of those things, go that they could be no otherwise ignorant but by willful obstinacy."

Ans. First, These were indeed such means of conviction as that their sin and unbelief against them had no real excuse, as himself everywhere expresseth, John xv. 22, xii. 47, 48, x. 36-38. Secondly, Nothing is allowed unto this ignorance, but that it left their repentance possible and their sin pardonable. Thirdly, This it will do until God hath used all the means of conviction which he intendeth, and no longer. This as yet he had not done. He had yet two farther testimonies unto the truth which he would graciously afford: First, His resurrection from the dead, Rom. i. 4, which was always afterward pleaded as the principal evidence of God's approbation of him; Second, The effusion of the Holy Spirit in his miraculous operations, Acts ii. 32, 33, v. 32; 1 Tim. iii. 16. But where at any time God hath granted all the means of conviction that he pleaseth, be they ordinary or extraordinary, if they are rejected, there is no hope, Luke xvi. 29-31. On the other side, this sin of rejecting Christ and the gospel after profession is absolutely willful and with a high hand, against all the light and conviction that God will give of the truth unto any of the children of men in this world.

2. These persons had an experience of the truth, goodness, and excellency of the gospel, which those others had not, nor could have; for they had "tasted of the good word of God, and the powers of the world to come," and had received great satisfaction in the things they were convinced of, as was before at large declared. Wherefore, in their rejection of him and them, an unconquerable hatred and malice must be granted to be predominant. And let men take heed what they do when they begin to sin against their own experience, for evil lies at the door.

3. In and under the crucifying of the Lord Christ God had yet a design of mercy and grace, to be communicated unto men by the dispensation of his Spirit. Therefore there was a way set open unto those who were guilty of that sin to repentance and pardon. But now, having made use of this also, that being sinned against, there is no place left for any thing but severity. Wherefore, --

4. There was in the sin of these persons blasphemy against the Holy Ghost; for they had received in themselves, or seen in others, those mighty operations of his whereby he gave attestation unto Christ and the gospel. Therefore they could not renounce the Lord Christ without an ascription of these works of the Holy Ghost unto the devil, which the devil acted them unto. So saith our apostle, "No man speaking by the Spirit of God calleth Jesus anathema," or "accursed," 1 Cor. xii. 3. To call him anathema is to declare and avow that he was justly crucified as an accursed person, as a public. This was done by these persons who went over to the Jews, in approbation of what they had done against him. This no man can do speaking by the Holy Ghost, -- that is, whosoever doth so is acted by the spirit of the devil; and if he have known the testimony of the Holy Spirit to the contrary, he doth it in despite of him, which renders the sin irremissible.

Footnotes:

2. "Solenne est hæreticis alicujus capituli ancipitis occasione adversus exercitum sententiarum Instrumenti totius armari." -- Tert. de Pudicit. "Utique æquum, incerta de certis, obscura de manifestis præjudicari, ut ne inter discordiam certorum et incertorum, manifestorum et obscurorum, fides dissipetur." -- Id. de Resur. Hapanta ortha enopion ton sunienton, phesi he graphe, tout' esti, ton hosoi huper autou saphenistheisan ton graphon exegesin kata ton ekklesiastikon kanona ekdechomenoi diasozousi, kanon de ekklesiastikos he sunodia kai sumphonia nomou te kai propheton te ten tou kuriou

parousian paradidomene diatheke. -- Clem. Alex., Stromat. vi. Eu oida hoti rheta tina paralepsontai tes graphes hoi kai tauta boulomenoi tolman phaskein apo Theou gegonenai, me dunamenoi hen huphos apodeixai tes graphes aitiomenes men tous hamartanontas, apodechomenes de tous eu prattontas, kai ouden hetton kakeina legouses hatina perispan dokei, oliga onta, tous amathos ta theia grammata anaginoskontas. -- Origen. adv. Cels. lib. vi. -- Ed.

3. Apostles? -- Ed.

Chapter II – Partial apostasy from the gospel — Pretenses of the church of Rome against the charge of this evil examined and rejected

Apostasy from the gospel is either total or partial. Of the former we have treated in a high and signal instance. When men willfully and maliciously (for they cannot do it willfully but they must do it maliciously) renounce Jesus Christ as a seducer and malefactor, going over in their suffrage unto the Jews, by whom he was crucified, they enter into that part of hell and darkness which properly constitutes this sin. It were well for such persons if their guilt had no other aggravation than theirs who actually "with wicked hands slew him, and hanged him on a tree." But rising up unto a contempt of all the means of conviction and evidences of truth that God will grant us in this world, they cast themselves without that line of divine mercy and pardon which some of the others were encompassed withal. So is it with many at this day in the world, who with wicked hearts and blinded minds, in the pursuit of carnal lusts, voluntarily and obstinately embrace Mohammedanism, with an open renunciation of Christ and the gospel Unto such persons there is nothing left but "a fearful looking for of judgment and fiery indignation which shall devour the adversaries." Not that I would cast all persons who may be actually hurried into this abomination under the same dreadful doom, seeing the case in general will admit of many circumstantial differences, if not altering the nature of the crime, yet disposing of things unto various events. Not only surprisals by mighty temptations, with dread and terror, so shaking the powers of nature as to intercept the influence of light and convictions of truth, do claim an exemption from a decretory determination under this sentence; but other cases may also be attended with some such alleviating circumstances as, preserving their minds and souls from willful malice, leave room for the exercise of sovereign grace. I myself knew one, yea, was conversant with him, and assisting of him in the concerns of his soul, who in the Indies turned Mohammedan, was actually initiated by circumcision into their superstition, and lived in its outward practice a year or two, who yet was sincerely recovered unto repentance, and died in the faith of the Son of God.

Partial apostasy is every crime against the gospel which partakes of the nature of the other in any measure or degree; and whatever doth so makes an accession towards the guilt of "crucifying the Son of God afresh, and putting him to an open shame:" for it is in his gospel and church alone wherein he can now suffer from the sons of men. When any important principle of evangelical truth is forsaken and renounced, especially when many of them are so; when the rule of obedience which the gospel prescribeth is habitually neglected; when men believe otherwise than it teacheth, and live otherwise than it requireth, -- there is a partial apostasy from it, whose guilt and danger answer the degrees and measures which in each kind it proceeds unto.

And this is that which we may charge, yea, which the Lord Christ in his word doth charge, on every nation under heaven where the gospel is publicly professed. Men are apt to please themselves, to approve of their own state and condition, wherein they have framed unto themselves rest and satisfaction. Churches content themselves with their outward order and administrations, especially when accompanied with secular advantages, and contend fiercely that all is well, and the gospel sufficiently complied withal, whilst their outward constitution is preserved and their laws of order kept inviolate. About these is the world filled with endless digladiations, wherein the most aim at no more but success in their especial contests. Only a few remain who fruitlessly complain that, under all these conflicts, the glory, power, and purity of Christian religion are lost in the world. And it is known that the judgment of Christ concerning churches, as unto their good or bad spiritual estate, is ofttimes very distant from their own concerning themselves. It was not only for their sakes, but as a warning unto all others in all ages, that it is entered on an everlasting record, that when the church of Laodicea judged and declared without hesitation that she was "rich, and increased with goods, and had need of nothing," the Lord Christ, "the Amen, the faithful and true witness," pronounced her "wretched, and miserable, and poor, and blind, and naked." That things at this day are in no better a condition in many, in most churches in the world, is too evident to be denied with any pretence of reverence to the word of God, and it will be afterward made to appear.

Certainly the Lord Christ may say to the churches and nations among whom his name is yet owned in the world, what God said of old concerning that of the Jews, then his only church, "I had planted thee a noble vine, wholly a right seed: how then art thou trained into the degenerate plant of a wild vine unto me?" Jer. ii. 21. Yea, to most of them as in another place, "How is the faithful city become an harlot! it was full of judgment; righteousness lodged in it; but now murderers. Thy silver is become dross, thy wine mixed with water," Isa. i. 21, 22. The greatness of the evil complained of, the secret mystery of its accomplishment, the unreasonableness, folly, and ingratitude of the fact, the strangeness of the event, make the complaint to be formed into a scheme of admiration. And, indeed, if a man be able to consider the nature of the gospel, with the benefits communicated thereby unto mankind, he cannot but be astonished to find the generality of them to be so soon weary of it, and so ready on all occasions to relinquish it; for as future glory and a blessed immortality are attainable only thereby, so all that true freedom, tranquility, peace, and blessedness, whereof our nature in this life is capable, are by no other means communicable unto the souls of men. In brief, whatever is of advantage in any gracious communication from God unto us, -- without which we are nothing but the very worst and most malignant product of sin and misery, -- it is all confined unto the gospel and the contents thereof. Wherefore, the carelessness of men in neglecting of it, their wickedness in its relinquishment as to its principles and obedience, may well be expressed as God doth in the inferior instance of the apostasy of the Jewish church: Jer. ii. 11, 12, "Hath a nation changed their gods, which are yet no gods? but my people have changed their glory for that which doth not profit. Be astonished, O ye heavens, at this, and be horribly afraid, be ye very desolate, saith the Lord." Yet thus is it, and no otherwise, as we shall afterward manifest, amongst the generality of them that are called Christians in the world.

The church of Rome violently pleads an exemption from this charge by virtue of special privilege; -- not an internal privilege of efficacious grace into their minds and wills, to preserve it and all that belongs unto it always in saving faith and obedience, wherein alone a compliance with the gospel consists; but an outward privilege of indefectibility, keeping them in the state the gospel requireth they know not how, but, as it were, whether they will or no!

But there is no party or society of men under heaven (considering the notoriety of matter of fact to the contrary) but can with less violence unto common modesty make use of this pretence. So when the Jews of old were charged by the prophets with apostasy from the law and the obedience which it required, with threats of destruction for their sins, they warded themselves from a conviction of guilt and fear of punishment by an unreasonable, yea, outrageous confidence in church privileges, then not only appropriated but confined unto them, crying out, "The temple of the Lord, The temple of the Lord, The temple of the Lord, are these." This they thought sufficient to repel the charge of the prophets, to vindicate their innocency, and secure their peace. The reply of the prophet unto them will equally serve in both cases, "Behold, ye trust in lying words, that cannot profit. Will ye steal, murder, and commit adultery, and swear falsely, and burn incense unto Baal, and walk after other gods whom ye know not; and come and stand before me in this house, which is called by my name, and say, We are delivered to do all these abominations?" Jer. vii. 8-10. A plea of innocency and hope of impunity, under an evident guilt of the highest immoralities and the vilest of superstitions, do equally participate of folly and impudence.

It is fallen out with this church of Rome somewhat in like manner as it did with him from whom she falsely pretends to derive her wonderful privilege of indefectibility; for when our Lord Christ foretold that all men should forsake him, he alone, with the highest confidence and in a singular manner, undertook the contrary for himself. But all the prerogative which he pretended unto issued only in this, that when all the other disciples forsook their Master and fled, according to his prediction, he alone forsook him and denied him. And that impossibility of failing which this church appropriates unto itself as its singular and incommunicable privilege hath possibly been a means of, but assuredly is accompanied with, a peculiar apostasy, above all other churches in the world. Nothing, certainly, can be more vain in itself, nor more pernicious unto the souls of them who are under the power of such an apprehension, than this pretence, when all evidences in matter of fact do openly testify to the contrary. The principal nations of its communion are at this day engaged in fierce, bloody, and causeless wars, and these so managed as to be accompanied with a confluence of all those evils and flagitious wickednesses which have a tendency to make mankind sinful and miserable. Is this that love and peace which, according to the rule of the gospel, ought to be among the disciples of Christ, and without which it is impossible they should have any evidences in themselves, or give any testimony unto the world, that so they are? Doth this answer the promises to be accomplished in the days of the Messiah, Isa. ii. 2-4, or the innumerable precepts given by Jesus Christ himself as to unity, love, and peace? "But wars," they say, "are lawful, and so no argument that those engaged in them are revolters from the rule of the gospel." I say, It may be so; but it is far safer to judge all war unlawful than to justify all the wars that rage in Christendom, or to suppose them consistent with the rule or doctrine of the gospel. The truth is, many things must concur to reconcile any of them unto that obedience which we owe to the Prince of Peace; nor is any of them of that nature or necessity, but that, if the gospel had its proper efficacy on the minds of all that are called Christians, and its due authority over their consciences, they would be all prevented. However, in a church pretending to be no way fallen off or apostatized from the evangelical rule, it is justly expected that another representation be made of the religion taught by Jesus Christ than that which appears in the desolations that are wrought in the earth through the lusts and rage of the members of it. The state of things amongst them seems not to constitute that kingdom of righteousness, love, and peace, which Christ came to set up in the world, and which indeed at present, by reason of the general apostasy of the nations, is little elsewhere to be found but in the souls of his sanctified ones; and those particular churches are blessed in a peculiar manner who endeavour, in their profession and obedience, in any measure to rise up unto an expression thereof.

Besides, the lives of the generality of them who adhere unto the communion of that church, [and] of the most who preside therein, are openly contradictory unto the evangelical rule of obedience. It may for the most part be said concerning them with respect unto the whole, as one of them said of a part of the New Testament, "Either this is not gospel, or we are not Christians." In brief, if the kingdom of Christ, -- which was once a kingdom of light, and truth, and holiness; of separation, in principles, affections, and conversation, from the world; of communion with God and loving-kindness among men; of righteousness, peace, and joy in the Holy Ghost, -- may become, and is become, a kingdom of darkness, pride, ignorance, ambition, persecution, blood, superstition, and idolatry, then and not else doth it visibly remain among them, and they have nothing apostatized from the laws and government of it.

But they can easily discharge themselves of the guilt of this imputation: for notwithstanding that the things mentioned be in part acknowledged to be so, (as to what purpose is it to deny the sun to shine at noonday?) yet the peace, love, and unity, the holiness and righteousness, that ought, according to the gospel, to be and reside in the church, are found amongst them on other accounts; -- for the whole body of the church and all the members of it agree and are united in one head, even the pope of Rome, which is the only evangelical unity required of the disciples of Christ! and the holiness of the worship, with that of the saints that have been among them, as also of their present retired devotionists, and the charity of many, testified by magnificent works of piety and bounty, do sufficiently answer that sanctification, holiness, and love, that conformity unto Christ in heavenly-mindedness and obedience, which the gospel requireth. But this is no other but an account of the true nature of that apostasy of the latter times which is foretold by the apostle, 2 Tim. iii. 1-5, "In the last days perilous times shall come. For men shall be lovers of their own selves, covetous, boasters, proud, blasphemers, disobedient to parents, unthankful, unholy, without natural affection, truce-breakers, false accusers, incontinent, fierce, despisers of those that are good, traitors, heady, high-minded, lovers of pleasures more than lovers of God; having a form of godliness, but denying the power thereof." Under the power of the most filthy and outrageous lusts, men frame to themselves an outward shape, image, and representation of holiness; they delineate a form of religion by a substitution of other things in the room of the life and substance of it, which are lost. The power of Christianity is openly denied in their being acted by the power of all those lusts which are contrary unto it; for the grace of God in the gospel teacheth them by whom it is received to "deny all ungodliness and worldly lusts, and to live soberly, righteously, and godly in this present world." This men cannot more perfectly renounce than in being "foolish, disobedient, deceived, serving divers lusts and pleasures, living in malice and envy, hateful, and hating one another;" such persons being sufficiently remote from being "saved by the washing of regeneration, and renewing of the Holy Ghost." Whilst men live in this state and condition, wherein a complete denial or renunciation of the power of godliness or religion doth consist, if, to supply the absence thereof, they draw and take on themselves a scheme, form, and appearance of it, by the application of the names, offices, and properties of gospel effects unto outward, lifeless duties, or appearances of them, the apostasy foretold is completely accomplished. This is to let David go, and to foist an image covered with goats' hair in his stead; or at best, like Rehoboam, to make brazen shields in the room of those of gold taken away by Shishak. No otherwise doth the church of Rome deal in this matter. The power of faith, love, peace, holiness, conformity unto Christ, self-denial, and all the principles of a heavenly conversation, being lost and denied among the generality of its members, and all the real glory of Christianity thereby forfeited and despised, they have set up a form or image of it, wherewith they content themselves, and attempt to deceive others. Instead of that mystical, spiritual union with himself and among themselves which Christ prayed for and purchased for his disciples, they have substituted the morphosis or mormo of an agreement in professing subjection to the pope of Rome. For that heavenly love of one another in him, and for his sake, which he renews the souls of believers unto by his grace, we are presented in their profession with outward works of charity and bounty, measured and valued by the advantage which redounds unto the principal actors in this show. Peace (the great legacy of Christ unto his followers) with God in their own minds, with the whole creation not shut up under the curse, that comprehensive grace and mercy wherein is comprised all the blessedness which in this world we can be made partakers of, is preserved in the flourishing prosperity and temporal successes of the court of Rome. The internal, effectual operations of the Spirit of grace have the outward dispensations of ordinances shuffled in their place and stead; regeneration is baptism; growth in grace is episcopal confirmation; the application, by faith, of the blood of Christ, once offered in a holy sacrifice for us, must give way unto the daily sacrifice of the mass offered for the sins of the quick and the dead; disciplines and some outward bodily severities must supply the place of the mortification of sin, the power whereof is never more lost and denied than it is under the highest external pretences of it. So the whole work of the Spirit as a Spirit of grace and supplication in the church must be, and is unto themselves, satisfactorily represented by reading, saying, chanting with voices and musical instruments, prayers and praises invented and composed by they know not whom, and in a language which the most of those who are obliged to comply with them understand not at all.

And even the worst part of their image is in what they have fixed on as the delineation and representation of the rule and discipline of Christ in the gospel; for, rejecting that humble, holy, meek, diligent endeavour to preserve all the faithful in obedience, love, unity, and fruitful walking, by the application of the commands of Christ unto their souls and consciences through his Spirit, and with his authority, they have erected a worldly domination over God's heritage, in whose exercise more force, fraud, extortion, oppression, violence, and bloodshed, have been acted and perpetrated, than it may be in the secular government of any tyrannical state in the world.

Other instances of the like nature might be given. This is that morphosis tes eusebeias, or aletheias tes kat' eusebeian, that figure and representation of evangelical truth and holiness wherewith these men would countenance themselves in, and cover from others, that apostasy from the gospel which predominant lusts have cast them into and keep them under the power of, according as it was foretold it should come to pass in the latter days.

It is yet replied, "That whatever apprehensions others may have, or whatever judgment shall be made, of the predominant evils reigning among the generality of them, and their seeming inconsistency with the doctrine of the gospel, yet the promise of the Spirit to lead into all truth is not only granted but confined unto them, so as that they are eternally secured as to faith and belief, whatever other miscarriages they may fall into." And the nature of this plea is so effectual, that if it could be made good and confirmed on their behalf, notwithstanding I see not as yet how it is possible to solve other difficulties that occur in this case, yet would it with me determine all things in controversy between them and us. Let them but evince that they alone do inherit the promised Spirit of Christ exclusively unto all others, -- that he dwells, resides, works, guides in and among them alone, -- and in other things we will spare them the trouble of farther pleading their cause. But their pretence hereunto is impotent and contemptible; for what they insist upon amounts to no more but this, that they being "the church," the promise of giving the Spirit is made and fulfilled unto them alone; which only begs the matter that is in principal difference between us, and the disputes about it are endless. If, indeed, they argued, on the other hand, that they are the only church of Christ because they alone enjoy the promise of the Spirit, as the inference were undoubtedly certain (for it is the presence of Christ by his Spirit that gives being or existence unto the church), so the truth of the assertion were capable of an easy trial and a satisfactory determination; for where the Spirit doth so reside, according to the promise of Christ, and abide with any, as he doth with no others in the same kind, he will infallibly manifest his presence by his operations, and sufficiently evidence them with whom he is to be the church of Christ, seeing, as he is the promised Spirit of truth, the world cannot receive him. His operations are all of them either in a way of grace or gifts; and his gifts are either extraordinary or ordinary. When, therefore, those of the church of Rome can manifest that they enjoy such gracious operations of the Spirit as others enjoy nothing of the same kind, or that they are furnished and supplied with such spiritual gifts, either ordinary or extraordinary, as no others do participate of with them or besides them, -- not proving it by saying they alone are "the church," and therefore it must be so, but by the evidence of the things themselves, as it was in the primitive times, -- they shall not only free themselves from the charge of any dangerous apostasy from the gospel, but enjoy moreover all that their hearts can wish.

But this pretence hath been so often and so fully evinced of falsehood, and that by all means of conviction, in the examination of causes and effects (it being undeniably demonstrated that as no such promise was ever peculiarly made unto them, much less on such terms of security as they imagine, and that in the issue, as unto matter of fact, instead of being "led into all truth," they have departed almost from all), that it needs not again to be insisted on. And, indeed, such a promise as is pretended is altogether inconsistent with the glory and honour of the gospel of God. The word of the gospel, -- that is, the truth contained therein, -- is the sole external instrument of the reconciliation of sinners unto God, and of their walking before him in obedience unto his glory; other end and use it hath none. To give by irrevocable grant the possession of this truth, and not in order unto that end, and so to continue it whether ever that effect be produced or no, yea, where it is not, corresponds not with other fruits of the wisdom of God in the dispensation of his grace. And whereas the gospel, as to the nature of its doctrine, will and may be interpreted by its fruits and effects in the lives of men, to allow them the security of its truth on a supposition of a course of sin, and a continuance in a state of irreconciliation or enmity against God, is to expose the doctrine of it, and the law of obedience contained in it, to just censure and reproach.

Wherefore, notwithstanding these or any other pretences of an alike nature, we may safely proceed to show how the generality of Christians have partially apostatized from the gospel, and to inquire into the ways, means, causes, and reasons thereof.

Chapter III – Apostasy from the mystery, truth, or doctrine of the gospel — Proneness of persons and churches thereunto — Proved by all sorts of instances

There are three things in the gospel which are as the essentially constitutive parts of it:-- 1. The mystery of its doctrine, which is the object of faith; 2. The holiness of its precepts, which are the matter of our obedience; and, 3. The purity of its institutions of worship, which is the trial of our faith and obedience as to their profession. With respect unto these we are to make our inquiry, both as unto matter of fact, and as unto the reasons, causes, and occasions of it, in the apostasy from them that is in the world. Instances hereof, in every one of the particulars mentioned, we shall find in our own days, and those both deplorable and of ill abode. [4] But I shall not confine myself unto the present age, nor unto what is done or come to pass among ourselves, but consider things with respect unto the whole course and progress of religion since the first preaching and declaration of the gospel.

First, The mystery of the truth or doctrine of the gospel, which is the object of our faith, is the foundation of its precepts and institutions, of the holiness it requireth and of the worship that it appointeth. Where this is forsaken, the others cannot be retained. Men may profess the truth, and yet not yield obedience unto it, Tit. i. 16, 2 Tim. iii. 5; but without the real belief of it, no man can be obedient as he ought. The obedience which the gospel requireth is the "obedience of faith," Rom. i. 5, or being "obedient to the faith," Acts vi. 7. It is this "grace of God" alone which "teacheth men to deny all ungodliness and worldly lusts, and to live soberly, righteously, and godly in this present world," so as to find acceptance with God therein, Tit. ii. 11, 12. Wherever, therefore, this is rejected, renounced, forsaken, declined from by any, so far as it is so, so far there is and will be an apostasy from all other concernments of the gospel. This, therefore, we are to inquire into. And we shall find in our inquiry that all sorts of persons, all churches, are, and always have been, exceedingly prone to turn aside from the mystery and truth of the doctrine of the gospel, that they have done so accordingly, and that those which are now in the world continue to be of the same temper and inclination. And as it will appear that no evil practices are indulged unto on this supposition, so it is desirable that those who are secure in this matter, on such principles as wherewith they are satisfied, would not with too much severity reflect on them who cannot but be jealous over themselves and others. The great apostle himself makes this the principal ornament in the preparation of his triumph upon the success of his ministry, that he had "kept the faith:" 2 Tim. iv. 6-8, "I am," saith he, "now ready to be offered, and the time of my departure is at hand. I have fought a good fight, I have finished my course, I have kept the faith: henceforth there is laid up for me a crown of righteousness, which the Lord, the righteous judge, shall give me at that day." Of all that made way for that triumphant glory which he now had a prospect of, he insists on this only in particular, that he had "kept the faith;" which he did not do without a severe warfare and conflict: so great a matter was that in his esteem, which most suppose so common, so easy, that little diligence or watchfulness is required thereunto. And the frequent solemn charges, with pathetical exhortations, which he gives unto his son Timothy to be careful herein, manifest both the weight he laid upon it, the difficulty that was in it, and the danger of miscarriage wherewith it was attended: 1 Tim. vi. 20, 21, "O Timothy, keep that which is committed to thy trust, avoiding profane and vain babblings, and oppositions of science falsely so called: which some professing have erred concerning the faith." 2 Tim. i. 13, 14, "Hold fast the form of sound words, which thou hast heard of me, in faith and love which is in Christ Jesus. That good thing which was committed unto thee keep by the Holy Ghost which dwelleth in us." And the same apostle expressly mentions the proneness of some to relinquish the truth of the gospel; whom, therefore, he would have rebuked sharply, "that they might be sound in the faith, not giving heed to Jewish fables and commandments of men, turning from the truth," Tit. i. 13, 14. Neither would there be any need that some should "earnestly contend for the faith once delivered unto the saints," Jude 8, but that others are very ready to corrupt it and turn away from it.

Examples of this state and event of things among all the churches in the world, since the first planting of them in and by the doctrine of the gospel, will give more evidence unto the truth of our assertion, and a clear account of that matter of fact, whose reasons and causes we are to inquire into. And because I would confine myself unto the full declaration of the mystery of Christ, I shall not insist on the church of the Jews under the old testament. But it is known unto all how, from their first transgession in making the golden calf, -- whereon, as God complains, they quickly, in a few days, turned out of the way, -- they were continually prone unto all sorts of apostasy; and in the issue, the generality of them fell off from the promise and covenant of Abraham by their unbelief, as the apostle declares, Rom. xi.. And it is to be feared that the appearance and pretence of some Christian churches unto better success have this only advantage, that their ways and practices are not recorded by the Spirit of God, as theirs were. But I shall not insist on that instance.

Of all the churches that are or ever were in the world, those gathered and planted by the apostles themselves had the greatest advantage to know the mystery and truth of the gospel, and the most forcible reasons unto constancy and perseverance therein. Considering the ability of their teachers to reveal unto them "all the counsel of God," with their faithfulness in "withholding nothing that was profitable unto them," Acts xx. 18-21, 26, 27; their authority, as being sent immediately by Jesus Christ, and their absolute infallibility in all that they delivered; a man would rationally think that there were no room, no pretence, left for any to decline in the least from the doctrine wherein they were instructed by them, nor any advantage for Satan or seducers to practice upon them. There is no doubt but most of us suppose that had we been so taught by the apostles themselves, nothing could ever tempt us to doubt or waver, much less to relinquish any truth wherein we were so instructed. But, alas! this thought is not unlike the apprehension of the rich man in hell, who judged that if one rose from the dead to warn his brethren, they would repent and be converted unto God. But as Abraham told him, "if they would not believe Moses and the prophets, neither would they believe should one rise from the dead," no more would we, if we be not constant and steadfast in the doctrine of the gospel as revealed in the Scripture, be so, if we had been taught it by all the apostles together. An example of this proneness to relinquish evangelical principles we have in most of the churches called and gathered by them, whose faith and practice are recorded in their writings.

The church of Corinth was planted by the apostle Paul, and watered by Apollos, that great evangelist; and none can question but that they were fully instructed by them in all the principles of the gospel; which is evident also from that abundance of spiritual gifts which, above any other church, they bad received. But yet, within a few years, before the writing of his first epistle unto them, which was not above five or six years at the most, many of them fell into that fundamental error of denying the resurrection of the dead; whereby they wholly annihilated, as the apostle declares, the whole death and resurrection of Christ, rendering what appeared to remain of their faith altogether vain, 1 Cor. xv. 12-18.

The churches of the Galatians are yet a more pregnant instance. Converted they were unto the faith of Christ and planted in their church-state by the ministry of the same apostle; and although he instructed them in the whole counsel of God, yet it may be justly supposed that he laboured in nothing more than to establish them in the knowledge and faith of the grace of God in Christ, and the free justification of believers by faith in him or his blood alone: for this he everywhere declareth to have been his principal aim and design, in the whole course of his ministry. The doctrine hereof they received with so much joy and satisfaction that they valued the apostle as an angel of God, received him as Jesus Christ, and esteemed him above the sight of their own eyes, chap. iv. 14, 15. But yet after all this, upon a sudden, so as that he was surprised with it and amazed at it, they fell from the doctrine of grace and justification by faith alone, to seek after righteousness as it were by the works of the law: Chap. iii. 1, "O foolish Galatians," saith he, "who hath bewitched you, that ye should not obey the truth, before whose eyes Jesus Christ hath been evidently set forth, crucified among you?" Notwithstanding the evident demonstration of the troth which they had received, and experience of the power of the word, which he mentions, verse 2, yet all on a sudden they apostatsized from it. And as the foundation hereof lay in the uncured folly and vanity of their minds (as we shall see afterward that it doth in all alike cases), yet the strangeness of the manner of it, that it should be so sudden, and, it may be, universal, makes him ask if there were not some strange fascination or spiritual witchcraft in it. So have we seen persons among ourselves, who in a day or two have renounced all those principles of truth wherein they have been instructed, and embraced a system of notions diametrically opposite unto them, insomuch as some have supposed that there hath been a real diabolical fascination in the matter. Now, this apostasy of the Galatians was such as the apostle peremptorily declares that Christ and all the benefits of his death were renounced therein.

Wherefore, although we may be troubled at it and bewail it, that sundry persons are so ready to fall off from the same truth in the same manner, yet ought we not to think strange of it or be moved by it, seeing that whole churches called and instructed therein, and that particularly, by the apostle himself, did so fall in a short time after their first plantation.

It is more than probable that those who endeavoured to make a spoil of the

Colossians "by philosophy and vain deceit, after the tradition of men," chap. ii. 8, had no small success among them. And such things they were wherewith they were attempted and beguiled as took them off from "holding the Head," turning them aside unto the curious speculations of men "vainly puffed up by their own fleshly minds," verses 18, 19. Things of the like nature may be observed in most of the other churches unto whom the epistles are directed.

And in those unto particular persons, as unto Timothy and Titus, he warns them of this readiness of all sorts of persons to apostatize from the truth, giving express instances in some by name who had done so themselves, and sedulously endeavoured the overthrow of the faith of others. The holy apostle John lived to see more of these woful turnings aside from the truth and relinquishments of evangelical mysteries. Hence in his epistles he gives an account expressly of the apostasies that were among professors of the gospel, of the seducers, and their pretences whereby they were promoted, warning believers of the danger thereof, and of sundry duties incumbent on them necessary to their preservation. And the Epistle of Jude is written to the same purpose. It is known, also, how most of the churches unto whom the Lord Jesus Christ granted the favour of his visitation, wherein he tried and judged their state and condition, their stability in and declensions from the truth, were found guilty by him as to some degrees of backsliding and apostasy, for which they were severely reproved.

Certainly we can never enough admire the profound negligence and security of most churches and professors in the world with respect unto a due adherence unto the mysteries and truths of the gospel. Some think that they have such a privilege as that they can never decline from them or mistake about them, nor have done so in the long tract of sixteen hundred years, although they have been plunged into all manner of wickedness and carnal security. Others are wanton and careless under their profession, making little difference between truth and error; or, however, suppose that it is no great achievement to abide in the truth wherein they have been instructed. And these things have brought most churches and places under the power of that apostasy which shall afterwards be discovered. But if the churches thus planted by the apostles themselves were liable unto such defections, and many of them did actually, at least for a season, fall away from most important doctrines of the gospel (from whence, it may be, they had never been recovered if healing bad not been timely applied by apostolical authority and wisdom), can we, who have not their advantages, nor some of the evidences of the truth which they enjoyed, having all the same causes of apostasy, inward and outward, which they had to be tried withal, expect that we shall be preserved, unless we watchfully and carefully attend unto all the ways and means whereby we may so be? But these things will be spoken unto afterward.

We may, in the next place, inquire what was the state of the churches after the ending and finishing of the sacred records, and the death of the apostles with all other persons divinely inspired. Here some would have us believe that all things were well, at least for a long season, and some that they are so to this very day. All that was believed and practised among them must be esteemed almost as sacred as the gospel itself, and be made a part of the rule of our faith and worship. It seems those very churches which, during the days of the apostles, and whilst they were under their inspection, were so prone to mistakes, to follow their own imaginations, or comply with the inventions of others, yea, in sundry instances so as to apostatise from the most important doctrines of the gospel, were all on a sudden, on no other advantage but being delivered from apostolical care and oversight, so changed, established, and confirmed, that they declined not in any thing from the truth and rule of the gospel. For my part, I pay as great a respect and reverence unto the primitive churches of the first, second, and third centuries, as I think any man living can justly do; but that they did in nothing decline from the grace, mystery, truth, or rule of the gospel, that they gave no admittance unto "vain deceit, after the tradition of men, after the rudiments of the world," there are such evidences unto the contrary as none can believe it but those who have a great mind it should be so, and [have] their credulity at their disposal. I shall therefore briefly inquire what was foretold that would ensue among those churches, and what came to pass accordingly.

The apostle Paul tells the elders of the church of Ephesus that "he knew that after his departing grievous wolves would enter in among them, not sparing the flock," Acts xx. 29. Though he compares them to devouring wolves, yet are they not bloody persecutors by external force that he doth intend; for that expression, "Shall enter in among you," denotes an admission into the society and converse of the church, under pretence of the same profession of religion. They are, therefore, heretics and seducers, who lie in wait to deceive through various sleights and cunning craftiness, being not (whatever they pretended) really of the church, not of the flock of sheep, no, not in profession, but devouring wolves. The same persons are intended who by Peter are called "false teachers," such as should "privily bring in damnable heresies, denying the Lord that bought them," 2 Pet. ii. 1. But the apostle adds, moreover, in the next place, "Also of your own selves shall men arise, speaking perverse things, to draw away disciples after them," Acts xx. 30. I do not think that the apostle in that expression, "Also of your own selves," intended precisely any of those who were then personally present with him, or at least it is not necessary that we should so judge; but some that were quickly to succeed in their room and office are intended. And all the perverse things which they would teach, being contradictory to the doctrine of the gospel, contained some degrees of apostasy in them. That they prevailed in this attempt, that the church was leavened and infected by them, is evident from hence, that not long after that church is charged by our Saviour to be fallen in sundry things from its first purity, Rev. ii. 4, 5. So he assures Timothy that the time would come, and that speedily, as appears by the prescription he makes for its prevention, 2 Tim. iv. 1, 2, that men "would not endure sound doctrine; but after their own lusts should heap to themselves teachers, having itching ears;" whereby they should "be turned from the truth, and be turned unto fables," verses 3, 4; -- a plain prediction of that defection from evangelical truth and purity which was to befall the churches, and did so. And this, with the danger of it, he doth more vehemently urge, as from a spirit of prophecy, 1 Tim. iv. 1, 2, "Now the Spirit speaketh expressly, that in the latter times some shall depart from the faith, giving heed to seducing spirits, and doctrines of devils." By that phrase of speech, "The Spirit speaketh expressly," the apostle understands not a plain, distinct revelation made thereof unto himself alone, but that the infallible Spirit of God, whereby himself and the rest of the apostles were guided, did everywhere testify the same. It is an expression not unlike that he useth, Acts xx. 23, "The Holy Ghost witnesseth in every city;" that is, in all places those who were divinely inspired agreed on the same prediction.

And I judge the apostles did everywhere, by joint consent, acquaint the churches that after the gospel had been received and professed for a while, there would ensue a notable apostasy from the truth and worship of it. So Jude tells them, verses 17, 18, that "the apostles of our Lord Jesus Christ told them that in the last time there should be mockers, who should walk after their ungodly lusts." This all the apostles agreed in the prediction of, and warned all the churches concerning it, So John expresseth it, 1 John iv. 3, "This is that spirit of antichrist, whereof ye have heard that it should come." He speaks of the coming of antichrist, and therewithal an apostasy from the faith, as that which they had been fully instructed in. And the apostle Paul mentioneth it as that which not only they were forewarned of, but also acquainted with some particulars concerning; which it was not, it may be, convenient in those days to mention publicly, for fear of offence. "There must," saith he, "be a falling away," or an apostasy from the faith, under the leading of "the man of sin." And saith he, "Remember ye not, that, when I was yet with you, I told you these things? and now ye know what withholdeth," 2 Thess. ii. 3, 5, 6. He had both told them of the apostasy, and also acquainted them with one particular about it, which he will not now mention. This being the great testimony of the Spirit of God in those days, that the visible church should so fall away from the faith, one of the chief ways whereby Satan brought it to pass was by the advancing of a contrary revelation and principle, -- namely, that this or that church, the church of Rome for instance, was infallible and indefectible, and could never fall away from the faith. By this means he obliterated out of the minds of men the former warnings given by the Spirit unto the churches, so rendering them secure, defeating the ends of the prediction; for hereby he not only led men insensibly into the greatest apostasy, but taught them to adhere invincibly unto what they had done, and with the highest confidence to justify themselves therein. But all those and many other warnings did the Holy Ghost give concerning the defection from the mystery of the gospel which the churches would in succeeding times fall into; which being neglected by secure professors, whilst their faith was weakened and undermined by innumerable artifices, issued in their apostasy. For these things being thus expressly foretold by the Spirit of God himself, we may briefly inquire into the event of the predictions mentioned, and whether indeed they came to pass or no.

An account in general of the state of the church after the days of the apostles we have given us by Hegesippus, who lived in the next age after them, as his words are recorded by Eusebius, lib. iii. cap. 32. Relating the martyrdom of Simon, the son of Cleopas, he adds: "Unto these times the church continued a pure and incorrupted virgin, those who endeavoured to corrupt the rule of saving truth, where any such were, lying hid in obscurity. But after that the holy company of the apostles came to their several ends, and that generation was past who heard the divine Wisdom with their own ears, a conspiracy of wicked error, by the seductions of those that taught strange doctrines, began to take place; and when none of the apostles were remaining, they began to set up their science, falsely so called, with open face against the preaching of the truth." We have already seen that there were many declensions in the clays of the apostles themselves; but as they were jealous over all the churches with godly jealousy, -- for having "espoused them to one husband," they took care "to present them as a chaste virgin unto Christ" (the words which Hegesippus alludes unto), and thereon watched against all ways and means whereby as "the serpent beguiled Eve through his subtlety, their minds should be corrupted from the simplicity that is in Christ," by the teaching of other doctrines than what they had received from them, as Paul speaks, 2 Cor. xi. 2-4, -- so by their wisdom, diligence, and watchfulness, they were for the most part soon reduced from their wanderings and recovered from their mistakes. Hence this holy man pronounceth the church a pure virgin during the days of the apostles and their inspection, at least comparatively as to what ensued thereon, for immediately after he acknowledgeth that they were much corrupted and defiled, -- that is, fallen off from "the simplicity that is in Christ," -- intending, probably, those very things wherein after ages made them their example; for things quickly came unto that state in the world, and which yet with the most continueth therein, that men desired no greater warranty for their practice in religion than the shadow or appearance of any thing that was in use or prevailed among those churches, though themselves therein went off evidently from the simplicity that is in Christ.

This account and unquestionable testimony we have in general of the accomplishment of the predictions before mentioned, concerning a declension that was to ensue from the power, purity, and simplicity of the gospel. But whatever is here intended, it must be looked on as the very beginning and entrance of the apostasy that ensued; which can scarce be taken notice of in comparison of that excess which it quickly proceeded unto. In particular, the parts of the sacred predictions mentioned may be reduced unto four heads:-- 1. "Men from among themselves speaking perverse things." 2. "Grievous wolves entering in, not sparing the flock." 3. Weariness, and "not enduring of sound doctrine," but turning the mind unto fables, and from the truth. 4. A gradual, secret, mysterious work of a general apostasy in the whole visible church. And it might be easily demonstrated by instances how all these had their particular accomplishment, until the whole apostasy foretold was formed and completed. We may give some short remarks upon them all:--

1. It cannot be denied but that many of the principal teachers in the first ages of the church after the apostles, especially among those whose writings remain unto posterity, did, in a neglect of the gospel and its simplicity, embrace and teach sundry things, perverse, curious, and contrary to the form of wholesome words committed unto them; whilst, for any thing that appears, they were not so duly conversant in evangelical mysteries, with reverence and godly fear, as it was their duty to have been. It is known how instances hereof might be multiplied out of the writings of Justin Martyr, Irenæus, Clemens, Origen, Tatianus, Athenagoras, Tertullian, Lactantius, and others; but I shall not reflect with any severity on their names and memories who continued to adhere unto the fundamental principles of Christian religion, though, what by curious speculations, what by philosophical prejudices and notions, by wrested allegorical expositions of Scripture, by opinions openly false and contradictory to the word of God, they much corrupted and debased the pure and holy doctrine of Jesus and his apostles.

2. The "grievous wolves" foretold of, who were to "spoil the flock," I look on as heretics in their various kinds. And on this account it would seem to exceed all belief what multitudes and shoals of all sorts of persons fell off from the mystery and truth of the gospel, after they had been declared unto them and professed by them, which is a full confirmation of the assertion before laid down. But they may in general be reduced unto two heads:--

(1.) Of those who, in a regardlessness and contempt of the gospel which they had received and professed, fell away unto foolish, extravagant, heathenish imaginations, unintelligible endless fancies, for the most part (as is supposed) accompanied with wicked practices, whereby, although they would retain the name of Christians, they completely and absolutely fell off from Christ and his gospel. Such were the Gnostics in all their branches and under their several appellations, Marcionites, Manichees, and others almost innumerable, with whose names, rise, opinions, and course of lives, Epiphanius, Austin, and Philastrius, have filled up their catalogues. It may be said, "They were all of them persons of so great abominations that they deserve no consideration among such as own Christian religion." But the greater the abominations were which they fell into, the more wild, senseless, and wicked were their imaginations, considering the multitudes of professed Christians which fell into them, the more effectual is the testimony they give unto the truth of our assertion; for were there not an inexpressible proneness in the minds of men to relinquish the mystery of the gospel, were it not promoted by unutterable folly and secret enmity against the truth, would it have been possible that so early in the church, taking date immediately from the decease of the apostles, such multitudes of professed Christians should openly renounce those sacred truths for such noxious, foolish imaginations? These are they who are expressly prophesied of, that they should "bring in damnable heresies, denying the Lord that bought them, and bringing upon themselves swift destruction, many following their pernicious ways; by reason of whom the way of truth was to be evil spoken of," 2 Pet. ii. 1, 2: for all their impious opinions and practices were by the heathen objected unto, and charged on Christian religion, as is evident in Origen's reply to Celsus, among others; and so by reason of them "the way of truth was evil spoken of."

(2.) There was another sort of heresies, and so of real apostasy from the mystery of the gospel, whose authors and followers yet pretended an adherence unto and profession thereof. And these may be reduced to two heads:-- [1.] Concerning the person; and, [2.] Concerning the grace of Christ. Of the first sort, the principal and most prevalent was that of the Arians in denying his deity; of the latter, that of the Pelagians in opposing his satisfaction, merit, and grace. The first of these was poured out as a flood from the mouth of the old serpent, and bare all before it like a torrent; the latter insinuated itself as poison into the very vitals of the church. The first, as a burning fever, carried present death with it and before it; the latter, as a gangrene or hectical distemper, insensibly consumed the vital spirits of religion. In the flint we have a most woful evidence of the instability of professors, and their readiness to forego the saving mysteries of the gospel; for in little more than half an age after its first rise, the generality of Christians in the world, bishops, priests, and people, fell under the power of it, and in their public confessions renounced and denied the true eternal deity of the Son of God: for, having obtained the patronage of some emperors, as Constantius and Valens, and the suffrage of innumerable prelates, who jointly promoted this heresy by force and fraud, almost the whole world, as to outward profession, was for a season led into this apostasy, wherein some whole nations (as the Goths and Vandals) continued for sundry ages afterward. And for the latter, or Pelagianism, it secretly, subtilely, and gradually, so insinuated itself into the minds of men, that, for the substance of it, it continues to be no small part of that religion which the generality of Christians do at this day profess, and is yet upon a prevalent progress in the world.

This is the second way of the apostasy of professors which was foretold by the Holy Ghost, which so came to pass as that the wounds which Christianity received thereby are not healed unto this day.

3. Another way was, that men should grow weary of sound doctrine, and not being able, for the reasons afterward to be insisted on, to endure it any longer, should hearken after fables, and be turned away from the truth. And this no less eminently came to pass than any of the former. About the third century it was that monkish fables began to be broached in the world. And this sort of men, instead of the doctrines of the grace of God, of justification by the blood of Christ, of faith

and repentance, of new obedience and walking before God according to the commands of Christ and rule of the gospel, which men grew weary of and could not well longer endure, filled their minds and satisfied their itching ears with stories of dreams and visions, of angelical perfection in themselves, of self-invented devotions, of uncommanded mortifications, and a thousand other foolish superstitions. By such fables were innumerable souls turned from the truth and simplicity of the gospel, thinking that in these things alone religion consisted, despising the whole doctrine of our Lord Jesus Christ and his apostles in comparison of them. These are particularly prophesied of and declared, 1 Tim. iv. 1-3. By the hypocrisy and lies, fabulous stories and doctrines of devils, of this sort of men, the body of the Christian people was so leavened and infected with the belief of vain delusions and the practice of foolish superstitions that little or nothing was left sound or wholesome among them.

4. Lastly, The secret working of the "mystery of iniquity," in, under, and by all these ways, and other artifices innumerable, which the subtlety of Satan, with the vanity of the minds and lusts of the hearts of men, made use of, wrought out that fatal apostasy which the world groaned under and was ruined by when it came unto its height in the Papacy. The rise and progress of this catholic defection, the ways, means, and degrees of its procedure, its successful advance in several ages, have been so discovered and laid open by many, so far as the nature of so mysterious a work is capable of a discovery in this world, that I shall not need to repeat here any instance of it, In brief, the doctrine of the gospel was so depraved, and the worship of it so far corrupted, that the waters of the sanctuary seemed, like the river Jordan, to run and issue in a dead sea, or, like those of Egypt, to be turned into blood, that would yield no refreshment unto the souls of men. So was that prophetical parable of our Saviour fulfilled, Luke xix. 12-15, etc.

Before I proceed to particulars among ourselves in this kind, I shall yet farther confirm our assertion in general by the consideration of the second venture, if I may so say, that God gave the gospel in the world, the second trial which he hath made of many churches and nations, and what hath been the event and success thereof.

During the season spoken of the church was driven into the wilderness, as to its visible profession, where it was secretly nourished by the Spirit and word of God, and the few witnesses unto the truth which yet remained prophesied in sackcloth, ofttimes sealing their testimony (whereby the world was disquieted and tormented) with their blood. But when the time came that God would again graciously visit the remnant of his inheritance, he stirred up, gifted, and enabled many faithful servants of Christ, by whom the work of reformation was successfully begun and carried on in many nations and churches. It is true, they arrived not therein at the purity and peace of the apostolical churches; nor was it by some of them absolutely aimed at. And this quickly manifested itself by the great differences that were among them both in doctrine and worship; whereon those mutual contests and divisions ensued which proved the principal means of obstructing the progress of their whole work, and continueth to do so to this very day. But a state of a blessed and useful recovery it was from that apostasy into errors, heresies, superstitions, and idolatries, which the whole professing church of these parts of the world was fallen into. And many ways did it manifest itself so to be. For, --

1. The doctrine taught by them generally was agreeable to the Scripture, which they strenuously vindicated from the corruptions of the foregoing apostasy, and the

worship of the churches was freed from open idolatry.

2. The consciences of men, pressed, harassed, and distorted with innumerable vain affrightments, superstitions, foolish imaginations, and false opinions, whereby they were brought into bondage to their pretended guides of all sorts, and forced unto services, under the name of religious duties, merely subservient unto their carnal interests, were set at liberty by the truth, and directed into the ways of gospel obedience.

3. Multitudes had it given unto them on the behalf of Christ, not only to believe in him, but also to suffer for him; so that no less numbers sealed their testimony with their blood, under the power of those who undertook the patronage of the present apostasy, than did under the rage of the heathens at the first introduction of Christian religion into the world.

4. The fruit which it hath brought forth in many nations, by the real conversion of multitudes to God, their edification and holy obedience, their solid spiritual consolation in life and death, with many other things, do give testimony unto this work that it was of God.

It cannot therefore be denied but that many churches were by the reformation brought into a state of revalescency or recovery from that mortal disease they had been under the power of. But all men know what care and diligence is required to attain perfect health and soundness in such a condition, and to prevent a relapse; which if it should fall out, the last error would be worse than the first. It might therefore have been justly expected from them, and it was their duty, to have gone on in the work of reformation until they had come to a perfect recovery of spiritual health. But instead thereof, things are so fallen out (by whose default God knows) that not only the work hath received little or no improvement among themselves, in the increase of light, truth, and holiness, nor been progressive or successful in the world towards others, but also hath visibly and apparently lost its force, and gone backwards on all accounts. Wherefore, we have here also another sad evidence of the proneness of men to forego the truths of the gospel after they have been instructed in them. I shall instance only in the known doctrines of the reformed churches, aiming especially at what is of late years fallen out among ourselves in a sort of men whom the preceding generations were unacquainted withal, which I shall therefore insist on apart and by itself afterward.

It is not unknown how ready many, yea, multitudes, are in all places to desert the whole protestant faith and religion, casting themselves into the baffled, prostituted remainders of the old apostasy. Every slight occasion, every temptation of pleasure, profit, favour, preferment, turns men unto the Papacy; and some run the same course merely to comply with the vanity of their minds in curiosity, novelty, and conformity unto what is in fashion among men. Some flee unto it as a sanctuary from guilt, as that which tendereth more ready ways for the pacification of conscience than that faith and repentance which the gospel doth require. Some having lost the sense of all religion in the pursuit of their lusts, finding themselves uneasy in their atheism, or disadvantaged by the reputation of it, take shelter in the Roman dress. Some are really entangled and overcome by the power and subtlety of numerous seducers who lie in wait to deceive. By one way and means or another, on motives known to themselves and him who useth them as his engines to subvert the faith, many in all places fall off daily to the Papacy, and the old superstition seems to be upon a new advance, ready to receive another edition in the world; yea, it is to be feared that there is in many places such a general inclination unto a defection, or such an indifferency to all religion, that multitudes want nothing but a captain to conduct them back into Egypt: for whereas they have lost all sense of the power, use, and excellency of that religion, or profession of truth, wherein they have been educated and instructed, and that by giving up themselves unto their lusts and pleasures, which will not fail to produce that cursed effect, they either embrace the Roman religion, to supply the place of that no religion which they had left unto themselves, or if they pretend to soar to such a pitch of reason as to disown the vanity and folly of that profession, and its inconsistency with all the principles of free, generous, and rational minds, they betake themselves for a while unto a kind of skeptical atheism, which, having given them a sorry talkative entertainment for a little space, by debasing and corrupting their minds, gives them up again unto what they did before despise. By such means are the numbers of apostates multiplied amongst us every day.

But there are yet other instances of the proneness of men in foregoing the faith that the church was retrieved unto at the first reformation. How great an inroad hath been made on our first profession, at least an alteration made therein (whether for better or for worse the great day will discover), by that system of doctrines which from its author, and for distinction's sake, is called Arminianism! I am not bound to believe what. Polinburgh affirms in his preface to the second part of Episcopius' works, namely, "That the most of the prelates and learned men in England are of their way and judgment," which, as stated by Episcopius, hath many Racovian additions made unto what it was at first; nay, I do believe that what he asserts is false and calumnious unto the persons he intends; -- but yet I wish withal that too much countenance were not given by many unto his insinuation.

A late writer, [5] in a treatise which he calls "A sober and compassionate Inquiry," etc., among other things of the like nature, fancieth that some dislike the church of England on the account of its doctrine; and this they do, as he farther supposeth, because it "doth not so punctually agree with the synod of Dort as they could wish." To evidence the unreasonableness hereof, he informs us, "That no one father or writer of the church, whether Greek or Latin, before St Austin's time, agreed in doctrine with the determinations of that synod; and as for St Austin, he was a devout, good man, but whose piety was far more commendable than his reason;" -- and therefore he rejects it with indignation (as he well may), that "a novel Dutch synod should prescribe doctrines to the church of England, and outweigh all antiquity;" and so closeth his discourse with some unworthy calumnies cast on the divines of that assembly, which were esteemed of the best that all the reformed churches of Europe (that of France alone excepted) could afford at that time.

But the interest of the present design which he had in hand was more regarded in these assertions than that of the truth. It is but a pretence, that those whom he reflects upon do dislike the doctrine of the church of England; for, look upon it as it is contained in the Articles of Religion, the Books of Homilies, and declared in the authenticated writings of all the learned prelates and others for sixty years after the reformation, wherein the doctrine taught, approved, and confirmed in this church was testified unto all the world, and the generality of those reflected on by him do sacredly adhere unto it. It is a defection from this doctrine that is by some complained of, and not the doctrine itself. And how the doctrine of the person before mentioned, or of Curcellæus, -- of whose works Limborch, in his preface unto them, boasts that they were so earnestly desired in England, -- can be brought into a consistency with that of this church so confirmed and declared, will require a singular faculty in the reconciliation of open multiplied contradictions, and those in the most weighty points of religion, to declare. Let but the doctrine established at the first reformation, as explained and declared in the writings of the principal persons who presided, lived, and died in the communion of this church, -- which are the measure of it in the judgment of all other churches in the world, -- be continued and adhered unto, and there will be neither difference nor complaint on this matter. For the disputes which have been, and which it may be always will be, among learned men, concerning some abstruse and philosophical notions about the order of the divine decrees, predetermination, the nature of human liberty, and the like innumerable, neither ever did nor ever will much disturb the peace of the church; for as they are understood by very few, if by any at all, so the community of Christians are altogether unconcerned with them, either as to their faith or obedience. Differences about them will be ended at the last day; and it may be, as to the great end of the gospel, that is time enough.

But the pretence of this author, "That no one father or writer of the church, Greek or Latin, before St Austin's time, agreed with the determinations of the synod of Dort," is of little importance in this cause; for as I suppose he may not speak this absolutely on his own trial and experience, but rather on the suggestions of others, so it is no more than what is strongly pretended concerning the doctrine of the holy Trinity itself with respect unto the determination and declaration made of it at the council of Nice. And it were to be wished that too much countenance had not been given unto this imagination by Petavius and some others, whose collections of ambiguous expressions out of the ancient writers of the church, and observations upon them, are highly boasted of by our present Photinians. And as, it may be, it will not be easy for this author positively to declare what was the judgment of any one ancient writer on all points of Christian belief, especially on such as had not received an especial discussion from oppositions made unto them in their own days or before them: so it is confessed by all that an allowance is to be given unto general expressions of such writers as seem occasionally to declare their present thoughts on any particular doctrines about which there had never been any controversy in the church; for the proper signification of words themselves, whereby men express their minds, is never exactly stated until the things themselves which they would signify have been thoroughly discussed. Hence the same words have had various uses and divers significations in several ages. And by this rule, whatever be supposed that none of the ancients before Austin were of the same mind with those who assembled at Dort, it may with more truth be affirmed that none of them were otherwise minded but Origen only, and those who were influenced by him, he being by many, on evident grounds, accused to have prepared the way and opened the door both unto Arianism and Pelagianism.

The censure passed on Austin, namely, "That his piety was far more commendable than his reason," is at least as novel as the Dutch synod; for it is not the commendation of his piety, but the disparagement of his reason, that is intended. And I must take the liberty to say, that either this author hath not been much conversant in the writings of this great and holy person, or he is a very incompetent judge of the rational abilities of them in whose writings he is conversant. This confidence in pronouncing a censure so contrary to the concurrent sense of the generality of learned men of all sorts in the church for twelve hundred years savours too much of partiality and prejudice. But it is some relief, that the adversaries of the truth with whom he had to do were never able to discover nor make advantage of the weakness of his reason. It was sufficient for the work whereunto God designed him; which was, not only to check and suppress the many instances wherein sundry crafty persons apostatized from the truths of the gospel, both in his own days and before, but also to give over the light of truth, clearly discovered and strenuously vindicated, unto posterity, for the benefit of the church in all ages. Persons may freely despise the men of their present contests, against whom they have all the advantages which may prompt them thereunto, and they have so much countenance in casting contemptuous reflections on the principal first reformers as not to think therein they invade the bounds of Christian modesty; but what will be the apology for their confidence in such censures of the rational abilities of Austin I cannot conjecture, though the reason of it I can easily guess at. However, it needeth not be much taken notice of, seeing a censure somewhat more severe hath not long since been passed on St Paul himself, by a writer of the same strain and judgment.

There is little ground of fear, as I suppose, that a "novel Dutch synod," as it is called, though consisting of persons delegated from all the principal reformed churches of Europe (that of France only excepted), "should prescribe doctrines to the church of England," seeing in that synod the church of England did rather prescribe doctrines to the Dutch than receive any from them; for the divines which had the pre-eminence of suffrage and authority in that assembly were those of the church of England, sent thither by public authority to testify the doctrine of this church, and to lead the Dutch into the same confession with themselves.

But to return; it is to be feared that as Pelagianism, in its first edition, did secretly and gradually insinuate itself into the animal and vital spirits of the body of the church in those days, proving a poison unto it, so under its new varnish and gilding it will be received, until it diffuse itself into the veins and vitals of the present reformed church-state in the world. This I know, that some pretending a zeal for holiness and reformation of life do yet, with a shameful partiality, charge those doctrines as a principal means of the decay of piety, which they cannot but know were generally believed and avowed then when piety most flourished in this nation. But this is part of that entertainment which the church of England meets with at this day from her degenerate offspring. The doctrine of all the ancient bishops must be traduced, as the means of the decay of piety; and, which increaseth the wonder, it had not this effect till it began to be publicly deserted and renounced I for whether they are the one the cause of the other or no, yet there is a demonstrative coincidence between the originals of our visible apostasy from piety and the admission of these novel opinions, contrary to the faith of the first reformed churches, and that they both bear the same date among us.

But there is yet a greater abomination effectually taking place among us, to the utter overthrow of the faith of some, and the corrupting of the minds of others from the truth of the gospel. This is the leprosy of Socinianism, which secretly enters into the walls and timber of the house, whence it will not be scraped out. It commenced in the world some time before the other spring of a partial apostasy before mentioned; but for a good space it lay fermenting in some obscure places of Poland and the countries adjacent. When the books and writings of the authors and promoters of the opinions called by that name came once to be known and read in other places, they were continually all of them abundantly answered and confuted by learned men of all sorts, so as it was justly hoped it would obtain no great success or progress in the world. But, --

"Latius excisæ serpit contagio gentis
Victoresque suos natio victa premit."

The vanity of the minds of men, their weariness of sound doctrine, which they will endure no longer, whatever they embrace, have given it admission, either in part or in whole, among multitudes who once professed the faith of the gospel: for whereas the whole system of the opinions of those men is but a collection of such errors as formerly perplexed the church and overthrew the faith of many, the principal and most material of them may be referred unto two heads, -- 1. Photinianism; and, 2. Pelagianism. Unto the first are referred their denial of the Trinity, and consequently of the divine person and incarnation of the Son of God. Under the latter, their opposition unto the satisfaction of Christ, the true nature of his priesthood and sacrifice, justification by faith in his blood and the imputation of his righteousness, the efficacy of his grace, and the corruption of our nature by the fall, may be comprised. The denial of the resurrection of the same bodies, the eternity of the punishment of the damned in hell, with other of their imaginations, were also traduced from some of old. The first part of their heresy as yet takes no great place but only among themselves, the doctrine opposite unto it being secured by law, and the interest of men therein who have advantage by the public profession. But yet it is to be feared that the coldness of many in asserting and defending those fundamental doctrines of the gospel which they oppose, yea, their indifferency about them, and the horrid notions, with strange expositions, that some have embraced and do use concerning the person of Christ, do proceed from some secret influence on the minds of men, which the venom of their opinions and sophistical disputes have had upon them. And from a just improvement of their sentiments have proceeded those bold efforts of atheistical imaginations and oppositions unto the Scripture, both the letter and sense of it, which have of late been divulged in public writing; which, being brought from the neighbour nation, do find no slack entertainment by many among us.

But as to the latter branch of their profession, or their Pelagianism, it hath diffused itself among multitudes of persons who were some time of another persuasion, and have yet engagements on them so to be. All that unreasonable advancement of reason in matters of religion which we have amongst us; the new notions men have of the satisfaction of Christ, pretending to the acknowledgment of it, indeed destructive unto it; the noisome conception of the little use of the person of Christ in religion beyond the revelation and confirmation of the gospel; doctrines of the possibility, yea, facility of yielding acceptable obedience unto all evangelical commands without the aids of effectual grace, of the powers and incorruption of our nature, of justification by and upon our own obedience, of the suitableness of all gospel mysteries to unrenewed reason or an unsanctified mind, of regeneration as consisting only in the reformation of our lives; with a rejection of all internal real efficacy in converting grace, and the substitution of morality in the room of grace; with the denial of any influences of grace from Jesus Christ unto the holiness of truth; and many other opinions wherewith men even pride themselves, to the contempt of the doctrine received and established in the reformed churches of old, -- are borrowed out of the storehouses of their imaginations, shall I say, or raked out of their dunghill. And whither the infection may diffuse itself I know not. The resurrection of the same bodies substantially, the subsistence and acting of the soul in its separate state and condition, the eternity of hell torments, the nature of Christ's sacerdotal office as distinguished from his regal, begin to be either questioned or very faintly defended amongst many. And many other noisome opinions there are, about the Scriptures, the nature of God, his attributes and decrees, the two covenants, our union with Christ, the gifts and operations of the Spirit, which some vent as pure mysteries and discoveries of truth, and value themselves for being the authors or maintainers of them, that came all from the same forge, or are emanations from the same corrupt fountain of Socinianism.

We have, as I suppose, sufficiently demonstrated the truth of what we before observed concerning the proneness and readiness of mankind to relinquish and fall off from the mystery and doctrine of the gospel, after it hath been declared unto them and received by them. Withal we have stated the matter of fact, -- namely, that such a defection there hath been, and is in the world at this day; the reasons and causes whereof we are now to inquire into. Only I must premise, that the principal instance designed, and which is among ourselves, I have referred to an especial consideration by itself, wherein we shall inquire into the especial reasons of it, which are superadded unto those more general, which equally respect apostasies of this kind.

Footnotes:

4. Of evil omen. -- Ed.

5. Dr Goodman, rector of Hadham, who published, in 1674, "An Inquiry into the Causes of the Present Separation from the Church of England." He was answered by Vincent Alsop in his "Melius Inquirendum." -- Ed.

Chapter IV – The reasons and causes of apostasy from the truth or doctrine of the gospel, and the inclination of all sorts of persons thereunto in all ages, inquired into and declared — Uncured enmity in the minds of many against spiritual things, and the effects of it in a wicked conversation, the first cause of apostasy

For an entrance into the ensuing discourse, I shall lay down that principle which, I presume, all men will give their assent unto, -- namely, that a defection from the truth of the gospel once professed is a sin of the highest guilt, and that which will issue in the most pernicious events. God himself did frequently complain, by his prophets of old, that his people "had forsaken him," and were gone away from him, -- that is, from the doctrine and institutions of his law, the only means of conjunction and communion between him and them, Deut. xxviii. 20; 1 Sam. viii. 8; 2 Chron. xxxiv. 25; Jer. v. 7, 19, xvi. 11. To convince them of their horrible folly and iniquity herein, he demands of them what iniquity they had seen in him, what inequality in his ways, what disappointments they had met withal, that they should grow weary of his laws and worship, so as to relinquish them for such things and ways as would end in their temporal and eternal ruin, Jer. ii. 5, Ezek. xviii. 25: for if there were nothing in them whereof they had cause to complain; if they were all holy, just, and good; if in the observance of them there was great reward; if by them God did them good and not evil all their days, -- there was no apology or excuse to be made for their folly and ingratitude. That so it was with them, that their defection from the law and institutions of God was the highest folly and greatest wickedness imaginable, is by all acknowledged: yea, it will be so by them who at the same time are under a greater guilt of the same kind; for the judgments of men are ofttimes so bribed by their present interests, or corrupted by the power of depraved affections, as to justify themselves in worse evils than those which they condemn in others.

But as it was with the people of old, so it is at present with them who decline from the mysteries or renounce the doctrines of the gospel, after they have been received and professed by them, or have done so at any time: yea, their guilt hath greater aggravations than accompanied the idolatrous revolts of the Jews of old; for the gospel is a clearer revelation of God, and much more glorious, than that which was made by the law. There is therefore no reason to be taken from itself why men should desert it, either in its doctrines and precepts or the worship which it doth require. Nothing can be charged on the gospel, nothing on any thing contained in it or produced by it, which should countenance any in a defection from it. It is in itself a blessed emanation from the eternal Fountain of wisdom and truth, and hath more impressions and characters upon it of divine excellencies than the whole creation besides. Neither hath it any proper operations or effects on the souls of men but what are means and causes of deliverance from their original apostasy from God, with all the evil that ensued thereon, which is all that is evil; for the recovery of lost mankind from a state of darkness, bondage, and misery, into that of liberty, light, and peace, the present favour and future enjoyment of God, with order and mutual usefulness in this world whilst they continue therein, is the great and immediate design of the truths of the gospel. Neither is there any thing that is truly good, holy, just, benign, or useful among men, but what is influenced by them and derived from them. Some there have been, indeed, perhaps in all ages, who, pretending unto the liberty of it, have really been servants of corruption, and have turned the grace of God into lasciviousness; and some have charged the principal doctrines of it as those which give men a discharge from a necessity of holy obedience and the utmost use of their own endeavours therein. And there are those who, being given up to sensuality of life, living under the power of darkness, in the pursuit of secular ends, have no other thoughts of it But what the devils in the possessed man had of our Lord Jesus Christ, -- that it comes to "torment them before the time." And there are not wanting some who fear no evil But from the gospel, who suppose that the minds of all men would be serene and peaceable, that all things would be quiet, flourishing, and orderly in the world, if the gospel were out of it; for whatever disturbances men make themselves, in envy, wrath, malice, persecution of others, the guilt and blame of them shall be charged on the gospel itself. And it is notoriously known how a false pretence of some grants made in, and appointments settled by, the gospel, hath been made use of to countenance some sorts of men in the crafty acquisition and violent possession of worldly power, grandeur, and wealth, venting themselves in ambition, cruelty, luxury, and pride of life. But the iniquity and folly of all these abominations, cursed artifices of the father of lies and fountain of malice, shall be, if God will, elsewhere discovered. At present I shall take it for granted that in itself it is a glorious representation of divine wisdom, goodness, grace, and love; neither doth it produce any effects but whereof God is the immediate author, and will be the everlasting rewarder. Wherefore the reasons and causes of apostasy from the part of the gospel under present consideration, -- that is, the mysteries and truth of its doctrine, -- must be searched for in the minds of them by whom it is forsaken, with the external furtherances that do accompany them.

It is not unnecessary such an inquiry should be engaged into; for things are in that posture and condition in the Christian world in this present age, that if it should be supposed that the lives of professed Christians do make a due representation of the gospel, that the generality of men were led and influenced into that course of life and conversation which they openly pursue by the doctrines and principles of it, it could scarce stand in competition with heathenish philosophy for usefulness unto the glory of God and the good or advantage of mankind. It is not, therefore, the gospel, but it is apostasy from it, which hath produced so many deplorable effects in the world, and which, by drenching mankind in wickedness, makes way for their misery and ruin. And this, in the vindication of the gospel, will be made in some measure to appear in the discovery of the causes and reasons of this apostasy; for let men pretend what they please, unless they have first forsaken the gospel in their hearts and minds, they would not, they could not, forsake all rules of holiness and morality also in their lives.

Again; the prevalency of this defection is so great, and the neglect of men (either intent on their private occasions, desires, and interests, or captivated under the power of it unto the approbation of the greatest and most dangerous evils) so visible and shameful, as that every sincere attempt to warn them of their danger, to excite them unto their duty, or direct them in its performance, whereby the progress of this product of the counsels of hell may be obstructed and themselves defeated, ought to have a candid reception of all those who have a due regard unto the interest of Christ and the gospel in the world, or the everlasting concernments of their own souls.

These are the general ends which are aimed at in the ensuing discourses; and if any one of greater abilities for this work shall be hereby provoked, or take occasion from hence, to make a more diligent inquiry into the causes and reasons of that defection from the glory and power of Christian religion which prevails in the world, and shall thereon prescribe more suitable and effectual remedies for the healing of this epidemical distemper, I shall rest abundantly satisfied in the success of this attempt and essay. And the reasons which present themselves to my thoughts are these that follow.

I. That rooted enmity which is in the minds of men by nature unto spiritual things, abiding uncured under the profession of the gospel, is the original and first spring of this apostasy. So the apostle tells us that "the carnal mind is enmity against God," Rom. viii. 7; -- that is, unto the revelation of the will and mind of God in Christ, with the obedience which he requireth thereunto; for of these things doth he there discourse. The nature of this enmity, and how it operateth on the minds of men, I have elsewhere [6] declared at large, and shall not here again insist upon it. It is sufficient unto our present purpose that men, on various accounts, may take upon them the profession of the truths of the gospel whilst this enmity unto spiritual things abides uncured, yea, predominant in their minds. So was it with them of whom the apostle complains that under their profession they manifested themselves, by their wicked lives, to be "enemies of the cross of Christ," Phil. iii. 18; as those also are who, "professing that they know God, do yet in works deny him, being abominable, and disobedient, and to every good work reprobate," Tit. i. 16.

Thus, upon the first preaching of the gospel, many were convinced of its truth, and took upon them its profession, merely on account of the miracles that were wrought in its confirmation, whose hearts and minds were not in the least reconciled unto the things contained in it. See John ii. 23, 24; Acts viii. 13.

Some are so far prevailed with as to acknowledge its truth, by the efficacy of its dispensation as an ordinance of God for their conviction and instruction, and yet do not part with their enmity against it. Thus John was among the Jews as "a burning and a shining light," and they rejoiced for a season in his ministry, John v. 35, insomuch that the body of the people were initiated into his doctrine by the token and pledge of it in baptism, Matt. iii. 5, 6; but though all of them confessed their sins, according to his direction, very few forsook them, according to their duty.

When both these concurred, preaching and miracles, in an eminent manner, as when our Saviour preached on his feeding five thousand with five barley loaves and two small fishes, being prepared in their minds by the miracle they saw, they were so affected with his doctrine about "the bread of life that came down from heaven," that they cried out, "Lord, evermore give us this bread," John vi. 34; but, their natural enmity unto spiritual things being yet uncured, upon his procedure to instruct them in heavenly mysteries, they put in exceptions to his doctrine, verses 41, 52, 60, and immediately forsook both him and it, verse 66. And our Saviour assigns the reason of their defection to have been their unbelief, and that it was not given unto them of the Father to come unto him, verses 64, 65, or the enmity of their carnal minds was yet unremoved. Hence what they esteemed a hard and unintelligible saying, verses 52, 60, his true disciples understood to be "the words of eternal life," verse 68.

In process of time, many are prepossessed with notions of the truth of the gospel in their education, by the outward means of instruction that have been applied unto them; but yet, notwithstanding this advantage, they may still abide under the power of this depravation of their minds.

Evangelical truths being by these or the like means entertained in the minds of men, which are also variously affected with them, they will move and act towards their proper end and design. And hereof there are three parts:--

1. To take off the soul of man from rest and satisfaction in itself, as unto present peace in the condition wherein it is, and hope of future blessedness by its own endeavours; for neither of these are we capable of in our depraved, apostate state. Wherefore the first work of the gospel is to influence, guide, and direct the minds of men to renounce themselves as to these ends, and to seek after righteousness, life, peace, and blessedness, by Jesus Christ.

2. The renovation of our minds, wills, and affections, into the image or likeness of God, is another part of its design. And this it doth by presenting spiritual things unto us in that light and evidence, with that power and efficacy, as to transform us into their likeness, or to bring the substantial image of them upon our whole souls, 2 Cor. iii. 18; Eph. iv. 23, 24; Col. iii. 10.

3. It engageth the whole soul, in all its powers and faculties, through the whole course of its activity, or in all it doth, to live unto God in all holy obedience, Rom. xii. 1.

But when this work, or any part of it, is urged on the consciences and practice of men, they like it not in any measure. The uncured enmity whereof we speak riseth up in opposition unto them all. It begins to suppose that it hath admitted a troublesome inmate, that came in, as it were, to sojourn, and will now be a judge. Whilst the mind is exercised only about the notions of truth in speculation and reasonings, it is satisfied and pleased with them; yea, it will come unto a compliance with its guidance in sundry things and duties which it may perform, and yet abide upon its old foundations of self-sufficiency and satisfaction, Mark vi. 20. But when, in pursuit of the ends before mentioned, the gospel presseth to take men off wholly from their old foundations and principles of nature, to work them unto a universal change in powers, faculties, operations, and ends, to make them new creatures, it proves irksome unto that enmity which is predominant in them; which therefore stirreth up all the lusts of the mind and the flesh, all the deceitful policies of the old man and powers of sin, all carnal and unmortified affections, in opposition unto it. Hence spiritual truths are first neglected, then despised, and at last, on easy terms, parted withal. For men, by conviction, and on rational grounds or motives, whether natural or spiritual, may receive that as truth, and give an assent unto it, which, when it should be reduced unto practice, the will and affections will not comply withal. So it is said of some, that ouk edokimasan ton Theon echein epignosei, Rom. i. 28, -- "it liked them not," it pleased them not, they approved not of it, "to hold," retain, or keep, "God in their knowledge," or to continue in that acknowledgment of him whereof they were convinced. The inbred notions which they had by the light of nature, with their consideration of the works of creation and providence, gave them conceptions and apprehensions of the being and power of God, verses 19, 20. Hereby they are said to "know God," as they did with respect to the things mentioned; that is, the essential properties of his nature, -- "his eternal power and Godhead," verse 21. This knowledge, these notions and conceptions, did immediately direct them to "glorify him as God," in holy worship and obedience, as it is expressed in the same verse; but this, through the depravation of their minds and affections, they liked not, and therefore would not retain this knowledge of him, but gave themselves up unto all abominable idolatries and brutish lusts, which were inconsistent therewithal, as the apostle at large declares. Wherefore, even as unto divine things that are conveyed unto us by natural light, and such as is unavoidable unto all mankind, the will, the affections, and the practical understanding are more vitiated and corrupted than are the preceptive and directive powers of the mind; and hence it was that all the world, who had nothing to conduct them but the light of nature, apostatized from its guidance, and lived in contrariety unto it. They were all rebels against that light which they had; and so will all mankind be without the especial grace of God.

It is so also with respect unto truths communicated by supernatural revelation. It is given as the character of those who were to carry on the great apostasy from the mysteries and worship of the gospel, that "they received not the love of the truth, that they might be saved," 2 Thess. ii. 10. The truth itself, as to the profession of it, they did receive and own for a time; but such an approbation of it, such a love unto it, as should incline them unto obedience, or the improvement of it unto its proper ends, that so they might be saved, they neither had nor endeavoured after. This made them prone, on all occasions and temptations, to forego and relinquish the profession of it, to change it for the vilest errors and grossest superstitions; for in such a posture of mind, men's corruptions will prevail against their convictions. First they will stifle the truth as to its operation, and then reject it as to its profession. Let other notions be proposed unto them more suited unto the vanity of their minds or the sensuality of their affections, and they will not fail of a ready entertainment.

There are instances among all sorts of men, how, when they have imbibed persuasions and opinions, even such as are false, vain, and foolish, and have them riveted in their minds by powerful interests or inveterate prejudices, neither the evidence of truth nor the fear of danger can prevail with them for their renunciation or relinquishment. All false ways in Christianity, and that of Mohammedanism, give us examples hereof. But we have two general instances of it that may well fill the minds of men with astonishment. The first is of the Jews, who for so many successive generations, under all manner of difficulties and calamities, continue obstinate in the most irrational unbelief and apostasy from the faith of Abraham their forefather and the expectation of all their ancestors that can enter into the heart of any man to imagine. For many generations, those who from among them have been so convinced of their folly as really and sincerely to embrace the gospel do scarce answer one unto a century of years. The other is in the church of Rome. It is known how that communion aboundeth with men otherwise wise and learned, what kings and rulers of the earth do adhere thereunto; and this they continue to do, and will do so, notwithstanding that the errors, impieties, superstitions, and idolatries of that church are so many and so manifest. Other instances there are sufficiently pregnant to evince that no opinions in religion can be so foolish or contemptible but that some will be found pertinaciously to adhere unto them against all endeavours for their relief, either in the way of God by rational and spiritual convictions, or in the way of the world by persecution.

It may be more may and will be found to be obstinate in error upon trials, with difficulties, dangers, and oppositions, than will on the like trials be constant in the profession of the truth, -- I mean among them who together with its external profession have not received its internal power and efficacy, with the love of it in their hearts: for both sorts receive their notions and apprehensions of things in the same way, and on the same grounds of appearing reasons, though the understanding be imposed on and deceived in the one and not in the other; but error once received under the notion of truth takes firmer root in the carnal minds of men than truth doth or can whilst their minds are so carnal. And the reason of it is, because all error is some way suited unto the mind as thus depraved, and there is nothing in it that is enmity thereunto. Neither in itself nor any of its effects doth the mind dislike it, for being fallen off from the first Truth and Goodness, it wanders and delights to wander in crooked or by paths of its own; for "God made man upright, but they have sought out many inventions," Eccles. vii. 29. These it pleaseth itself withal and is conformed unto; for there is somewhat in every error to recommend itself unto the vanity, or curiosity, or pride, or superstition of the carnal mind. But it is otherwise with evangelical truths, which the mind disrelisheth because of its innate enmity unto the things which they propose and exhibit. Hence it is easier, for the most part, to draw off a thousand from the profession of it, who have no experience of its power and efficacy in their souls, than to turn one from an erroneous way, especially if he be confirmed in it by interest and prejudice. And so it is at present in the world. Every sort or party of false professors, as Papists and others, do carry off multitudes of common professors from the truth which they had owned, but seldom do we hear of any one recovered from their snares. Nor need any seducers desire a greater advantage than to have admittance unto their work where persons live in an outward profession of the truth and inward enmity unto it. They shall be filled with proselytes unto satiety.

This was the fundamental cause of that apostasy from the doctrine and truths of the gospel which has prevailed in almost the whole visible church. Had the generality of men received the truth in the love thereof, had they not had a secret enmity in their hearts and minds against it, had not things vain, curious, and superstitious been suited unto the prevailing principles of their minds and affections, they would not, they could not, upon any suggestions or temptations, so easily, so universally, have forsaken the gospel for the traditions of men, nor gone away from Christ to follow after Antichrist, as we know them to have done. But when an external profession of the truth became to be transmitted from one generation to another, the spirit and power of it being wholly neglected, men did but wait for opportunities gradually to part with it, and give it up for any thing else that was suggested unto them, many in the meantime setting their wits on work to find out inventions suited to their lusts and corrupt affections. That it was thus with them who were carried away with the great apostasy, that they did by all outward ways and means, in their lives and conversations, manifest that so it was with them, shall be afterward declared; and had it not been so with them, the event complained of had not ensued.

And herein lies the present danger of the persons, churches, and nations, which at this day make profession of the gospel: for if a pressing trial or vigorous temptation, if a coincidence of various ways and means of seduction, do befall them who have received the truth, but not in the love and power of it, they will be hardly preserved from a general apostasy; for when any attempts shall be made from without upon them, they have treachery from the deceitfulness of their own hearts at the same time working in them, for their uncured enmity against the truth doth but watch for an opportunity to part with it and reject it. Any thing that will but free them from the efficacy of those convictions or power of the traditions under which they are held captive unto the profession of the truth, as it were whether they will or no, shall be cheerfully embraced and complied withal. And the danger hereof doth sufficiently evidence itself in that open dislike of the rule and conduct of the truth which most men testify in the whole course of their lives.

It is plain, therefore, that unless this enmity be conquered or cast out of the mind; unless the mind be freed from its corrupt agency and effects; unless the truth obtain its real power and efficacy upon the soul; unless it be so learned "as it is in Jesus," whereby men, "put off concerning the former conversation the old man, which is corrupt according to the deceitful lusts, and are renewed in the spirit of their minds, putting on the new man, which after God is created in righteousness and true holiness;" unless they love and value it for the effects of spiritual peace, power, and liberty, which it produceth in them, -- there will be found among them little constancy or perseverance in their profession when temptations shall concur with opportunities for a revolt: for who can give security that what hath formerly fallen out amongst the generality of mankind shall not in any place do so again, where the same causes of it do again concur?

Having discovered this first cause of defection from the gospel, we may easily discern what are the only true effectual ways and means of the preservation and continuance of the true religion in any place or among any people where it hath been professed, especially if temptations unto a revolt should abound, and the season be made perilous by advantageous opportunities. Love of the truth, and experience of its power in the hearts of men, will produce this effect, and nothing else [will.] All other means, where these have been wanting, have failed in all places in the world, and will do so again when a time of trial shall come. True religion may be established by law, countenanced by authority, have a prescription of a long profession, or be on other accounts so fixed on the minds of men as that multitudes shall promise the firmest stability in the profession thereof; but there is no security in things of this nature, and we shall quickly see all the hopes that are built upon them vanish into nothing. Convictions or traditions, unto whose power a secret enmity is retained, may make a bluster and noise for a season, but every breath of temptation will carry them away before it. Were it not so with the most of men, had it been possible that so many nations in less than an age should fall into Arianism, after the truth had been so long known and professed among them; or that the body of this nation after a blessed reformation should again relapse into Popery, as in the days of Queen Mary, when many who had professed the gospel east others into flames who continued so to do?

It is greatly complained of that Popery doth increase in this nation; and some express their fears of its farther prevalency, and that perhaps not without cause. And although there are several other ways whereby men may and do apostatize from the truth, yet all those who take any other measure of things besides their own secular interests, with the corrupt affections of their minds, in wrath, envy, and revenge, do look on this as far the most dangerous, as that which will be most compliant with the predominant lusts of the present age, and most comprehensive to receive the community of men. Besides, by what it hath done formerly, it sufficiently instructs what it is likely enough to do again. Wherefore very many industriously attempt its prevention, as that which would prove (if it should prevail) deplorably ruinous unto the nation and their posterity therein. To this end some implore the aid of authority for the enacting of severe laws for the prohibition of it. This, according to the opinion of late ages, some suppose the most effectual means for the preservation of the truth; for if they can but destroy all that are otherwise minded, the rest of mankind will have the face of peace unto them who are advantaged thereby. Some write books in the confutation of the errors of it, and that to very good purpose. But in the meantime, if there be any thing of truth in reports, the work is as effectually progressive as if no opposition had been made unto it; and we may assure ourselves that these and such like means as these, if they are alone, will never keep Popery out of England, if it should ever have an advantage and opportunity for a return, nor prevent the entrance of any other false way in religion.

As for the use and severity of penal laws, I meddle not with it, as that which is to be referred to the wisdom of our governors. But I must needs say, it seems not to be unto the advantage of truth, or, at least, not unto the reputation of them by whom it is professed, that they should no otherwise be able to preserve its station amongst men. Neither can it be honourable unto any religion, that where it pretends unto all the advantages and rights of truth, and [is] in the real possession of all outward emoluments and supportments, yet that it cannot secure itself or maintain its profession without outward force and violence, things so remote from the first introduction and planting of truth in the world. But these things are not of our present consideration. [As] for the confutation of the errors, superstitions, and idolatrous practices of the church of Rome, in books of controversy, it is no doubt a work good, useful, and necessary in its kind; but when all is done, these things reach but a few, nor will many divert from other occasions to the serious consideration of them. Wherefore some other way must be fixed on and engaged in to secure the truth and interest of protestant religion among us; and this is no other but the effectual communication of the knowledge of it unto the minds, and the implantation of the power of it on the hearts of the people. This is that alone which will root out of them that enmity unto evangelical mysteries and spiritual things which betrays the souls of men into apostasy.

Unless men know what they are to value religion for, and what benefit they really receive by its profession, it is irrational to expect that they will be constant therein when a trial shall befall them. If once they come to say, "It is in vain thus to serve God," or, "What profit is it that we have kept his ordinances?" they will easily admit the yoke of any falsehood or superstition that pretends to gratify them with greater advantages. And at one time or other it will be no otherwise with them with whom this enmity is predominant.

But, on the other side, when God by the gospel "shines in the hearts of men, to give them the light of the knowledge of his glory in the face of Jesus Christ;" when they find their consciences set free thereby from the intolerable yokes of superstition and tradition; and that by the word of truth which they do profess they are begotten anew unto the hope of eternal life, their inward man being renewed and their lives reformed thereby; that their expectation of a blessed immortality is well founded on it and safely resolved into it, -- they will, through the effectual supplies of the Spirit of Christ, abide constant in the profession of it, whatever may befall them.

On these terms, on these experienced evidences of truth and goodness, was the gospel first entertained among men, and the reformation of religion first introduced into this nation; for although sundry other things concurred unto its reception and establishment, yet if the minds of multitudes had not received an experience of its power and efficacy unto the ends mentioned, it would never have been of any permanency among us. The mere outward form of true religion is not able to contend with that appearance which error and superstition will represent unto the minds of men, as knowing how much they stand in need thereof.

These things I know are by some despised. They suppose they have surer ways and better expedients for the preservation of the profession of the gospel amongst us than its own power and efficacy. What those ways are we need not conjecture, seeing themselves declare them continually; but they shall not be here spoken unto. But it is to be feared that they may be filled with the fruit of their own imaginations when those things shall fail them wherein they have placed their confidence. Wherefore, if there be a neglect about these things in the ministry and others whose duty it is to promote them, the issue will be sad, it may be beyond what is feared: for if the body of the people be suffered to live without any evidence of an acquaintance with the power of that truth which they do profess, or any demonstrative fruits of it in a holy conversation, we may cry out, "Popery, Popery," as long as we please; but when temptations, opportunities, and interests do concur, their profession will fall from them as dry leaves from a tree when they are moved with the wind. The apostle tells us that those who "went out from them were not of them, for if they had been of them they would have continued with them," 1 John ii. 19. They were among them by the profession of the truth, or they could not have gone out from them; -- but they were "not of them" in the participation of the power of the truth, and "communion thereby with the Father and the Son;" for if they had, "they would have continued with them," -- that is, steadfast in their profession.

This is that which ought to be fixed on the minds of all persons concerned, of all that are zealous for the truth of the protestant religion, or are obliged, what lies in them, to provide for its preservation. When things are come unto the appointed season, when they are issuing in that period which they have a natural tendency unto, all other expedients and devices will be of none effect. A diligent communication unto the body of the people, through the dispensation of the word, or preaching of it, of the power of the truth they profess in all its blessed effects, -- whereon they will have an experience and witness within themselves of the reasons why they ought to abide constantly in its profession, -- will alone secure the continuance of the gospel in succeeding generations. All other means will be ineffectual unto that end; and so far as without this they are or may be effectual, it will be of no advantage unto the souls of men.

That there is a danger at all times of a defection among professed Christians from the truth hath been before evinced. That this danger at present hath many especial circumstances rendering it dangerous in a peculiar manner is in like manner acknowledged by all such as call these things into serious consideration. And it will not, I presume, be denied but that every man, according as he is called and warranted by especial duty, is obliged to his utmost endeavours for the prevention of a revolt from the truth. The whole inquiry is, What is the best way, means, or expedient, to be plied unto this end? And this, I say, is only by the diligent ministerial dispensation of the word, with such an exemplary zeal and holiness in them by whom it is dispensed, and all other things requisite unto the discharge of that work, as may reconcile the hearts of the people unto evangelical truths, beget in them a delight in obedience, and implant the power of the word in their whole souls. Want hereof was that which lost the gospel in former ages, and will do so wherever it is, in this or those which are to come. And I shall not, in my own thoughts, blamably digress from my present subject, if I confirm this opinion with some few obvious considerations; for, --

1. It is the way, the only way, which God hath ordained, and which he blesseth to this end and purpose. None will pretend, as I suppose, that God hath appointed any other way to bring men unto the profession of the truth but by the preaching and dispensation of the word alone. When they are wrought upon or convinced thereby, so as to give up themselves unto the profession of it, it will be hard to find an ordinance of God of another kind for their preservation therein. When the apostle took his last farewell of them who were converted by his ministry at Ephesus, he "commended them to the word of God's grace, which," as he judged, "was able to build them up, and to give them an inheritance among all them which are sanctified," Acts xx. 32.

A man would think it were a more difficult work to convert men from Judaism or Paganism, or any false religion, unto the profession of the gospel, than to retain them in that profession when they are initiated thereinto: for in that first work there are all sorts of prejudices and difficulties to be conflicted withal, and not the least advantage from any acknowledged principles of truth; but as to the preservation of men in the profession of truth which they have received and owned, the work on many accounts seems to be more expedite and easy. If, therefore, the dispensation of the word, as it is God's ordinance unto that end, hath been a sufficient and effectual means for the former, what reason can be assigned that it should not be so for the latter also, without farther force or violence?

It will be said that the first preachers of the gospel were furnished with extraordinary gifts, whereby their ministry was rendered effectual unto the first conversion of the nations; but whereas now those gifts do cease, the efficacy of the ministry doth so also, and therefore stands in need of such outward assistance as the former did not. I say, for my part, I wish it all the assistance which those unto whom it is committed can desire, so that no force be offered to the consciences or persons of other men. But why shall we not think that the ordinary gifts of the ministry are as sufficient for the ordinary work of it as the extraordinary were for that which was extraordinary? To speak the truth, the difference lieth in persons in the discharge of their duty, and not in the things, gifts, or duties themselves. Were all those who are called, or profess themselves to be called, unto the preservation of the truth of the gospel in the work of the ministry, as conscientiously diligent in the discharge of their duty, as well fitted, according to the rules of the gospel, with those ordinary spiritual gifts which are necessary unto their work and calling, did as fully represent the design and nature of their message unto men in a holy conversation, as those first appointed unto the conversion of the nations were and did, according to their larger measures of grace and gifts, the work would have a proportionate success in their hands unto what it had in the beginning. But whilst those unto whom this charge is committed do neglect the use of this means, which is the ordinance of God unto this purpose, that the truths of the gospel be preserved amongst men; whilst either they judge that the principal end of their office is to capacitate them for secular advantages, and to give them outward rest therein, with the enjoyment of those things which unto the most in this world seem desirable; and therewithal think meet to betake themselves unto other expedients for the preservation of the truth, which God hath not appointed nor sanctified to that end, -- it is no wonder if faith and truth fail from amongst men.

The apostle Paul foresaw that a time would come wherein some men would "not endure sound doctrine, but after their own lusts would heap to themselves teachers, having itching ears," who should "turn them away from the truth, and turn them unto fables," 2 Tim. iv. 3, 4; and we may see what course he prescribeth for the prevention of this evil, that it might not proceed unto a general apostasy. It must also be observed that the advice he gives in this case, though originally directed unto one individual person, who was immediately concerned, yet it lies in charge on all that are or shall be called unto the rule of or ministry in the church. This course he proposeth, verses 1, 2, 5, of that chapter: "I charge thee before God, and the Lord Jesus Christ, who shall judge the quick and the dead at his appearing and his kingdom; preach the word; be instant in season, out of season; reprove, rebuke, exhort with all long-suffering and doctrine. Watch in all things, endure afflictions, do the work of an evangelist, make full proof of thy ministry." This is that course and way which he prescribeth for the preservation of the truth against the corruptions of men's minds and the craft of seducers; and the charge of this duty he giveth with so great a solemnity, and urgeth with so many motives emphatically expressed, as manifest of how great moment he conceived it to be.

Perhaps this way of the preservation of the truth and the salvation of the souls of men, by continual labouring in the word and doctrine, with an undergoing of all those difficulties which attend it, is not esteemed so advisable as formerly; for what good would men's lives or preferments do unto them if they should be obliged thus to labour in this sweaty kind of preaching? But if it be so, they must at one time or another be contented to part with the truth and all the advantages they have by the profession of it; for let men turn themselves which way they please, let them traverse their methods and multiply their counsels, to secure religion according to their apprehension, however they may hereby chain their idols, as the heathens did their gods of old to prevent their departure from them, and fix a profession of lies, the truth of the gospel, as unto any useful end of it, will be no otherwise preserved in a nation, church, or people, but by this means of God's appointment.

2. This is such a way and expedient for the preservation of the truth and the profession of the gospel as none can have the impudence to complain of or except against. There is in all places, among all sorts of persons, a pretence of zeal for the retaining of what they conceive to be the truth or right in religion. But the ways which, for the most part, they have chosen unto that purpose have been full of scandal unto Christian religion; so far from being rational means of preserving men in it as that they are effectual to deter them from it. Such is that outward force which hath been now tried in this nation, as elsewhere by all sorts of persons; and wise men may easily observe what it is arrived unto. In the meantime, it is openly evident that, let the end aimed at be never so good, the means used for the attaining of it are accompanied with much evil. What peace or satisfaction they have in themselves who are the prosecutors of this way I know not. It is above my understanding to apprehend that the minds of any Christians can be thoroughly at ease, rejoicing in God through Jesus Christ, whilst they cause others to be terrified, pursued, ruined, and destroyed, merely for that which is their faith and hope in Christ Jesus. But I know not the principles of the minds of other men, the make or constitution of their consciences, nor the rules of their walking before God, much

less their prevailing prejudices and interests, that influence them beyond all evidence of reason to the contrary; and therefore they may have a satisfactory peace in this way, though I understand not how. On the other side, those who are practised upon and forced to suffer in this course of proceeding are filled with alienation from them and their profession by whom they suffer. Hence it is known what mutual animosities, hatreds, contentions, severe reflections, and dreadful scandals, this way is attended withal. We see at this day what clamours and contests are raised about it, what pleas are managed against such procedures, how uncouth it is unto human nature to suffer all extremities for that which men are fully persuaded they deserve well in of mankind; nor can any man give assurance but that, at one time or other, the wheat shall be plucked up instead of tares.

But as to the way now proposed, of preserving the truth by the diligent, effectual dispensation of the word of the gospel unto the generality of the people, who can pretend a provocation by it or take offence at it? No mortal man will be prejudiced by it in any thing that he dares own a concernment in. The devil, indeed, will be enraged at it, not only as that which is designed unto the ruin of his interest and kingdom in the issue, but as that wherein he hath no share, nor can interpose his endeavours; for he is a spirit as restless and active as he is malicious, and loves not to be excluded out of any business that is on foot in the world. Wherefore, although he equally hates the truth in the management of all men, yet in the way of preserving of it before mentioned he can and doth so apparently immix himself and his effectual workings that he is very well satisfied with it; for what he may possibly lose on the one hand in point of truth, he gains ten times more on the other in the loss of love, peace, holiness, with all the fruits of goodness, meekness, and benignity, which ought to be among men. And let him have but his hand effectually in the promotion of this loss, and have the contrary fruits to feed upon, he is little concerned with the profession of truth in this or that way of worship amongst men. Be it, therefore, that he is or will be enraged at this way of preserving the truth, we know that the kingdom of Christ will be no otherwise maintained in the world but by a conquest of his rage; and for those who manage the same design with him, their wrath and envy, which they dare not manifest, will but torment and consume themselves.

3. Setting aside some few instances of violence and blood, consuming the persons of men, as among the Waldenses, Bohemians, and some others, which yet were never totally prevalent, and revolutions of government attended with the like cruelties, as in the days of Queen Mary in England, which was but of short continuance, no instance can be given of the defection of any church or nation from the truth but where there was a neglect of implanting the power of the gospel on the minds and hearts of men by those unto whom that charge was committed. This sinful neglect was that which constantly opened the door unto all apostasy. Wherefore on this foundation the weight of all useful profession of the gospel among us doth depend. And if God will be pleased to put it into the hearts of all them who are concerned in this duty to labour effectually therein, and to give unto the people an example of the power of the gospel in their own holy, humble, useful, fruitful conversation among them, and shall be pleased, moreover, to furnish them with the gifts of his Spirit, enabling them unto a successful discharge of their duty, evangelical truth would certainly receive an unconquerable establishment among us. And it may be it is not suited unto the exigence of this season that any of those who are called and enabled unto this work, being willing to engage their utmost in defence of the truth, especially in this way of its

preservation, by leavening the minds of men with a sense of its power and worth, should be prohibited the discharge of their duty. But the purposes of God in all things must stand, and himself be humbly adored, where "his judgments are unsearchable, and his ways past finding out."

Again: this innate and yet uncured enmity unto things spiritual and heavenly becomes a cause and means of apostasy from the truths of the gospel, by filling the hearts of men with a love of sin, and their lives with the fruits of it in wicked works; for men are "alienated and enemies in their mind," in or "by wicked works," Col. i. 21. The enmity which is in their minds doth operate and manifest itself in wicked works. And the alienation wherewith this enmity is accompanied is from the "life of God:" Eph. iv. 18, "Having the understanding darkened, being alienated from the life of God;" that is, from the spiritual, heavenly life of faith and holiness, which God requireth, and whereof he is the end and object. Of this life the truths of the gospel are the spring, rule, and measure. See Acts v. 20; Eph. iv. 20, 21. Wherefore, when men are "alienated from the life of God," and through the love of sin are given up unto wicked works, they cannot but secretly dislike and hate that truth, that spiritual and heavenly doctrine, which is the spring and rule of holiness, and whereby both the love of sin and the fruits of it in wicked works are everlastingly condemned. Let, then, men pretend and profess what they please, whilst this enmity is in them as a predominant principle of sin and wicked conversation, they are practically and really enemies unto the gospel itself; and where any persons are so, it is easily imaginable how ready and prone they will be to part with it on any occasion, for none will retain that in their minds which is useless to them, and troublesome unto their principal inclinations, any longer than they have a fair opportunity to part with it. That this frame of mind is an effectual obstruction unto the due receiving of the gospel, our Saviour expressly declares: John iii. 19, 20, "This is the condemnation, that light is come into the world, and men loved darkness rather than light, because their deeds were evil. For every one that doeth evil hateth the light, neither cometh to the light, lest his deeds should be reproved." Wherever the power of sin abideth, and men are engaged in the practice of it, so as that their deeds are evil, they will not receive the light of the gospel, -- that is, in its own nature and power, and for its proper ends; and when they are, by conviction or any other means, wrought unto a compliance with it, yet they do it but partially and hypocritically, nor can do it otherwise whilst their deeds are evil. So was it with them who are said to believe in Christ. Being some way convinced of the truth of his doctrine, yet would they not confess him, because "they loved the praise of men more than the praise of God," John xii. 42, 43. By the reigning power of this one sin of ambitious hypocrisy most of them were kept off from any assent unto the gospel; as our Saviour speaks unto them, "How can ye believe, which receive honour one of another, and seek not the honour that cometh from God only?" John v. 44. With the residue, who were not able wholly to withstand their convictions, it prevailed so far as that they should not receive it sincerely, but partially and hypocritically. Now, that which so effectually keeps the most from giving any admission at all unto the gospel, and which suffers none to receive it in a due manner, will easily prevail, where it abides in its power, unto a total relinquishment of it when occasion is offered.

Seeing, therefore, that all those whose deeds are evil, who through the enmity that is in their minds do give up themselves in their lives unto wicked works, are really alienated from the truths of the gospel, they are and will be ready at all times for a defection from them; for being kept under the dominion of sin, they have no real benefit by them, but rather find them inconsistent with their principal interests and chiefest joys.

Hence is that description which the apostle giveth of those who were evangelically converted unto God: Rom. vi. 17, 18, "God be thanked, that ye were the servants of sin, but ye have obeyed from the heart that form of doctrine which was delivered you. Being then made free from sin, ye became the servants of righteousness." There is no obedience from the heart unto the gospel, no possibility of being cast into the mould of the doctrine delivered in it, unless we be made free from the service of sin.

We may therefore, without scruple, fix [on] this as one principal means and cause of that apostasy from the truth of the gospel which hath been in the world, and which is yet deplorably progressive. Men who love sin and live in sin, whose works are wicked and whose deeds are evil, are all of them in their hearts alienated from the spiritual, holy doctrines of the gospel, and will undoubtedly, on any occasion of temptation or trial, fall away from the profession of them.

What reason have we to hope or judge that drunkards, swearers, unclean persons, covetous, proud, ambitious, boasters, vain, sensualists, and the like enemies of the cross of Christ, should adhere unto the truth with any constancy if a trial should befall them? "Look diligently," saith the apostle, "lest there be any fornicator, or profane person, as Esau, who for one morsel of meat sold his birthright," Heb. xii. 15, 16. Esau's birthright was his right unto and interest in the promise of the gospel made unto Abraham. This he, being a profane person, when he was pressed with a little hunger, parted withal for one morsel of meat. And if others, saith the apostle, are like him, profane persons, fornicators, or such as live in any course of sin, if a temptation befall them, and their lusts call to be satisfied, they will for morsels of bread, for the smallest earthly advantages, part with their interest in and profession of the gospel. So he tells us of them who, having put away a good conscience, did make shipwreck of the faith, 1 Tim. i. 19. After men have debauched their consciences by living in sin, they may for a while speed on their voyage with full sails of profession; but if a storm come, if a trial befall them, if they meet with a rock or shelf in their way, they quickly make shipwreck of the faith, and lose that, whatever else they labour to preserve.

What should secure such persons unto any constancy in profession for whilst they are in this condition, it is altogether indifferent unto them, as to their present or future advantage, what religion they are of, or whether they are of any at all or no. It is true, one way of religion may more harden them in sin, lay more prejudices against and hinderances of their conversion, than another; but no religion can do them good or yield them the least eternal advantage whilst they abide in that condition. It will be all one at the last day what religion wicked and ungodly sinners have been of, unless it be that the profession of the truth will prove an aggravation of their sins, Rom. ii. 11, 12.

Besides, when a temptation unto the relinquishment of the truth doth befall them, it hath nothing but a few traditional prejudices to contend withal. When they are taken off from them, and begin to search themselves for reasons why they should adhere unto the truth which they have outwardly professed, they quickly find in their own hearts a predominant dislike and hatred of that light and truth which they are solicited to part withal; for every man, as our Saviour testifieth, hateth the light whose deeds are evil.

This is that which abroad in the world hath lost the gospel so many princes, nobles, and great men, who for a while made profession of it. This is that which is of such dismal abode at this day as to the danger of a general apostasy. All sorts of persons do give up themselves unto the service of sin. The complaint of the prophet is not unsuited to our occasion, Isa. i. 4-6. Many are openly flagitious, beyond precedent or example among the heathen. Worldliness, pride, ambition, vanity, in all its variety of occasions and objects, with sensuality of life, have even overrun the world. And that which is of the most dreadful consideration is, that the sins of many are accompanied with the highest aggravation of all provocations, -- namely, that they proclaim them like Sodom, and hide them not, but glory in their shame. In all these things men do really, though not in words, proclaim that they are weary of the gospel, and are ready to leave it; some for any pretence of religion, some for none at all.

And this is the most dangerous posture that any place, church, or people can be found in; for whereas men are of themselves ready and prone unto a spiritual revolt and defection, when this ariseth from and is promoted by the love of sin and a life therein, God is ready also penally to give them up unto such delusions as shall turn them off from the gospel. So the apostle expresseth it, 2 Thess. ii. 10-12, "They received not the love of the truth, that they might be saved. And for this cause God shall send them strong delusion, that they should believe a lie: that they all might be damned who believed not the truth, but had pleasure in unrighteousness." Where men, under the profession of the truth, will continue profligate in sin, and take pleasure in unrighteousness, God will not always suffer the gospel to be prostituted to give them countenance in their wickedness, but will judicially give them up unto such delusions as shall flood them away into an open apostasy from it.

This was the great cause of that general and almost catholic apostasy that was in the world before the reformation. The body of the Christian people, by such means and on such occasions as shall be afterward declared, were grown worldly, sensual, wicked, and obstinate in sin. The complaints hereof are left on record in the writings of many in those days. And in vain it was for any to attempt to reduce them unto a conformity unto the gospel, especially considering that the most of their guides were no less infected than themselves. Chrysostom was almost the only person, at least he was the most eminent, who set himself in his ministry to stem, if it were possible, the rising tide of impiety and wickedness among all sorts of persons; but instead of any success, his holy endeavours ended in his own banishment and death. All degrees and orders of men undertook the patronage of public sinning against him, and to his ruin. Wherefore there remained but two ways of dealing with the generality of men in such a condition. The one was, according to the advice of the apostle, to "turn away" or withdraw from them, 2 Tim. iii. 5, so leaving them out of the communion of the church; the other was, to accommodate religion unto their temper and lusts, whereby a face and appearance of Christianity might be preserved among them. And the generality of their leaders preferring their interest before their duty, the latter way was chosen and gradually promoted.

Hence were opinions and practices invented, advanced, and taken into religion, that might accommodate men in their lusts, or give countenance and pretended relief unto them who were resolved to live in their sins. Such were auricular confession, penances, absolutions, commutations of all sorts, missatical sacrifices for the living and the dead, the church's treasury of merit and power of pardon, suffrage and help of saints, especially purgatory, with all its appendages.

Hereby was the apostasy completed; for men being grown carnal and wicked, there appeared no way to keep them up unto the profession of the gospel but by corrupting the whole doctrine and worship of it, that their lusts might be some way accommodated. To this end external things were substituted in the room of things internal, having the same names given unto them; ecclesiastical things in the room of things spiritual; outward offices, orders, and multiplied sacraments, with their efficacy by virtue of the work wrought, in the place of real conversion unto God, purity of heart, with strict universal holiness; disciplines and corporeal severities in the room of evangelical repentance and mortification; -- nor could the lusts of men have possibly a higher accommodation, whilst any pretence of religion was necessary to be preserved. So formerly did wickedness of life lead the way unto apostasy from the truth. And the whole of the papal apostasy may be reduced unto these two heads:-- First, An accommodation of the doctrine and worship of the gospel unto the carnal minds and lusts of men, with the state of their consciences that ensued thereon; and, secondly, The accommodation of the lusts, ignorance, and superstition of men unto the interests and worldly advantage of the pope and his clergy.

And herein lieth the danger of this age. The great design of the generality of men is, to live in sin with as little trouble at present, and as little fear of what is future, as they can arrive unto. And there are but two ways whereby such a posture of mind may be attempted.

The one is by obliterating all notions of good and evil, all sense of future rewards and punishments, or of God's government in the world. This some in all ages have endeavoured: for "the fool hath said in his heart, There is no God;" and thereon are "they corrupt, and do abominable works," Ps. xiv. 1. And no age could ever give more instances of this affected atheism than that wherein we live. Neither do any deceive themselves into it, but merely with this design, to live in sin without control from themselves; which is the last restraint they can acquit themselves of. And some of them do please themselves with the attainment of them in the psalmist: "The wicked, through the pride of his countenance, will not seek after God: God is not in all his thoughts," Ps. x. 4. But God hath inlaid the minds of men, antecedently unto all actings of their wills and affections, with such a tenacious and unanswerable witness to the contrary, that it is very difficult for any to bring themselves unto any tolerable satisfaction this way: for "that which may be known of God is manifest in themselves," whether they will or no, Rom. i. 19; neither can they free themselves from prevailing apprehensions that it is "the judgment of God, that they who commit sin are worthy of death," verse 32. Wherefore we have not many instances of men who pretend a senselessness of these things out of principle, or that find no disquietment on the account of sin. And by the most of them this is but pretended. Their outward boasting is but a sorry plaster for their inward fears and vexations; nor will the pretended security of such impious persons endure the shock of the least of those surprisals, calamities, and dangers, which human nature is obnoxious unto in this life, much less of death itself. The end therefore mentioned, be it never so earnestly desired, is not this way to be attained.

Another way, therefore, must be found out unto the same end, and this must be by a religion. Nothing but religion can convert men from sin, and nothing but religion can secure them therein. To this purpose is that of our apostle: "In the last days perilous times shall come. For men shall be lovers of their own selves, covetous, boasters, proud, blasphemers, disobedient to parents, unthankful, unholy, without natural affection, truce-breakers, false accusers, incontinent, fierce, despisers of those that are good, traitors, heady, high-minded, lovers of pleasures more than lovers of God; having a form of godliness, but denying the power thereof," 2 Tim. iii. 1-5. Had they the power of religion in them, they could not give themselves up unto the pursuit of such brutish lusts; and had they not some form or other of it, they could not be secure in their practice: for, --

Sin and conscience are stubborn in their conflict whilst immediately opposed, conscience pleading that there should be no sin, and sin contending that there may be no conscience; but, as nature is corrupted, they will both comply with an accommodation. Wherefore a device to satisfy sin and to deceive conscience will not fail of a ready entertainment; and this is the design in part or in whole of every false way in religion that men apostatize unto from the purity and simplicity of the gospel. See 2 Peter ii. 18, 19. One way or other is proposed to take men off from the necessity of regeneration and the renovation of their nature into the image of God, in the first place; for this is that lion in the way which deters all sorts of sluggards from attempting any thing seriously in religion. And whereas our Lord Jesus Christ hath placed the necessity of it at the first entrance into the kingdom of God, there is no false way of religion but its first design is to destroy its nature or take away its necessity. Hence some would have it to be only baptism, with the grace it confers by the work wrought; some substitute a moral reformation of life in the room of it, which, as they suppose, is sufficiently severe; and the light within makes all thoughts of it useless; -- for if this point be not well secured, all ensuing attempts to accommodate men with a religion will be in vain; it will still be returning on them, that "except they be born again, they cannot enter into the kingdom of God." Internal sanctification of the whole person, the mortification of all the motions of sin that are in the flesh, with that universal obedience which is required unto the life of God, must also be provided for or against, and yet conscience be satisfied therewithal. Wherefore, if you can obtain that persons who live in sin, and are resolved so to do, not troubling themselves about these things, shall suppose that they may be secured eternally in such a way of religion as you propose unto them, -- that what is wanting in themselves shall be done for them by absolutions and masses, and various supplies out of the church's treasury, with the great reserve of purgatory when things come to the worst, -- there is no great fear (especially if some other circumstances fall in also to promote the design) but that you will find them very ductile and pliable unto your desires. Add hereunto, that the ways whereby any may be interested in these efficacious means of eternal salvation, -- namely, by confession, penances, and alms, -- are possible, yea, easy to persons who never intend to leave their sins. Of this sort are the most of those visibly who every day fall off to the Roman church. And it were to be desired that the wickedness of men did not give grounds of fearing additions to their number; for if there be no assurance of the constancy of men in the profession of the truth, unless their souls and lives are transformed into the image of it (as there is not), certainly those ways wherein men are furiously engaged in the pursuit of their lusts must needs be perilous, and may, without the especial help of divine grace, bring forth a fatal defection.

Footnotes:

6. See the treatise on Indwelling Sin, vol. vi. -- Ed.

Chapter V – Darkness and ignorance another cause of apostasy

II. The second spring or cause of defection from the gospel in any kind, is that spiritual darkness and ignorance which abides in the minds of men under the profession of the truth.

The gospel may fall under a double consideration: First, Of the things themselves that are contained, revealed, and proposed therein; -- these are the material objects of our faith. Secondly, With respect unto the doctrinal way of their declaration. With respect unto the first, there is a spiritual darkness on the minds of all men by nature, so as that they cannot discern them in their own native form and beauty. With respect unto the latter, men are said to be ignorant, namely, when they do not in a due manner understand and comprehend the doctrines of the gospel, and so perish for want of knowledge. These things being of a distinct consideration, and of different influence into this pernicious event, the first shall be first spoken unto.

1. That there is such a spiritual darkness on the minds of men by nature, and wherein their depravation by sin cloth principally consist, is fully testified in the Scripture, as I have at large elsewhere evinced. [7] Hence all men grant, so far as I know, that there is need of spiritual illumination to enable us to discern spiritual things in a due manner, though all are not agreed in the nature and causes of that illumination. But to deny the thing itself is to deny the gospel, and to make the promises of God of none effect. Now, where illumination is needful, there darkness is to be removed; for the end of the bringing in of light is to dispel darkness. Wherefore, such a depravation of the minds of men in spiritual darkness must be acknowledged, or the gift and grace of God in illumination must be rejected; and they by whom it is done do by their own blindness give new evidence unto the truth which they do oppose, there being no more certain demonstration of the power of darkness in any than for them to affirm that they stand in no need of light to be communicated unto them by the effectual operation of the Spirit of God. As to the nature of this illumination I shall not here dispute, but take it at present for granted that it is an act of His power who of old "commanded light to shine out of darkness, shining in our hearts, to give us the knowledge of his glory in the face of Jesus Christ," 2 Cor. iv. 6.

There is a glory and beauty in those spiritual things which are the subjects of the truths of the gospel. There is in them the wisdom of God, "the wisdom of God in a mystery," 1 Cor. ii. 6, 7, yea, "the manifold wisdom of God," Eph. iii. 10; the glory of the Lord, which is represented unto believers in the glass of the gospel, 2 Cor. iii. 18, or "the glory of God in the face of Jesus Christ," chap. iv. 6; -- things expressly beyond discovery by the use of any means whatever merely natural, 1 Cor. ii. 9, 10. Even the philosophers of old contended that there was a beauty in all truth, which would engage the minds and affections of men unto it were they able to discern it; and if they saw and granted this in things natural and moral, which are earthly and exposed unto the common reason of mankind, how much more must it be granted of the truth of things heavenly, spiritual, and divine! See John iii. 12. In brief, whatever there is of divine glory or excellency in the divine nature itself, in any or all of its holy properties, in the great and most glorious effect of them in the person and grace of Christ, in the renovation of our nature into the image of God, in the divine life of faith and obedience, it is proposed unto us in the truths of the gospel.

2. Whatever doctrinal proposition may be made of these things unto the minds of men, yet the things themselves cannot be comprehended nor spiritually discerned without the illumination of the Holy Ghost before mentioned. Hence it follows that men may be instructed in the doctrines of truth, yet, continuing under the power of natural darkness, not discern the things themselves in their own spiritual nature and glory, nor have any experience of their power and efficacy. This all the prayers of holy men in the Scripture for spiritual light and instruction, all the promises of God savingly to enlighten the minds of men, and the descriptions given of that work of his grace whereby he doth effect it, do undeniably evince. One consideration will be sufficient unto our purpose. Whosoever hath a spiritual view and knowledge of these things, his mind will be, and is, certainly changed and transformed into the image of them. So the apostle tells us expressly, 2 Cor. iii. 18, "We all, with open face beholding as in a glass the glory of the Lord, are changed into the same image." They are cast into the same mould with the doctrine whereunto they are given up, Rom. vi. 17. The mind is united unto the things so discerned, and the image of them is so brought forth therein as that there is an exact conformity between them. But we see by open and palpable experience, that notwithstanding the knowledge which many have of spiritual things, their minds continue carnal and fleshly, filled with corrupt and depraved affections, and are no way changed into the image or likeness of the things themselves. There needs no farther demonstration that men have never had a spiritual view of or insight into the glory of gospel truths, be their doctrinal knowledge of them what it will, than this, that their minds are not renewed thereby, nor transformed into the likeness of them.

Where it is thus with men, they have no stable grounds whereon to abide in the profession of the truth against temptation, opposition, or seduction; for their steadfastness must be an effect of such an assurance in their minds of the truth of the things which they do believe, as will be prevalent against all that force and artifice wherewith they may be assaulted, and such as will not suffer their own minds to be indifferent, careless, or negligent about them. But whence should this arise? Assurance from outward natural sense in spiritual things we are not capable of, nor are they evidenced unto our minds by rational demonstration All the full persuasion or assurance we can have of them, which will be prevalent against temptations and oppositions, ariseth from such a spiritual view of them as gives an experience of their reality, power, and efficacy upon our minds: and this respects both the renovation of the mind itself in light and faith; the adhesion of the will unto the things known and believed, with a holy, heavenly, unconquerable love; and the constant approbation of the good, acceptable, and perfect will of God in all things. Hence this assurance, though it be neither that of sense nor that of reason, yet in the Scripture is compared with them and preferred above them, as that which giveth the mind a more certain satisfaction than they can do, although it be of another kind. And without this it is impossible that men should attain any such evidence or full persuasion of that evangelical truth which they may profess, as to secure them in their profession in such a juncture of circumstances and occasions as they may fall into.

Here, therefore, I place another means and cause of apostasy from the truth of the gospel after it hath been received and professed. Multitudes in all ages have been instructed in the truth, some have been learned and knowing in the doctrines of it; but whereas, by reason of their darkness, as being destitute of spiritual illumination, they did not discern the things themselves which they assented unto, in their supernatural, heavenly nature and glory, and therefore had no experience of their proper power and efficacy on their own minds, affections, and lives, they could not have any such evidence of their truth as would upon trials confirm their adherence unto them or secure them from apostasy.

Had the minds of men been transformed in their renovation to "prove what is the good, and acceptable, and perfect will of God," -- had they by beholding of spiritual things "been changed into the same image from glory to glory, by the Spirit of the Lord," -- they would not have abandoned the most important doctrines of the gospel, as we know them to have done, nor have embraced foolish imaginations in their stead, on every plausible courtship and address unto their fancies How came men under the papal apostasy gradually to desert the principal truths of the gospel and all the spiritual glory of its worship? Not discerning the internal glory and beauty of things evangelical and purely divine, not having an experience of the power of them in and upon their own minds, they chose to comply with, and give admission unto, such things whose outward painted beauty they could discern, and whose effects on their natural and carnal affections they had experience of.

We have seen, in all ages, men learned and skilled in the doctrines of the truth, so as that they might have been looked on as pillars of it, yet to have been as forward as any unto apostasy from it when they have been tried; yea, such have been the leaders of others thereinto. So many of this sort fell into Arianism and Pelagianism of old, as some have done into Socinianism, and many into Popery in our days When such fall away, usually they overthrow the faith of some, and shake the confidence of others.

But the apostle gives a double relief against this temptation:-- first, The stability of God's purpose in the preservation of the elect; and, secondly, The means of preservation in holiness of them that believe, 2 Tim. ii. 19. And we may be assured concerning them all, that they never had that intuition into nor comprehension of spiritual things which alone could secure their stability. They never saw so much or that in them for which they should be preferred above all other things. No man who forsakes the truth ever saw the glory of it, or had experience of its power. "They went out from us, but they were not of us," saith the apostle of such persons; "for if they had been of us" (whose fellowship is with the Father, and with his Son Jesus Christ), "they would no doubt have continued with us: but they went out, that they might be made manifest that they were not all of us," 1 John ii. 19.

Thus when the apostle had described the woeful apostasy of some among the Hebrews, he adds concerning them whose preservation he believed, "But, beloved, we are persuaded better things of you, and things that accompany salvation," Heb. vi. 9. Whatever knowledge men may have of the doctrines of the gospel, and whatever profession they may make, unless they have withal those things which are inseparable from salvation, such as is the saving illumination of the Holy Ghost, whereby the darkness of our minds is removed, there can be no assurance that they will always "quit themselves like men," and "stand fast in the faith." And this consideration doth not a little evidence the danger of a defection from the truth which attends the days wherein we live.

For, first, it is from hence that we have such a numerous generation of sceptics in religion among us, -- a sort of men who pretend not to renounce or forsake the truth, only they will talk and dispute about it with the greatest indifferency as to what is true or false. The Scripture, the holy Trinity, the person of Christ, his offices, the nature of justification and grace, whether it be or be not, this or that church, all or any in the world, as to their profession and worship, are weighed in the defiled, tottering scales of bold, irreverent discourses. For some reasons known to themselves, this sort of persons will own the public profession of religion, perhaps be teachers in it. But on all occasions they fully manifest that they are utterly ignorant of the fundamental difference between truth and error, and so give no firm assent unto what they do profess; for this difference lieth in their glory and beauty in themselves, and in their power and efficacy towards us. Spiritual, heavenly truth, by its relation unto the being, infinite wisdom, goodness, love, and grace of God, by the characters of all these things impressed on it and represented by it, is glorious, amiable, and desirable; -- all error, as an effect of darkness, and by its relation unto Satan as the head of the apostasy which drew off our minds from the original essential Truth, is distorted, deformed, and brings the mind into confusion. Truth is powerful and effectual to conform the soul unto God, and to principle it with a love of and power unto obedience; -- error turns the mind aside into crooked and by paths of folly or superstition, or pride and self-advancement. Were men practically acquainted with this difference between truth and error, it would take away that indifferency in their minds unto them which this sceptical humour doth discover. Truth so known in its nature and efficacy will beget that reverence, that love, that sacred esteem of itself, in the souls of men, as they shall not dare to prostitute it to be bandied up and down with every foolish imagination. And from this sort of men, who are commonly the most bold and forward in undertaking the conduct of others, by a pretended generous contempt of their narrow principles, groundless scruples, and pusillanimous fears, nothing is to be expected but a wise and safe compliance with any ways or means of apostasy from the truth which shall be advantageously presented unto them.

And by the means of this darkness, it is easy to conceive how uncertain and unstable the minds of the generality of men, who perhaps also are somewhat ignorant (whereof we shall treat afterward), must needs be in their assent unto the truth and the profession of it, They are no way able to discover it in such a way or manner as to give them an assurance which will be infallibly victorious against temptations and oppositions; nor can they have that holy love unto it which will secure their minds and affections from being enticed and ravished from it. But, all the difference between truth and error which they can discern lying in bare different notions and apprehensions, wherein also they are dark and unskilled, it is no wonder if at any time they make an easy transcursion from the one to the other. So did the body of the people lose the truth gradually under the papal defection without any great complaint, yea, with much complacency and satisfaction; and it is to be feared that multitudes are ready at once to steer the same course if occasion be offered unto them.

From this consideration we may rectify the seeming solecism that is in the profession of religion, or the professors of it. Truth in every kind is the only guide of the mind in all its actings; wherein it proceeds not according unto it, it is always out of the way. Divine truth is the sole conduct of the mind in all its actings towards God; it is the only fountain, immediate cause, and rule of all our obedience. But yet, whereas in other things men generally walk in the light of those sparks of truth which they have received, we see that many by whom divine truth is owned and professed in its greatest purity and highest discovery are ofttimes no less wicked and vicious in their lives, no less enemies unto holiness, no less barren and unfruitful in those good and useful works it guides and directs unto, than those who, having the greatest aversion from it, are, under the conduct of other principles, erroneous and superstitious. Thus the lives of the common sort of Protestants are no better than those of the Papists, nor are theirs to be compared with those of some of the Mohammedans; yea, by the power of false and superstitious apprehensions imposed on their minds and consciences, some are carried out unto greater and more frequent acts of bounty and charity, of the mortification of the flesh, the denial of its sensual appetites and satisfactions, than are to be found among the most who profess themselves to be under the conduct and rule of truth. Hence no profession of religion, be it never so corrupt or foolish, is advanced amongst us, but instantly (at least for a season, and while it is new) it pretends an advantage as unto life and conversation against the truth, measured by the lives of its common professors; yea, this is made the principal motive and argument to prevail with honest and well-meaning people unto a compliance with the profession of their way, because of the effects which (as it is pretended) it produceth in their lives and conversations above those which profess the truth. And how prevalent this pretence hath been among us is known unto all.

Wherefore, I say, we cannot allow that the lives of the common sort of professors should be esteemed a just and due representation of the doctrine which they do profess. It is true, that where it is not so men will have no benefit by their profession, nor will they be steadfast in it when a trial shall befall them. Where the mind is internally and really conformed unto the truth, there the actions of the life may be allowed to represent sincerely, though not perfectly, the truths which are believed; and he is no firm Christian in any kind, he is brought into no spiritual order, whose mind doth not receive by the Spirit of Christ the transforming influence of evangelical truth, and who exerts not the power of it in a holy conversation, so as that he is not unwilling that what he believeth may be impartially judged by what he liveth, as to sincerity, though not as to perfection. But if we should allow the lives of men in general to be a rule whereby judgment might be safely passed in these things, it cannot be denied but that sometimes, and in some ages and places, error would, at least for a season, carry it in glory and reputation from the truth, yea, the light of nature from grace, tradition from the Scripture, and the Alcoran from the Gospel.

But we have sufficient ground of exceptions unto this interpretation and exposition of the doctrine of our Lord Jesus Christ, and that without the least apology for the ungodly lives of its professors. Among these, that now insisted on is of the first rank and evidence. Multitudes of those who profess the truth never had a view of its spiritual glory because of the darkness of their minds, and therefore have no experience of its power and efficacy, nor are their hearts and lives influenced or guided by it; for the gospel will not have its effects on the minds of men unless it first communicates unto them those internal spiritual principles which are necessary unto all the operations that it doth require. Put this new wine into old bottles and all is lost, both bottles and wine also. The doctrine of the gospel, taken notionally into the old, unrenewed, corrupt minds of men, is utterly lost as unto all the proper ends of it. And wherever there is a reformation of life, with any diligent attendance unto duties moral or religious, wrought in persons by the light and dispensation of the gospel, they are the immediate effects of those doctrines which it hath in common with the light of nature and the law in its power, and not of those which are peculiarly its own. And this they seem to understand well enough who, finding, either in their own experience, or from the observation they have made of others, how ineffectual the truth of gospel mysteries is towards the minds of carnal men, have upon the matter abandoned the preaching of it, and have taken up only with those principles which are suited unto the light of nature and convictions of the law.

The holiness which the gospel requireth is the transforming of our whole souls into the image and likeness of God, with the actings of renewed nature in a universal approbation of his "good, and acceptable, and perfect will," Rom. xii. 2. But this will not be effected unless we can "behold the glory of the Lord" in it, whereby alone we may be "changed into the same image from glory to glory," 2 Cor. iii. 18. Nor can we so behold that glory unless he "who commanded the light to shine out of darkness do shine in our hearts to give us the knowledge of it," chap. iv. 6. Hence is the doctrine of it ineffectual in the hearts and upon the lives of many by whom its truth is openly professed.

It is otherwise with every false religion. The motives which they make use of, and the instruments they apply, unto the hearts of men, to effect the reformation of their lives, and to engage them unto such works and duties as they require, are all of them suited either unto their natural light, or unto their superstitions, fears, desires, pride, and other depraved affections. Those of the first sort, -- namely, such as are suited unto natural light, -- are common, in some degree or measure, unto all religion whatever, be it on other accounts true or false. Every thing that is called religion pretends at least unto the improvement of natural light, as did the philosophers among the heathen of old. It urgeth also the law so far as it is made known unto them, though by other presumptions and prejudices some do abate and take off from its force and efficacy, making void the commandments of God through their own traditions. Whatever change is wrought or effected on the minds and lives of men by virtue of these principles, and motives taken from them, doth not belong unto any one way in religion more than another; nor is it to be accounted unto the glory or advantage of any of them. In these things Mohammedanism and all false ways in Christianity have an equal share and interest, unless where, by some corrupt opinions of their own, men deprave the light of nature and the rule of the law itself.

Some finding, as they say, more of justice, temperance, veracity, righteousness in dealings, with common usefulness unto mankind, among Turks and Banians, [8] than among the common sort of Christians, do foolishly begin to think that their religion is better than Christianity. But as this scandal will be surely required at the hands of them who give it by their flagitious lives, so it is foolishly and wickedly taken by others; for those truths and laws which produce these effects in them are common unto all religions, and are equally suited unto the light and reason of all mankind, and have more evidence and efficacy communicated unto them by the gospel than by any other kind of religion whatever. And so it is with them among ourselves who would plead an advantage unto their profession by the effects of it in their lives as to a moral conversation, when they can pretend unto no real motive thereunto, -- namely, unto what is good and useful, and not mere affectation and hypocrisy, -- but what is owned and pressed in the doctrine of the gospel which we adhere unto. The differences, therefore, that are in this kind are not from the doctrines men profess, but they arise from the persons themselves who embrace them, with their various lusts, inclinations, and temptations.

It is evident, therefore, that whatever there is of moral good, duty, or usefulness among men in any false way of religion, it all proceeds from those principles and is the effect of those motives which are owned and improved in that which is true; and it may be easily evinced that they are more cultivated and cleared, have more evidence, life, light, and power given them, by the truths of the gospel, than by any other means or way whatever. And where they have not an equal effect upon those who profess that truth which they have on some by whom it is deserted, it is from the power of their own cursed lusts and carnal security. The difference on the part of religion itself consists in what is superadded unto these general principles by any notions of it. Now this, in every false religion, is what is suited unto the natural principles of men's minds, their innate pride, vanity, curiosity, superstition, irregular hopes and fears. Such among the Romanists are the doctrines of merit, of outward disciplines, of satisfactions for sin, of confession, penances, of purgatory, and the like. They were all of them found out to put some awe on the minds, and to have some influence on the lives of men, who had lost all sense of the principles and motives of gospel obedience, though some considerable respect was had unto the benefit and advantage of them by whom they were invented; for why should men labour and beat their brains merely for others, without some income and revenue of advantage unto themselves? And it is no wonder if they produce in many, as they have done, great appearing acts of devotion, many outward works of bounty and charity, yea, in some, real austerities of life and renunciations of the pleasures of the world. I doubt not but that the sensual, wicked paradise of Mohammed doth effectually prevail in the minds of many of his followers unto that kind of virtuous and devout life which they suppose may bring them unto its enjoyment.

The inquiry, then, on the whole matter is, wherefore the truths of the gospel do not produce, in all by whom they are professed, effects as much more excellent than those mentioned as truth is more excellent than error, heavenly light than superstition, faith than frightful apprehensions of feigned torments, true peace and tranquility of mind than outward reputation and glory. And the principal reason hereof is, because such persons as are barren in the knowledge of our Lord and Saviour Jesus Christ do not discern those troths in their spiritual nature, nor can therefore take in the power and efficacy of them on their souls.

There is a holiness, obedience, and fruitfulness in good works, wrought, preserved, and maintained by the truth of the gospel, in them who are truly regenerated and sanctified thereby, who receive the proper efficacy of it on their minds and souls, which differ in the whole kind and nature from any thing which the principles and motives before mentioned, which have their efficacy from their suitableness unto the depraved affections of men's minds, can produce; and this alone is acceptable with God. But it must be granted, that where men are ignorant of the power mad unacquainted with the internal efficacy of the gospel, their lives under the profession of the truth may be as bad, and it is a great wonder they are not worse than those of the Papists, of the most erroneous persons, or even of the Mohammedans themselves: for they have many superstitious imaginations and false principles that are suited to put some outward restraint upon their lusts, and to press them unto actions praiseworthy in themselves; but these being no way influenced by such apprehensions, and being not under the power of gospel truth, it is a wonder, I say, if they exceed them not in all manner of wicked conversation. It is not merely the outward profession of the truth, but the inward power of it, that is useful either unto the world or the souls of men.

And hence it is that the preaching of any person which principally dwelleth on and argueth from the things which the light of nature can of itself reach unto, and the convictions which are by the law, is better accepted with, and appears more useful unto, multitudes of common professors, than the declaration of the mysteries of the gospel is: for such things are suited unto the natural conceptions of men and the working of their own reason, which gives them a sense of what efficacy they have; but being in the dark unto the mysteries of the gospel, they neither see their excellency nor experience their power. Nevertheless, they and they only are the true spring, cause, and rule of all acceptable obedience, even "the power of God unto salvation to every one that believeth." From the whole it appears how prone such persons must be unto an apostasy from the truth who have no spiritual light to discern its glory nor to let in the power of it upon their souls.

If, then, we would be established in the truth, if we would stand fast in the faith, if we would be preserved from the danger of that defection from the gospel which the world is prone, disposed, and inclined unto, it must be our principal endeavour to have a spiritual acquaintance with the things themselves that are declared in the doctrine of truth which we do profess, and to have an experience of their efficacy upon our own souls. Mere notions of truth, or the knowledge of the doctrines of it, enabling us to talk of them or dispute for them, will not preserve us. And although this spiritual light be the grace, promise, and gift of God, yet is it that which we are to endeavour after in a way of duty; and the directions ensuing may contribute somewhat towards the right discharge of our duty herein:--

1. Pray earnestly for the Spirit of truth go lead us into all truth. For this end is he promised by our Saviour unto his disciples; and there are no teachings like his. If we learn and receive the truths of the gospel merely in the power and ability of our natural faculties, as we do other things, we shall not abide constant unto them in spiritual trials. What we learn of ourselves in spiritual things, we receive only in the outward form of it; what we are taught by the Spirit of God, we receive in its power. The apostle grants that "the spirit of man," his mind, reason, and understanding, is able to conceive of and apprehend "the things of a man," things merely natural, civil, or moral, which are cognate unto human nature; but saith he, "The things of God," the mystery of his wisdom, love, and grace in Christ Jesus, "knoweth no man, but the Spirit of God," and by him are they revealed unto them that do believe, 1 Cor. ii. 9-12. Without his especial aid, men may, by their natural sagacity and industry, attain an acquaintance with the doctrines of truth, so as to handle them (like the schoolmen) with incredible subtilty and curiosity; but they may be far enough for all that from an establishing knowledge of spiritual things. That horrible neglect which is among Christians of this one duty of earnest prayer for the teaching of the Spirit of Christ, that scorn which is cast upon it by some, and that self-confidence in opposition unto it which prevails in the most, sufficiently manifest of what nature is their knowledge of the truth, and what is like to become of it when a trial shall befall them. The least spark of saving knowledge inlaid in the minds of the poorest believers, by the gracious operation of the Holy Ghost, will be more effectual unto their own sanctification, and more prevalent against oppositions, than the highest notions or most subtle reasonings that men have attained in leaning unto their own understanding. Wherefore the Scripture abounds in examples, instances, and directions for prayer, unto this end, that we

may have the assistance of the Holy Spirit in learning of the truth of the mysteries of the gospel, without which we cannot do so in a due manner: Eph. i. 16-20, "Making mention of you in my prayers; that the God of our Lord Jesus Christ, the Father of glory, may give unto you the Spirit of wisdom and revelation in the knowledge of him: the eyes of your understanding being enlightened; that ye may know what is the hope of his calling, and what the riches of the glory of his inheritance in the saints, and what is the exceeding greatness of his power to usward who believe, according to the working of his mighty power, which he wrought in Christ, when he raised him from the dead, and set him at his own right hand in the heavenly places." Chap. iii. 14-19, "For this cause I bow my knees unto the Father of our Lord Jesus Christ, of whom the whole family in heaven and earth is named, that he would grant you, according to the riches of his glory, to be strengthened with might by his Spirit in the inner man; that Christ may dwell in your hearts by faith; that ye, being rooted and grounded in love, may be able to comprehend with all saints what is the breadth, and length, and depth, and height; and to know the love of Christ, which passeth knowledge, that ye might be filled with all the fulness of God." Col. ii. 1-3, "I would that ye knew what great conflict I have for you, and for them at Laodicea, and for as many as have not seen my face in the flesh; that their hearts might be comforted, being knit together in love, and unto all riches of the full assurance of understanding, to the acknowledgment of the mystery of God, and of the Father, and of Christ; in whom are hid all the treasures of wisdom and knowledge."

2. Rest not in any notions of truth, unless you find that you have learned it as it is in Jesus What it is to learn the truth as it is in Jesus, the apostle fully declares, Eph. iv. 20-25, "But ye have not so learned Christ; if so be that ye have heard him, and have been taught by him, as the truth is in Jesus: that ye put off concerning the former conversation the old man, which is corrupt according to the deceitful lusts; and be renewed in the spirit of your mind; and that ye put on the new man, which after God is created in righteousness and true holiness." This it is to learn the truth as it is in Jesus, -- namely, together with the knowledge of it, to have an experience of its power and efficacy in the mortification of sin, in the renovation of our nature, and transforming of the whole soul into the image of God in righteousness and the holiness of truth. When men learn that they may know, and are satisfied with what they know, without an endeavour to find the life and power of what they know in their own hearts, their knowledge is of little use, and their assent unto the truth will have no stability accompanying of it. The immediate end (with respect unto us) of the whole revelation of the mind and will of God in the Scripture is, that it may put forth a spiritual, practical power in our souls, and that we may do the things which are so revealed unto us. Where this is neglected, where men content themselves with a bare speculation of spiritual truths, they do what lies in them to frustrate the end, and "reject the counsel of God" in them. If, therefore, we would know any evangelical truths in a due manner, if we would have that evidence and assurance of them in our minds which may secure our profession against temptations and oppositions, let us not rest in any apprehensions of truth whose efficacy we have no experience of in our hearts, nor think that we know any more of the mysteries of the gospel than we find effectually working in the renovation of our minds, and the transforming of our souls into the image of the glory of God in Christ.

3. Learn to esteem more of a little knowledge which discovers itself in its effects to be sanctifying and saving, than of the highest attainments in notions and speculations, though gilded and set off by the reputation of skill, subtilty,

eloquence, wit, and learning, which do not evidence themselves by alike operations. We are fallen into days wherein men of all sorts, sects, and parties, are vying for the reputation of skill, ability, knowledge, subtilty, and cunning in disputes about religion. And few there are who are cast under such disadvantages by apparent want of learning, but that they hope to make it up one way or other, so as to think as well of their own knowledge and abilities as of other men's. He who hath learned to be meek, humble, lowly, patient, self-denying, holy, zealous, peaceable, to purify his heart, and to be useful in his life, is indeed the person who is best acquainted with evangelical truth. Wherefore, let this knowledge be esteemed, both in ourselves and others, above all that proud, presumptuous, notional, puffing knowledge, which sets up for so great a reputation in the world, and we shall have experience of a blessed success in our pursuit of it.

4. Be not satisfied without a discovery of such a goodness, excellency, and beauty in spiritual things, as may attract your hearts unto them, and cause you to cleave unto them with unconquerable love and delight. This is that necessary, inseparable adjunct, property, fruit, or effect of faith, without which it is not essentially differenced from the faith of devils. That knowledge, that perception and understanding of the truth, which doth not present the things known, believed, perceived, as lovely, excellent, and desirable unto the will and affections, is a "cloud without water," which every wind of temptation will scatter and blow away. Do not, therefore, suppose that you have learned any thing of God in Christ, of the mystery of his grace, of his acceptable and perfect will, unless you see therein such evidence of infinite wisdom, goodness, holiness, love, in all things so suited unto the eternal glory of God and advantage of your own souls, in the uttermost rest, peace, and satisfaction that they are capable of, as that you may admire, adore, delight in them, and cleave unto them with a holy, prevalent, unconquerable love. When you do so, then will you be established in the truth, and be able to bid defiance unto the artifices of Satan, with the solicitations of men, that would withdraw or separate you from it. But I will not farther digress in these discourses.

Ignorance is another occasion of apostasy from the truth, which was named under this head of the depravation of the minds of men. It is the want of a due perception, understanding, or knowledge of the principal doctrines of the gospel, with the evidence which is given unto them, and the use of them in the Scriptures, that we intend hereby. A general knowledge of some doctrines, without an acquaintance with their grounds and reasons, their use and effects in the life of God, is of no value in these things When persons know not in religion what they ought to know, as they ought to know it, or what it is their duty to know, and without the knowledge whereof they can perform no other duty of religion in a right manner, then are they culpably ignorant, and so as to be exposed unto all other evils that may befall them; for whether this be for want of due instruction from others, or want of diligence in themselves to learn, the event is equally pernicious. In the first way, the Holy Ghost assures us that "where there is no vision, the people perish," Prov. xxix. 18. The people will suffer where those whose duty it is so to do are not able to instruct them; for "if the blind lead the blind, both must fall into the ditch." And in general it is affirmed, that the "people are destroyed for lack of knowledge," Hos. iv. 6. Of such ruinous consequence, by one means or other, is the people's ignorance of what it is their duty to know; and by no one way doth it so effectually operate unto their destruction as by this of disposing them to a defection from the truth which they have professed when any trial or temptation doth befall them.

Multitudes, yea, whole nations, are often brought unto an outward general profession of the truth of religion, especially with respect unto the opposition of any other that is made thereunto. The influence and example of some that are in power and esteem among them, falling in with a season of encouraging circumstances, may produce this effect, where men have little knowledge of what they profess, and less sense of its power and efficacy. So the body of the people of old turned unto the profession of the true religion under the reformation made by Josiah; nevertheless, as the prophet observes, "they did it not with their whole hearts, but feignedly," Jer. iii. 10. They did it not out of love to the truth, or a cordial respect unto the ways of God, but in a hypocritical compliance with their ruler. The conversion of the northern nations after they had possessed the western parts of the Roman empire was a pledge of what their future profession was like to prove. The first conversion of the world was by the laborious preaching of apostles, evangelists, and others, accompanied with many miraculous operations, exemplified in holiness of life, and patience under all sorts of persecutions; and by this means none were received or admitted into the profession of Christian religion but such as were personally convinced of its truth, instructed in its mysteries, conformed in their lives to its precepts, and engaged unto its profession against persecution. But in these latter conversions, some kings, rulers, or potentates, being dealt withal by popes or other princes, and thereon (perhaps with no small influence from secular considerations) admitting of the Christian religion in opposition unto Paganism, their allies, kindred, and subjects, usually followed them therein; having indeed little more of Christianity than the administration of some external rites, and a relinquishment of their old idols for the new saints proposed unto them. By this means their first profession of Christianity was laid in profound ignorance of the principles and most important doctrines and duties of the gospel. Hence it became most easy for them who were looked on as their guides to lead them into all those foolish opinions, idolatrous practices, superstitious devotions, and blind subjection to themselves, whence at length issued the fatal apostasy. Knowing but little of what they ought to have known, and delighting not in obedience unto what they did know, they willingly embraced themselves, and God judicially gave them up unto, those strong delusions which turned them wholly from the gospel.

Thus the generality of this nation hath received and professed the protestant religion in opposition unto Popery; and no doubt many did so through a sincere and effectual conviction of its truth, upon the first reformation. But it is so come to pass, that what through their own supine negligence and carelessness about all things invisible and eternal, what through the sloth, ignorance, laziness, and wretched indifferency in religion, of some of those that should instruct them, multitudes are become shamefully ignorant of the rudiments and principles of that religion which they account themselves to profess. So hath it been almost in all ages and places after profession became national. Many will not make use of the means of instruction which they have, and more want that means in an effectual measure. Nor, it may be, can there be an instance given where there hath been sufficient care taken, or at least sufficient provision made, for the instruction of the body of the people in all parts of it; neither is that ordinary course of the ministry which is passant in the world sufficient to this purpose. Can any man who knows any thing of the gospel, or of the nature of men with respect unto spiritual things, once suppose that the reading of prayers unto a people, or the rehearsing of a sermon without zeal, life, power, or evidence of compassion for the souls of men, accompanied with a light, vain, worldly conversation (as it is with many), should answer the apostolical pattern of laying the foundation, and then carrying on of men by continual instruction unto perfection? From hence (as also from other reasons obvious unto all impartial observers) it is that "darkness covers the earth, and gross darkness the people," ignorance prevailing on all sorts of men. Some will not learn, some have none to teach them, some are engaged in the pursuit of sensual lusts and vanities, some swallowed up in the love of and cares about the things of the world; few in any age have been conscientiously diligent in the things which are of eternal concernment unto them.

This was that which facilitated the papal apostasy, from whence it took its rise, and by which it received its progress. Those who would on the motives mentioned be accounted Christians, and which it was the interest of the pretended presidents in religion to have so esteemed, being profoundly ignorant, they first accommodated the practices of religion unto their carnal, superstitious minds, and then gradually led them into all errors and fables; for they were blind, and knew not whither they went. So were the important truths of the gospel abandoned for monkish dreams, for legends of foolish, lying miracles, and other heathenish superstitions. It was by ignorance, I say, principally, that the people gave themselves up unto the power of seducers; which enabled the architects of the Roman apostasy to carry them into opinions, ways, and practices, suited unto their secular interest: and so sensible have they been of their advantage hereby, as that some of them have commended ignorance, as the most useful qualification of the people in religion!

We may therefore well fix this as another cause, or occasion at least, of apostasy. When men are ignorant of the religion which themselves profess, as to its doctrines, and the principal grounds of them; when they are like the Samaritans, who understood not their own religious worship, which they had received by tradition, but "worshipped they knew not what," John iv. 22, -- they are no way able to defend themselves against the least impressions of seducers. They may plod on in the old track of some formal outward duties, but if any one meet them in their way, it is easy for him to turn them out of it. So the apostle, showing the danger that professors were in because of apostatical seducers, assigns the means of their preservation to be "the unction which they had received, whereby they knew all things," 1 John ii. 19, 20, 27. Had they not been taught and instructed in the truth, they could not, at such a season, have persevered in the profession of the faith. Yea, such persons are very ready to think that there is something worthy their consideration in what is proposed unto them by the most corrupt seducers, whereas they have really found nothing in what themselves have so long professed; for no man can find any real benefit, profit, or advantage, in that whereof he is ignorant. So it is said that some by "good words and fair speeches deceive the hearts of the simple," Rom. xvi. 18. Every thing they say hath a plausible pretence and appearance unto persons under that character, so as that they are apt to be taken and pleased with it. Hence is that advice of the apostle unto them who design establishment in faith and order: "Brethren, be not children in understanding; howbeit in malice be ye children, but in understanding be men," 1 Cor. xiv. 20. Teleioi ginesthe tais phresi, Be ye complete, perfect," well instructed in your minds, fully initiated into the doctrines of the gospel. Such the apostle calls teleious, "perfect men," 1 Cor. ii. 6; Heb. v. 14. Those who, in opposition hereunto, are "children," -- that is, weak and ignorant, -- will also be uncertain and unstable. They will be as children, "tossed to and fro, and carried about with every wind of doctrine, by the sleight of men, and cunning craftiness, whereby they lie in wait to deceive," Eph. iv. 14.

For let some crafty papal emissaries come among this sort of people, and let them confidently tell them that they neither have, nor ever will have, any benefit by the religion they profess, and that they have no evidence or assurance of the truth of it; -- they tell them no more but what they will know to be true if once they take it into consideration; for whereas they have seemed to be "always learning," by resorting to church, and the like outward means whereby religion is expressed, yet they "never came to the knowledge of the truth." Wherefore, when by any means they are put unto a stand, and are forced to consider themselves, they are amazed to find how little it is that they believe of the religion which they profess, or know of the ground of what they would be thought to believe.

Let such persons add (as they will not fail to do) that with them of Rome is full assurance, that none ever mistook the way who accompanied them that are of the old religion, which their forefathers professed so many ages before this new-fangledness came up, which hath filled all things with confusion, disorder, sects, and divisions, whereas before all were of one mind (which was the most plausible argument of Paganism against Christianity), every troublesome personal circumstance of their present condition makes them inclinable to believe that it may be as they say. Let them tell them, moreover, of the power granted unto the priesthood of their church to pardon all sorts of sins; of the effectual intercession of saints and angels, among whom they may choose out particular patrons and guardians for themselves; of the mercy, grace, goodness, power, and interest in heaven of the blessed Virgin, all continually exercised in the behalf of Catholics; of the miracles that are daily wrought among them; of the wondrous sanctity and devotion which some among them have attained; -- they begin to think that there is somewhat in these things which they can feel or see, whereas in their own religion they can understand little or nothing at all. The "great things" of the gospel are "strange things" unto them; they neither do nor can understand them by all the diligence they think meet to use in this case. But the things now proposed unto them have the nature of tales, which the mind of man is accustomed unto, and apt both to receive and retain. And it is not imaginable how easy a transition will prove from a religion whereof men know little or nothing at all, unto that which at one view presents unto their fancies and senses all that they need believe or do that they may be eternally happy.

Suppose one of another sort to come among such persons, and at once call them off from the profession of that religion which they pretend unto, confidently requiring them to attend wholly unto a light within them, which will be their guide and direct them unto God; -- they find by natural experience that there is some such light within them as that which he seems to propose unto them; for there is so in all men, as the apostle declares, even the light of conscience, accusing or excusing as unto sin or duty, Rom. ii. 14, 15. Having, therefore, by reason of their ignorance, no experience of any power or efficacy in that religion which themselves profess, they begin to think there is a reality in what is proposed unto them, and so are easily inveigled; for there is no security of his constancy for one moment, when a trial or temptation shall befall him, who hath not light or knowledge enough of the truth to give him some inward experience of the efficacy of what he doth profess.

But it is no way necessary to insist any longer on that which is so evident, both in matter of fact and in the reasons of it. An apostasy from a traditional profession of those truths which indeed men understand not, is easy, and in a time of temptation unavoidable. In all ages, multitudes have thus perished for want of knowledge; for such persons are destitute of defence against any external cause or means of defection. They have nothing in their minds to oppose to force, nothing unto seductions or fraud, nothing to the examples of great leaders, nothing to conflict with the superstition of their own minds; and will therefore, when wind and tide suit the design, comply with any fair pretence for a revolt.

And herein lieth no small part of the danger of the public profession of the protestant religion among us. By whose defect principally God knows, but it is incredible how stupidly ignorant multitudes are. Such there are who know no difference in religion, whilst the same names of God and Christ are commonly used, and the same places frequented for worship. Yet will this sort of men show great zeal and earnestness against Popery and other heresies! None more forward to revile, contemn, and prosecute them to their power; as ready as Mohammedans are to persecute Christians, or Papists sincere believers, and that on the same grounds. But if at any time they are put unto a stand, and necessitated to give an account unto themselves of the reason of their own religion, what it is they believe, and why they do so, their confidence will fail them, and, like unto men fallen into cross-paths and ways, they will not know what to do. And on such occasions they are the readiest of all men, in a kind of shame of themselves, to give up the religion which they have professed for any other, wherein it is promised they shall have more skill, and by which they may have some benefit, as it is pretended, whereas by their own they have had none at all.

Whatever, therefore, is amongst us or elsewhere an occasion of ignorance among the people, it doth expose them unto a fatal defection from the truth If those upon whom it is incumbent to instruct them in the knowledge of the truths and mysteries of the gospel are unskillful or negligent in the discharge of their duty, they do what lieth in them to give them up bound hand and foot to the power of their spiritual adversaries; and they will be found chargeable with no less guilt who lay obstructions in the way of others who would willingly labour in the instruction of them unto their power. A man would think, from all circumstances, and all indications of the present inclinations of the minds of men, that it were the chief interest of all that really love the protestant religion to preserve its professors from apostasy or any disposition thereunto. That this will be done effectually without a continual instruction of them in the truths which are to be professed, with their grounds, reasons, and effects, is so fond an imagination as that it deserves no consideration. It is but to build castles in the air, to suppose that men will be kept constant in the profession of religion by outward laws, the observance of external forms, and the secular advantage of some persons by it, wherein they are not concerned. They will not be so, I say, when a trial shall befall them. There is no other means that is appointed of God, or is rational in itself, for the attaining of this end, but that those who are so concerned do what in them lies personally to instruct the people in the truth, encouraging them unto obedience by their own example; and to prevail with them who have the same design to be assisting with them therein. But to cry out of the great danger of protestant religion in the growth of Popery, and at the same time not only to be negligent themselves in the great duty of communicating the real effectual knowledge of it unto the souls of men, but also to lay needless obstructions in the way of others who would sincerely endeavour so to do, is an unaccountable solecism in religion. Either we are not in earnest in our pretended zeal for the truth and our fears of the prevalency of Popery, or we believe not that instruction in the truth is the only means to preserve men in the useful profession of it; which is to renounce the gospel and all rational consideration therewithal, or we are influenced by other things, which we far more esteem than evangelical truth and the purity of religion.

The reformation of the church consisted principally in the deliverance of the people from darkness and ignorance; and if through our neglect they should be reduced again into the same state and condition, they would be a ready prey for the Papacy to seize upon. The advice of the apostle, as to the duty of all gospel ministers and officers in such a season as we are fallen into, is that alone which will preserve us, 2 Tim. iv. 1-5.

But it may be supposed that so much labour and diligence in the instruction and teaching of the people, as some assert, is altogether unnecessary. It is enough if they be taught what are the general principles of religion, and do thereon comply with the conduct of the church whereunto they do belong. Besides, if this burden be incumbent on the ministry, that those called thereunto are to have no relaxation from constant, sedulous "labouring in the word and doctrine," and are moreover required to exemplify what they teach in the whole course of their conversation, who would ever take upon him that office that can advantage himself in the world any other way? It must needs prove very burdensome if we have a religion that will not be preserved in the minds of men without all this constant., endless toil and labour. In the Roman church we see how easy a thing it is to keep up the people unto its profession, whilst the clergy are at liberty to pursue and use the pleasures and honours of this world, nor are any of them obliged unto those irksome and endless pains which we seem to require; yea, they find by experience that ignorance in the people is the best expedient to keep them in subjection to the priests, and then all things are secure. I wish that such thoughts as these do not influence the minds of some unto a readiness for a change, if so be it might be effected without hazard. But if more pains, diligence, labour, with perseverance therein, be required by us in the ministers of the gospel and guides of the church, than the Holy Ghost in the Scripture doth plainly, positively, frequently enjoin, let it be rejected and despised. Alas! the best of us, of all that are alive, do come short in many things of the rules and examples that are proposed unto us therein, nor do I know on what grounds or by what measures the most of us do intend to give in our accounts at the last day. Nor is there any more impious opinion, nor more contradictory to the gospel, than that it is enough for the people to be instructed only in the general principles of religion, without any farther improvement or growth in knowledge: for those who are thus called "The people" are, I suppose, esteemed Christians, -- that is, disciples of Jesus Christ, and members of his mystical body; and if they are so, their growth in understanding, their edification in knowledge, their being carried on unto perfection, their acquaintance with the whole counsel of God, with the mysteries of his love and grace in Christ Jesus, are as necessary for them as the "saving of their souls," indispensably depending thereon, can render them. And if we will be ministers of the gospel, it will not be best for us to prescribe unto ourselves our rules and measures of duty. It will be our wisdom to accept of that office on the terms limited by the Holy Ghost, or utterly to let it alone. And we must know, that the more exactly our profession is suited unto the gospel, the less mixture there is in it of any thing human, the more difficult it is thoroughly to instruct men in the knowledge of it. The mind of man is far more apt and able to comprehend and retain fables, errors, and superstitions, than evangelical truths. The former are natural unto it; against the latter it hath a dislike and enmity, until they are removed by grace. Hence, some will make a more appearing proficiency in a false religion in four or five days than others will do in the knowledge of the truth almost in so many years. We may have well-grown Papists in a month's time, that shall be expert in the mysteries of their devotion; and there is another profession that two or three days will bring men unto a perfection in: but slow is the progress of most in learning the truth and mysteries of the gospel. If peculiar diligence and constant sedulity be not used in their instruction, they will be made a prey unto the next opportunity for a defection from the truth.

Footnotes:

7. See the previous volume of his works, page 244. -- Ed.

8. Idolaters in India, who believed in the transmigration of souls. -- Ed.

Chapter VI – Pride and vanity of mind, sloth and negligence, love of the world, causes of apostasy — The work of Satan, and judgments of God in this matter

III. The innate pride and vanity of the minds of men is another means whereby they are disposed and inclined unto an apostasy from the profession of evangelical truth. With respect hereunto the design and work of the gospel is, to "cast down imaginations, and every high thing that exalteth itself against the knowledge of God," taught therein, "bringing into captivity every thought to the obedience of Christ," 2 Cor. x. 4, 5. The mind of man is naturally lifted up with high thoughts in itself and of itself. That it is sufficient unto all the ends of its being, all the duties of its condition, without any special aid or assistance from above, is the prevailing principle whereby it is acted. Men do not only by nature say, "With our tongue will we prevail; our lips are our own: who is lord over us?" Ps. xii. 4, -- "We have a sovereignty over all our outward actions;" but also, that nothing is, or can, or ought to be required of us, but what we have power in ourselves to comprehend, comply withal, and perform. This in all ages of the church, under various forms and pretences, hath been contended for. The true state of all controversies about the powers of nature and grace is this, That, on the one hand, the minds and wills of men are asserted to be self-sufficient as to internal abilities unto all duties of obedience necessary unto eternal blessedness; on the other, that we have no sufficiency of ourselves, but that all our sufficiency is of God. See 2 Cor. iii. 5, ix. 8. This principle, which sprung immediately out of that pride whereby, aiming at an enlargement of our self-sufficiency, we utterly lost what we had, was never yet rooted out of the minds of the generality of professed Christians.

In all things the mind of man would be its own measure, guide, and rule, continually teeming with these two evils:--

1. It exalts imaginations of its own, which it loves, applauds, dotes on, and adheres unto. This is the original of heresy, this hath given birth, growth, and progress, to error; for "God hath made man upright, but they have sought out many inventions," Eccles. vii. 29. Seeking out and exalting inventions of our own, in things spiritual and religious, is the principal and most pernicious consequent of our fall from that state of uprightness wherein of God we were created.

2. It makes itself the sole and absolute judge of what is divinely proposed unto it, whether it be true or false, good or evil, to be received or rejected, without desire or expectation of any supernatural guidance or assistance; and whatever is unsuited unto its own prejudicate imaginations, it is ready to scorn and despise.

That, therefore, which we are now to demonstrate is, that where this pride and principle are predominant, where the one is not mortified by grace nor the other eradicated by spiritual light, there men can never receive the truths of the gospel in a due manner, and are ready to renounce them when they have by any means been brought unto the profession of them for a season; for, --

The gospel, -- that is, the doctrines of it and truths contained in it, -- is proposed unto us in the name and on the authority of God, having his image and superscription upon it. It hath such impressions of divine wisdom, goodness, grace, holiness, and power upon it, as manifests it to be the "glorious gospel of the blessed God," 1 Tim. i. 11. Hence it ought to be received with a holy reverence, with a due sense of the glory of God, and as his voice speaking unto us from heaven. Hence is the caution of the apostle, that we would "not refuse" or "turn away from him that speaketh from heaven," Heb. xii. 25. Without this it will never be duly received, truly understood, nor steadfastly believed. It is not to be received as "the word of men, but as it is in truth, the word of God," 1 Thess. ii. 13. It must be received with that frame of spirit, with that submission, that subjection of soul and conscience, which becomes poor worms of the earth when they have to do with the great and holy God, expressed Gen. xviii. 27. So our Saviour tells us that "unless we be converted, and become as little children, we cannot enter into the kingdom of God." Unless we deny ourselves and all our own imaginations, unless we become humble and teachable, we can never arrive at a useful acquaintance with the mysteries of it. And he convinced the learned Pharisees that by reason of their pride, vain-glory, and hypocrisy, they could not perceive or understand the doctrine which he taught.

God promiseth that he will teach the meek or humble in judgment: "The meek will he teach his way," Ps. xxv. 9. "The secret of the Lord is with them that fear him; and he will show them his covenant," verse 14. "Whom shall he teach knowledge? whom shall he make to understand doctrine? them that are weaned from the milk, and drawn from the breasts," Isa. xxviii. 9. Unless men become as weaned children, as David affirms of himself, Ps. cxxxi. 2, when "his heart was not haughty, nor his eyes lofty," verse 1, God will not teach them. There is, therefore, no such effectual obstruction of divine teachings as the pride of men's minds, which is utterly inconsistent with them. Hence it is that men come with carnal confidence in themselves, the ability and sagacity of their own minds, to the consideration of the gospel and the things contained in it, without the least peculiar awe or reverence of God from whom it is; and hence do they suppose themselves, without more ado, competent judges of the mind of the Holy Ghost in all divine revelations. Can men who have once read the Scripture imagine that this is the way to learn heavenly truth or to partake of the teachings of God? Will the same frame of spirit suffice them in this design as that which they have when they are exercised about their other occasions? When we consider how men for the most part learn the truth, we need not wonder to see how easily they unlearn and forsake it. If the truth at any time be entertained by a soul whose mind is unhumbled and whose affections are unmortified, it is a troublesome inmate, and will, on the first occasion, be parted withal. It is true, we ought to employ the utmost of our rational abilities in the investigation of sacred truth; but yet if therein we follow the conduct of our own minds, diving perhaps into subtilties and niceties, forsaking a humble dependence on the teachings of God, it may be under apprehensions of singular wisdom, we betray ourselves into ruinous folly. This was that which corrupted all the endeavours of the schoolmen, and left them, in the height of their inquiries, to wax vain in their imaginations. The way of handling spiritual things in a spiritual manner, in the words which the Holy Ghost teacheth, -- that is, not with curious, subtile reasonings and inventions of carnal, unsanctified minds, but with that evidence and plainness in argumentation, suited practically to affect the minds and consciences of men, which the Scripture giveth us both example and rule for, -- was despised by them; but they came to the study of sacred things with their minds stuffed and prepossessed with philosophical notions and conceptions, with sophisms, distinctions, and various expressions of the serpentine wits of men, which they mixed with divinity, or the doctrine of the Scripture, woefully corrupting, debasing, and perverting it thereby. Most of their disputes were such as had never had foundation nor occasion in the world, if Aristotle had not invented some odd terms and distinctions, remote from the common understanding and reason of men wiser than himself. To inquire into divine revelation with a holy, humble frame of heart, waiting and praying for divine teaching and illumination of mind, that themselves might be made wise in the knowledge of the mysteries of the gospel, and able to instruct others in the knowledge and fear of God, it never came into their minds; but being furnished and puffed up with a conceit of their own sagacity, philosophical ability, and disputing faculty, harnessed with syllogisms, distinctions, solutions, and most preposterous methods of craft, they came with boldness on Christian religion, and forming it to their own imaginations, dressing it up and exposing of it in foolish terms of art, under a semblance of wondrous subtilty they wholly corrupted it, and drew off the minds of men from the simplicity of the truth as it is in Christ Jesus. Not one article of religion did this proud, self-conceited generation of men leave, that (whether their conclusions were true or false about it) any man could come to the understanding of it who had not been a better proficient in the school of Aristotle than of Christ. To believe and teach the doctrine of the Scripture, though with sound reason and judgment, and in the way of the Scripture to affect the minds and consciences of men, without their philosophical notions, niceties, and distinctions, whereby they had carved a corrupt, depraved, monstrous image of all things, and the knowledge of them, was, among them, to be a heretic or a blockhead. By the pride, confidence, and pretended subtilty of these men was religion totally corrupted, and the fountains poisoned from whence others sought for the waters of the sanctuary. Even what was left of truth among them was so debased, so divested of its native heavenly glory, beauty, and majesty, was rendered so deformed and unsuited unto that spiritual light wherein alone it can be usefully discerned, as to render it altogether useless and inefficacious unto its proper ends. Nor are we ever in more danger to subduct ourselves from under the teachings of God than when we lean unto our own understandings in our inquiries into spiritual things, so as to forget that humble, lowly frame of heart wherein alone we are meet to be taught or to learn in a due manner. And this is one way whereby men, through the innate pride of their minds, are obstructed in the receiving and disposed unto the relinquishment of evangelical truths.

Again; it is confessed that there is nothing proposed unto us in the gospel that is contrary unto reason, as reason is the due comprehension and measure of things as they are in their own nature; for how should there be so, seeing it is in itself the principal external effect of the reason or wisdom of God, which hath given unto all things their natures, properties, and measures? But yet there are things revealed in it which are above the comprehension of reason, as planted in the finite, limited understanding of man; nor is the ground hereof the accidental corruption of our nature, but the essential constitution of its being. There are, I say, divine mysteries in the gospel whose revelation we may understand, but the nature of the things themselves we cannot comprehend. And this reason itself cannot but acknowledge;

for whereas it knows itself to be finite, limited, and bounded, how should it be able perfectly to comprehend things infinite, or all the effects of infinite wisdom? "Can we by searching find out God? can we find out the Almighty unto perfection? It is high as heaven; what can we dot deeper than hell; what can we know? The measure thereof is longer than the earth, and broader than the sea," Job xi. 7-9. These things so exceed the natural and duly proportionate objects of our understandings as that we cannot find them out to perfection. The reason of man hath nothing here to do, but humbly to comply with the revelations that are made of them.

Moreover, there are in the gospel things that are unsuited, yea, contradictory unto reason as it is corrupted. Reason in us is now no longer to be considered merely as it is finite and limited, but as, in the subject and exercise of it, it is impaired, depraved, and corrupted. To deny this, is to deny the fundamental principle and supposition that, in all things, the gospel proceedeth on; that is, that Jesus Christ came into the world to restore and repair our nature. In this state, as it is unable of itself to discern and judge of spiritual things in a due manner, so it is apt to frame unto itself vain imaginations, and to be prepossessed with innumerable prejudices, contrary unto what the gospel doth teach and require; and whatever it doth so fancy or frame, the mind esteems as proper acts and effects of reason as any it exerciseth or is capable of.

With respect unto both these, -- namely, the weakness of reason as it is finite and limited, and the depravation of reason as it is corrupted, -- it is the design of the gospel to bring every thought into captivity unto the obedience of faith; for, --

1. As to the former, it requires men to believe things above their reason, merely on the authority of divine revelation. Things they must believe which "eye hath not seen, nor ear heard, neither have they entered into the heart of man to conceive;" only they are "revealed unto us by the Spirit," 1 Cor. ii. 9, 10. It will not admit of an inquiry how those things may be which the mouth of the Lord hath spoken. The sense and meaning of the revelation it may inquire into, but cannot comprehend the things revealed. "Nobis curiositate opus non est post Jesum Christum, nec inquisitione post evangelium; cum credimus nihil desideramus ultra credere, hoc enim prius credimus, non esse quod ultra credere debemus," Tertull. Præscrip. adv. Hæres. And when of old the wise, the scribes, the disputers of this world, would not submit hereunto, under the supposed conduct of their reason, they fell into the most brutish unreasonableness, in judging the wisdom of God to be folly and his power to be weakness, 1 Cor. i. 18-25. And it is an unparalleled attempt of atheism which some in our days (who would yet be accounted Christians) have engaged in; -- they would exalt philosophy or human reason into a right of judicature over all divine revelations. Nothing must be supposed to be contained in them but what is measurable by its principles and rules. What pretends to be above them, they say ought to be rejected; which is to make itself infinite, or the wisdom and understanding of God finite and limited. Wherefore, as to the things that are revealed in the gospel, because many of them are absolutely above the comprehension of our minds or reasons, they are not the judges of them, but are the servants of faith only in bearing witness unto them; for "the things of a man knoweth the spirit of man which is in him; but the things of God knoweth no man, but the Spirit of God," 1 Cor. ii. 11. In brief, to affirm that we can be obliged to believe no more than we can comprehend, or nothing but what we can perfectly understand the nature of in itself, or that we may reject what is really above reason, on a supposition that it is contrary unto reason, is to renounce the gospel, and therewith all divine revelations. And this is spoken not of reason as it is corrupted,

but merely as it is human reason, finite and limited.

2. As in things infinite, spiritual, and heavenly, the gospel proposeth unto men things quite above their comprehension, supposing their reason to be pure and incorrupted, only allowing it to be that which is finite and limited; so in things which practically respect the obedience of faith which it doth require, it prescribeth things contrary unto our natural conceptions, or reason as it is in us depraved: for the natural conceptions of our minds about religious duties and the way of living unto God are all of them suited unto the covenant of works, for they are the effects of the remainders of that light which did direct us to walk with God thereby. But hereunto the disposal of things in the covenant of grace is diametrically opposed, so that their accounts will never intermix, Rom. xi. 6; yea, the carnal mind, -- that is, reason as it is corrupted, -- acts its contradiction unto the will of God as revealed in the gospel with enmity and hatred, chap. viii. 7. And [as] for those duties which are suited unto the light of nature, the gospel doth so change them, with the respect it gives them unto the mediation of Christ and the efficiency of the Holy Spirit, as that corrupted reason defies them, being so qualified, as foreign unto its conceptions. The duties themselves it can approve of, but not of their respect unto Jesus Christ, whereunto they are disposed by the gospel.

Hence it is that of old those who pretended such an absolute sovereignty of their own reason as to admit of nothing as truth but what its dictates complied withal, were of all men the slowest to receive and the forwardest to oppose the mysteries of the gospel; because they were above it in some things, and contrary unto it in more, as it is in most things corrupted, they looked on them as folly, and so despised them. This the apostle declares and records, 1 Cor. i. 2. Especially was it so among them who, unto the vain imaginations wherein in general "their foolish heart was darkened," had superadded some peculiar sect in philosophy which was of reputation among the wise men of the world; for they conceived and maintained all the maxims of their sect as the absolute dictates of right reason, though most of them were foolish fancies, either taken up by tradition or sophistically imposed on their understandings. Hence, every thing that was contrary unto such principles or inconsistent with them, they looked on as opposite unto reason, and so despised it. Nor is it much otherwise at this day with many Christians, who make the traditional principles of their sect or party the rule whereby every thing that is in religion proposed unto them may be examined. Thus, though the generality of philosophers and wise men at Athens rejected the doctrine of the apostle, yet were there none so forward and fierce in their opposition unto him, so contemptuously proud in their censures of him, as were the Epicureans and Stoics, Acts xvii. 18; and the reason hereof was, because the doctrine which he taught was eminently contrary to the maxims of their peculiar sects: for whereas the Epicureans denied the providence of God in the government of the world, the existence of the souls of men after this life, all eternal rewards or punishments, there was no admission of any one word of the apostle's doctrine without a renunciation of all their impious sentiments, and so the ruin of their sect. And as for the Stoics, the fundamental principle of their philosophy was, that a man should look for all blessedness or happiness in and from himself alone, and from the things that were in his own power, as being every way sufficient unto himself for that end. All that the apostle taught concerning the mediation of Christ and the grace of God by him was also diametrically opposite unto this principle. Wherefore those of these two sects opposed him in a peculiar manner, not only from the pride and darkness that are naturally in the minds of men, and are improved by the advancement of corrupted reason above its own proper place and dignity, but from the prejudicate opinions which, on the reputation of their sects, they adhered unto, as assured dictates of right reason in general. And when some such persons as these afterward, upon a general conviction of its truth, took upon them a profession of the gospel, they were the men who corrupted its principal mysteries by their vain philosophy, as the apostle intimates, Col. ii. 8. So Tertullian, "Hæreses a philosophia subornantur. Inde Æones et formæ, et nescio quæ, et Trinitas hominum apud Valentinum, [qui] Platonicus fuerat. Inde Marcionis Deus melior de tranquillitate, a Stoicis venerat; et ubi anima interire dicatur ab Epicuræis observatur; et ut carnis restitutio negatur, de una omnium philosophorum schola sumitur."

We may apply these things unto our present purpose. The design of the gospel, in all its especial truths and mysteries, is to bring every thought into subjection unto the obedience of faith. Hence is that direction which flesh and blood will never comply withal, "If any man among you seemeth to be wise in this world, let him become a fool, that he may be wise," 1 Cor. iii. 18. Unless men renounce their carnal wisdom, in all its principles, effects, and operations, they will never become wise with that wisdom which is from above; and he who knoweth not what it is so to become a fool, be he who he will, was never yet wise towards God. Wherefore, when men have taken on them the outward profession of the gospel, they begin to find, upon inquiry, that the mysteries and principles of its doctrine are unsuited unto the natural pride of their minds, and inconsistent with that absolute sovereignty which they would in all things give unto their own reason. Hereon "many inventions are sought out" to cast off the yoke of faith, and to re-enthrone reason in the room thereof; -- not that men depart from the faith with this express design, but this is that which secretly influenceth them thereunto. Hence the generality of those who forsake the truth on this ground and occasion are such as, trusting too soon to their own rational abilities, having neither will, nor humility, nor industry to inquire into the principles and reasons of truth in a due manner, do give up themselves unto the conduct and teaching of others, who have invented opinions more suited unto the innate pride of their minds and carnal reasonings; and some, by an over-earnest pursuit of the workings of their own rational faculties in spiritual things, having subducted their minds from that humble frame wherein alone they are capable of divine teaching, are betrayed into the same miscarriage. All ancient heresies sprung from this root, yea, those of them which are most absurd and foolish, and most diametrically opposite unto right reason, arose from a pretence thereof: for when men will have reason to have an absolute supremacy in religion, it is unavoidable but they must judge that their own is the reason which is intended; and that some may be led hereby into very foolish imaginations is easy to be conjectured, unless we shall suppose all men to be equally wise and sober.

I shall briefly exemplify these things in one instance, and that in a prevalent apostasy from the truth, and which at present is visibly progressive in the world; this is that of Socinianism. And I shall give an instance herein, because the poison of it is highly efficacious where it meets with the complexion and constitution of mind before described, and is more diffused than many are aware of: for although the name of it be generally condemned, and there are some opinions comprised under it whose profession is inconsistent with the interest of the most, yet all those deviations from the truth which we have amongst us, under several denominations, are emanations from that corrupt fountain; yea, the whole of it being a system of opinions craftily suited unto the first notions and conceptions of corrupted reason, and the inbred pride of men's minds, in them who on any account own divine revelation, the first proposal of them finds ready entertainment with many of those whose souls are not prepared and fortified against them by a spiritual experience of the excellency, power, and efficacy, of the mysteries of the gospel. They no sooner hear of them but they know they express what they would have, as gratifying all the corrupt desires and carnal reasonings of their minds.

There are, as was observed before, two sorts of things in the doctrines of the gospel:-- 1. Such as are above the comprehension and measure of reason in its best condition, as it is in us limited and confined; 2. Such as are contrary unto it as corrupted and depraved. And unto these two heads is this kind of apostasy reducible.

1. What is above reason, incomprehensible by it, those of this way do absolutely reject. Such are the doctrines of the Trinity and of the incarnation of the Son of God. Because the things taught in these doctrines are not comprehensible by their reason, they conclude that they are repugnant unto right reason. And by others the same doctrines are refused, as not compliant with the light that is within them; for the existence of the divine nature in three distinct persons, with the hypostatical union of the natures of God and man in the same person, they cannot acknowledge. These things, so fully, so plainly, so frequently revealed and asserted in the Scripture, so attested by the primitive catholic church, are rejected on no other reason but that they are against reason; nor is there any pretence that they are so, but because they are above it. When they have puzzled themselves with Nicodemus' question, "How can these things be?" they peremptorily deny their existence, because they cannot comprehend the manner of it.

2. As unto those things which are contrary unto reason as corrupted, these they deprave and wrest unto a compliance therewithal. So they deal with the doctrines of the attributes of God, of his eternal decrees, of the office and mediation of Christ, of justification by his righteousness, of the power and efficacy of the grace of the Holy Spirit in the conversion of sinners, and of the resurrection of the dead. Because they cannot bring their reason as corrupted and depraved unto a compliance with these truths, they will force, hale, torture, and rack the truths themselves, to bring them into slavery unto their own reasons, or carnal, fleshly conceptions of spiritual things; for, allowing the words, terms, and propositions wherein they are expressed, they put absurd senses upon them, destructive unto the faith and contrary to the whole scope and design of the Scripture. So do they endeavour expressly to bring every divine revelation into captivity unto the bondage of their own perverse reasonings and imaginations.

It is, therefore, evident that this kind of apostasy springs from no other root but the pride of the minds of men, refusing to admit of evangelical truths on the mere authority of divine revelation, where they are above reason as it is limited, or contrary unto it as corrupted. On these terms the gospel can nowhere keep its station, nor will it forego its prerogative by subjecting itself to be tried by these uncertain measures or weighed in these uneven, tottering balances. The humble, the meek, the teachable, those who are made free and willing to captivate their understandings unto the obedience of faith, are those alone with whom it will abide and continue.

But it may be said, that, this being only one private heresy, of no great extent or acceptation in the world, there is no danger of any influence from it unto a more general defection. So, it may be, it seems unto many; but I must acknowledge myself to be otherwise minded, and that for two reasons:--

1. Because of the advance which it maketh every day in the addition of new,

bold, proud imaginations unto what it hath already made its successful attempts in: for, in the pursuit of the same principles with those of the men of this way and persuasion, not a few begin absolutely to submit the Scripture, and every thing contained in it, to the judgment and sentence of their own reason; which is the true form and spirit of Socinianism, visibly acting itself with some more than ordinary confidence. What is suited unto their reason they will receive, and what is not so, let it be affirmed a hundred times in the Scripture, they will reject with the same ease and confidence as if they were imaginations of men like themselves. Both books that are written unto this purpose, and the common discourses of many, do fully testify unto this advance of the pride of the minds of men; and he is careless about these things who seeth not that the next stage is downright atheism. This is that dunghill which such blazing exhalations of pride do at last fall into. And herein do many countenance themselves with a false and foolish pretence that all those whom they differ from are fanatical enemies of reason, when they ascribe unto it all that any man in his wits can so do who believeth divine revelation, and doth not absolutely disavow the corruption of nature by the fall.

2. The poison of these principles is greatly diffused in the world; for hence it is that all those doctrines of the gospel which have any thing of spiritual mystery in them, which are constituent principles of, or do any way belong unto, the covenant of grace, and so not absolutely reconcilable unto reason as corrupt and carnal, are by many so laden with contempt and scorn that it is sufficient to expose any man unto the contumelies of "ignorant, irrational, and foolish," who dares to avow them. Such are the doctrines of eternal predestination, of the total corruption of the nature of men as unto spiritual things by the fall, of the power and efficacy of the grace of God in the conversion of sinners, of the nature and necessity of regeneration, of union with Christ, of justification by the imputation of his righteousness, of the nature of internal, inherent righteousness or evangelical holiness, of the necessity of continual supplies of the Spirit in actual grace unto all duties of obedience, of the power of the Holy Ghost evidencing the divine authority of the Scriptures in and by themselves, with sundry others. Many can see no reason for the admittance of these things, or they cannot see the reason of them; and therefore, although they are fully and plainly declared in the Scriptures, yet are they, by no small generation among us, so derided and exploded as that the very names of them are grown into contempt. But why all this scorn, all this severity? Men may do well to consider, that not long since all the prelates of England owned those doctrines as articles of faith which now they so deride; and although they are not obliged by any divine precept to be of the same judgment with them because it was theirs, yet it may be they are under some obligation from the laws of the land not to renounce the ancient doctrines of the church, and are certainly bound by the laws of Christian modesty and sobriety not to vilify and scorn the doctrines they owned, and all that do profess them.

But it is warrant sufficient unto some for the utmost detestation of any principles in religion, that they have a seeming incompliance with their reason, though apparently corrupted by prejudice and weakened by ignorance. Hence they will not admit that there can be a consistency between the unchangeableness of God's decrees and the freedom of our wills; that justification by the blood of Christ doth not render our own obedience needless; that the efficacy of God's grace and the necessity of our duty are reconcilable. And herein they seem to take along with them, as their security, these two principles, seeing without them they have no foundation to build upon:--

(1.) That reason as it acts in them is the same with right reason in general, -- that whatever respect is due to the one is so to the other. It were well, in the meantime, if prejudices, corrupt affections, and gross ignorance, did not, on great variety of occasions, manifest themselves among this sort of persons; and not only so, but such a course of conversation among some of them as none can think consistent with the divine teachings who believe the Scriptures. But it is so come to pass, that all that humility, meekness, self-diffidence, all that conscientious fear of sinning and practice of holiness, which the word of God makes so necessary unto them who would learn the truth as it is in Jesus, are by many (puffed up with a conceit of their own ability to know all things) utterly disregarded.

(2.) That there is no time or instance wherein those thoughts which seem to us most rational are to be captivated unto the obedience of faith; and yet without this there is no true knowledge of the mind of God in the gospel to be attained. What such principles will carry men out unto in religion were easy to conjecture, if experience did not render conjecture useless in this case.

Wherefore, this pride of the minds of men, refusing to bow or subject themselves unto the authority of divine revelation, designing to exalt self, in its intellectual and moral abilities, in its powers to know what it should and do what it ought, hath in all ages been a great principle of opposition unto and apostasy from evangelical truth: nor was it ever more rampant than in the days wherein we live; for besides that it hath openly spawned that whole brood of errors which some entire sects do espouse, it diffuseth itself in its effects among all sorts of professors of Christianity. An humble subjection of mind and conscience unto the authority of God in his word, -- which alone, upon trial, will be found to answer the experience of believers, -- is the only security against this distemper. This we may, this we ought to, pray for, not only for ourselves, but that it might be given of God unto them who scarce believe that God gives any thing that is spiritual and supernatural unto the souls of men, in any such way as that the effect should depend on the efficiency of grace, and not on their own wills.

Unto this pride, as inseparable from it, we may adjoin that vanity and curiosity that are in the minds of men. These are those which the apostle marketh under the outward sign and effect of them, namely, "itching ears," 2 Tim. iv. 3; for hence an inclination and hankering of mind after things novel, vain, and curious, doth arise. Under the power of these affections, men "cannot endure sound doctrine," nor will abide in the simplicity of the gospel They know not how to be wise unto sobriety, and to keep their speculations about spiritual things within the bounds of sober modesty; but they are still intruding themselves into things they have not seen, being vainly puffed up by their own fleshly minds, Col. ii. 18. And as this curiosity hath produced many of these needless, vain opinions, subtle, nice, philosophical disputations and distinctions, wherewith some have filled religion; so from the uncured vanity of mind doth proceed that levity and inconstancy which are in many, whereby they are "tossed to and fro with every wind of doctrine" that blows upon them, from the "cunning sleights of men who lie in wait to deceive."

Unto all we may add carnal pride and ambition (where the outward affairs of the church or the profession of religion are accompanied with such secular advantages of wealth, honour, and rule, as to stir up envy and emulation among men of earthly minds); which, as they have occasioned many scandalous outrages in religion, so they have been the rise and occasion of many heresies also.

IV. Careless security and groundless confidences do betray men into apostasies from the gospel when unexpected trials do befall them. To give evidence hereunto we may do well to consider the things that ensue:--

1. The Holy Spirit hath sufficiently warned us all that defections and backslidings from the truth would fall out among the professors of it. This hath been already abundantly manifested in the express instances of such warnings and predictions before produced and insisted on. And there is in the word a vehement application made of all these warnings unto us and our duties. Hence are those exhortations and precepts multiplied, to "watch," to "stand fast in the faith," to "be strong and quit ourselves like men" in this matter. Nothing but a diligent attendance unto all gospel duties and a vigorous acting of all gospel graces will preserve us, if the Scripture may be believed. And as for those by whom these things are despised, it is no matter at all what religion they are of.

2. We are foretold and forewarned of the great danger that will attend the professors of the gospel when such a season of apostasy shall by any means come upon them. So prevalent shall the means of it be as that many shall be deceived, and if it were possible even the elect themselves, Matt. xxiv. 11, 24. Such a season is an "hour of temptation that cometh on all the world, to try them that dwell upon the earth," Rev. iii. 10; and the woful event in them that shall be overtaken with the power of it, in their utter and eternal destruction, is in many instances set before us.

3. It is also plainly intimated that such a season of the prevalency of a defection from the truth shall be a time of great security among the generality of professed Christians. Churches shall be asleep, persons shall cry, "Peace, peace," when that day cometh as a snare.

We are not, therefore, left without sufficient warning in this case, both of the certainty of our trial, the greatness of our concernment, and the danger of security; and yet, notwithstanding all these means of excitation unto a vigorous attendance unto our condition, danger, and duty, it is evident unto every discerning eye how desperately secure are the generality of professors of the gospel with respect unto this evil and the consequents of it. Nothing can awake them unto the consideration of their own state, although their neighbours' houses are set on fire from hell. Love of the world, with prosperity and ease, on the one hand, or the cares and businesses of it on the other, do so take up the minds of men that they are not sensible of any concernment in these things. And we may briefly consider the various ways whereby this security puts forth its efficacy in disposing men unto apostasy when they fall into the occasions of it:--

(1.) It doth so by possessing and overpowering them with a proud, careless, supine negligence. Men hear of this evil and the danger of it, but, like Gallio, they "care for none of these things." They know not of any concernment they have in them, nor of any need they have to provide against them. Unto some others, perhaps, these things may belong, but unto them not at all. Those who would press them on their minds and consciences they look on as persons causelessly importunate, or troubled with groundless suspicions and fears. If there be any danger about religion, they doubt not but sooner or later provision will be made against it by law; but as unto any special duty incumbent on themselves with respect unto their own souls, they know nothing of it, nor will consider it, Had not the world been asleep in this security, had not men been utterly regardless of their interest in the truth, it had not been possible that religion should have been so totally corrupted as it was in the Papacy, and yet so few take any notice thereof. At some seasons God raised up among them witnesses for the truth, who not only declared and professed it, but also sealed their confession with their blood; but the generality of Christians were so far from being excited thereby to the consideration of their own concern and duty as that they opposed and persecuted them unto destruction, as the disturbers of the public tranquillity. And it is no otherwise at this day. Many complain of, more fear, a defection from the gospel. It is also evident in how many things the doctrine of it is already by some corrupted by whom it was formerly professed. Instances of as great apostasies as the name of Christianity is capable of are multiplied among us; and yet how few are there that do at all regard these things, or once consider what is either their duty or their danger in such a season!

(2.) It worketh and is effectual by a wicked indifferency as unto all things in religion. Men under the power of this security neither see, nor will understand, nor can be made sensible of, the difference that is between truth and error, piety and superstition, so as to value one more than another. "It is all religion, and it is no more but so. If persons change from one way to another, so as they do not utterly renounce Jesus Christ, they may be saved in the way they betake themselves unto." The profession of such persons attends on all occasions, and an apostasy from the mysteries of the gospel will be but a useful compliance with opportunity.

We judge no men, no party of men, as to their eternal state and condition, upon the account of their outward profession in religion, unless they are open idolaters or flagitious in their lives God only knows how it is between him and their souls The framing of churches (as the church of Rome) according unto men's minds, fancies, opinions, or interests, and then confining salvation unto them, is an effect of pride and folly, as contradictory to the gospel as any thing that can be imagined. But yet there is a wide difference to be made between apostates and others. "Better men had never known the way of righteousness, than, after they have known it, to turn from the holy commandment." Those who have been instructed in the truth of the gospel, and have made profession of it, are for the most part acted by such depraved principles, moved by such corrupt lusts, and do show so much ingratitude against the Lord Jesus Christ in their defection, "denying the Lord that bought them," that they put a peculiar character and mark upon themselves; and although we will not judge any, yet is it our duty to put men in remembrance of the danger that attends such apostasies. So the apostle expressly tells the Galatians, that upon their admittance of legal ceremonies, and falling from the grace of the gospel in the one point of justification, "Christ should profit them nothing," or they should have no benefit by what they yet retained of the profession of the gospel, chap. v. 2-6. And as to those who are carried away by the "strong delusion" of the grand apostasy, foretold 2 Thess. ii. 3-12, he says plainly that "they shall be damned," verse 12; and Peter also affirms that those who introduce "damnable heresies" do bring on themselves, and those that follow their pernicious ways, "swift destruction," 2 Pet. ii. 1, 2. So little countenance doth the Scripture give unto this effect of cursed security.

(3.) It likewise worketh by vain confidences. Most men think with Peter, and on no better grounds than he did (nor so good neither, as not being conscious unto themselves of so much sincerity as he was), that though all men should forsake the truth and purity of religion, yet they will not do so. But they understand not at all what it is to be preserved in an hour of temptation, nor what is required thereunto. They scorn to fall away, and yet they scorn all the means whereby they may be preserved from so doing. Tell them that they stand in need of the power of God for their preservation, of the intercession of Christ, of the constant supplies of the Spirit, of an experience of the goodness and efficacy of the truth, with the benefits which their own souls have received thereby; and that for this end they are to watch, pray, and live in a constant attendance unto all evangelical duties; and they despise them all through their pride, or neglect them through their spiritual sloth that they are given up unto. Such persons as these, if they meet with any thing that mates [9] their confidence, fall at once under the power of the next temptation they are assaulted withal.

Wherefore, whereas the generality of professed Christians are influenced, one way or other, by this woful security, it is no wonder if they are surprised and hurried away from their profession by seducers, or that they will be easily carried down the stream when they fall into a general inclination unto a defection.

V. Love of this present world and the perishing satisfactions of it betrays innumerable souls into frequent apostasies from the gospel. So the apostle assures us in the instance of Demas: 2 Tim. iv. 10, "Demas hath forsaken me, having loved this present world." And as he forsook the apostle, so also the work of the ministry, and it may be Christianity therewithal. I shall not insist on that love of the world which works by covetousness in the course of men's lives, though this be a means also disposing them unto apostasy; for our Saviour affirms that the "seed which falls among thorns is choked," -- the word which is received by men whose hearts are filled with the cares of this present world never comes to the perfection of fruit-bearing. I shall only make mention of two seasons wherein the predominancy of this love in the hearts of men multiplies apostates from the truth.

The first is that of persecution, wherein the professors compared by our Saviour unto the stony ground do presently fall away. "Such persons," saith he, "have no root in themselves, but, during for a while, when tribulation or persecution ariseth because of the word, they are offended," Matt. xiii. 20, 21. The first thing that persecution attacks the minds of men withal is their secular interests in this world; their wealth, their houses, lands, and possessions, are put into hazard by it. Willing, it may be, this sort of men are to follow Christ for a while, with the young man in the gospel; but when they hear that all they have will be hazarded, it may be must be parted withal, they go away sorrowful. Sorry they are for a while to leave that word or doctrine which before they had received with joy, as Matt. xiii. 20, but sorrowful as they are, love of the world overcomes all other considerations, and away they go. What multitudes such seasons have driven from the truth, what stars they have cast down from heaven, no nation hath had greater experience than our own in the days of Queen Mary. I pray God it never meet with another trial, and also hope that it is not likely so to do!

The other season when love of the world gives up men unto this fatal evil is, when and where superstition and error are enthroned. We may look into some foreign nations where the gospel had once taken great place, especially a great part of the nobles were obedient unto the faith; but the supreme power of the nations abiding in the hands of those of the Roman profession, and therewith the disposal of authority, riches, and honour, those vain bubbles of the world, and idols of corrupted minds, it is known what influence it hath had upon the profession of religion, most of the posterity of those great and truly noble persons which once professed the protestant religion being in most places fallen back into the old apostasy: for, their minds being filled with the love of this world, and precipitated by ambition into a fierce pursuit of their desires, finding the way to worldly honour and wealth shut up unto all that would steadfastly adhere unto the truth, they have generally sacrificed their convictions, consciences, and souls, unto this predominant lust. And such a season as this is more to be feared than persecution itself. Many have a generous stoutness not to be violently forced out of their persuasion and profession; but when these cursed baits are laid before men, with various pretences to stifle their consciences and advantages to keep up their reputation, there is no setting up a dam against the torrent of their love of this world. The warmth of the sun caused him to cast away his garment which the blustering of the wind did but wrap closer about him. The rays of power in honours and favours have made more cast away their religion in the neighbouring nations than persecutors ever could do. Whilst, therefore, the world is enthroned in the minds of men, whilst it is made their idol, whilst hopes of advance and fears of loss are the principal affections whereby their course of life is steered, profession of the truth stands upon very uncertain and ticklish terms. And therefore, whilst we see that the minds of multitudes are under the power of this lust, all the security which can be had of their continuance in the profession of the truth is their not being led into either of the temptations mentioned.

I shall not insist on other depraved affections of the minds of men. The truth is, there is no one prevalent lust, no one predominant sin no spiritual or moral disorder indulged unto, but it disposeth the soul first unto an under-valuation and then to a relinquishment of the truth, as occasions are offered.

VI. The hand of Satan is in this matter. He was the head of the first apostasy from God. Having himself fallen away from that place and order in the obediential part of the creation wherein he was made, the first work he engaged in (and he did it effectually) was, to draw mankind into the guilt of the same crime and rebellion; and ever since the revelation of the means of recovery for man (from which he was justly excluded), he hath pursued the same design towards all unto whom that way of recovery is proposed.

Thus he quickly carried away the whole old world upon the matter into idolatry. And ever since God hath been pleased to make known the way of life and salvation by Jesus Christ, his two great designs and works in the world have been to keep men off from receiving the gospel, and to turn them aside who have received it. The first he managed two ways, -- first, by stirring up raging, bloody persecutions against them that professed it, to deter others from engaging into the like way; and the other, by blinding the eyes of men, and filling them with prejudices against the truth, as the apostle declares, 2 Cor. iv. 4. By what ways and means in particular he carried on this first design, in both parts of it, belongs not unto our present inquiry. Failing herein, his principal design in the world hath been, and continueth yet to be, the corrupting of the minds of men about the truth, and drawing them off from it, in part or in whole. So the apostle intimates, 2 Cor. xi. 3, "I fear, lest by any means, as the serpent beguiled Eve through his subtilty, so your minds should be corrupted from the simplicity that is in Christ." It was the serpent by whom Eve was beguiled, but who is it the apostle is jealous that the Corinthians might have their minds corrupted by, from the simplicity that is in Christ; that is, by false doctrine, or, as it were, "another gospel," as he speaks, verse 4? It was the same serpent, by himself and in his agents, as he expresseth it, verses 14, 15. And he compareth his attempt to draw off professors from the gospel unto his attempt on Eve, whereby he began the apostasy from God in the state of nature. The tenor of the covenant was proposed unto our first parents in the prohibition of eating of the tree of knowledge of good and evil, and the threatening annexed thereunto; and he beguiled Eve by corrupting the threatening by his false interpretation of it, whereby he corrupted her mind. The tenor of the covenant of grace is proposed unto us principally in the promises of the gospel, which are the centre of the whole doctrine of it. These, therefore, he endeavours by all means to pervert, in opposition unto the wisdom and grace of God in them. Hereby he hopes to draw off men from the simplicity that is in Christ, or the plain declaration of the will of God in the gospel, unto false and foolish imaginations of his own suggestion. And what a hand he was to have in the great apostasy the apostle foretells, 2 Thess. ii. 9-11. There was to be the working of Satan in it, and strong or effectual delusions, unto the, belief of lies; which are all from him, who is the father of them. So men departed from the faith by "giving heed to seducing spirits," 1 Tim. iv. 1, -- that is, to the devil and his agents. It would be too long a digression, to engage into a particular inquiry how, by what ways and means, Satan prevails with men to turn them off from the truth, and turn them unto fables. How he blinds their minds, how he inflames their lusts, how he presents occasions, how he suggests temptations, with false and corrupt reasonings; what colours and pretences he puts upon his designs when he transforms himself into an angel of light; with what power, signs, and lying wonders, he gives countenance to his delusions; how he works on the minds of seducers, how on the minds of them that are to be seduced; how he stirs up persecution against the truth and its profession, -- would require a discourse, fully to declare, longer than the whole of this is designed to be. It may suffice to know that he is not weary nor wanting unto any of those manifold advantages which are administered unto him. He is at work in all places at this day; in some, making havoc of the churches; in others, by various wiles and artifices, filling the minds of men with prejudices against the truth, and turning them from it.

Lastly, God doth not look on all these things as an unconcerned spectator. He, indeed, "is not tempted with evil;" he tempteth none, he seduceth none; but he rules them all, and overrules all events unto his own glory. He will not suffer men first to undervalue and despise, and then to reject and forsake, the chiefest of his mercies, such as his word and truth are, without reflecting on them with some acts of his severity. Wherefore, when men, from the corrupt principles mentioned, seduced by the lusts of their own hearts and entangled by the deceits of Satan, do relinquish the truth, God, in his holy, righteous judgment, gives them up unto farther delusions, so that they shall complete their apostasy, and grow obstinate therein unto their destruction. When a people, a nation, a church, or private persons, have received the gospel and the profession thereof, not walking answerably thereunto, God may forsake them, and withdraw from them the means of their edification and preservation. The rule of his continuance with any people or church, as to the outward dispensation of his providence and the means of grace, is that expressed 2 Chron. xv. 2, "The Lord is with you, while ye be with him; and if ye seek him, he will be found of you; but if ye forsake him, he will forsake you." He judicially forsakes them by whom he is wilfully forsaken.

God may be forsaken by men in one way, and he may righteously forsake them in another. For instance; under the profession of the truth, men may give up themselves unto all ungodliness and unrighteousness, unto a flagitious course of life in all abominations, so holding the truth captive in unrighteousness. In this case God ofttimes, in a way of punishment, gives men up unto an apostasy from the truth which they have professed, to show that he will not always have it prostituted unto the lusts of men. So the apostle speaks expressly, 2 Thess. ii. 10-12. Although they received the truth in the profession of it, yet they loved it not; they yielded not obedience unto it, but took pleasure in sin: therefore God ordered things so that they should reject the truth itself also, and believe lies, unto their own destruction. Herein at this day lies the danger of a total and ruinous apostasy. Multitudes, the generality of all sorts, the body of the people, do yet assent unto and profess the truth; but, alas! what are the lives and conversations of many under that profession? How do all manner of sins abound among us! The profession of the truth by not a few is the greatest dishonour and disparagement that can be cast upon it. The best service many can do it is by forsaking it, and declaring that the belief of it is inconsistent with their cursed wicked lives. And may we not justly fear lest such persons should speedily be given up, by one means or other, to "strong delusion, to believe a lie," unto their just damnation? And on the other hand, also, God sometimes gives men up to sins and wickednesses in practice, because of the rejection of the truth which they have received. So he dealt with them who liked not those notions of truth which they had concerning him, his being and his providence, from the light of nature, Rom. i. 28. And so he usually deals with all apostates. If they will forsake the truth, they shall forsake righteousness and holiness, which are the proper fruits of it, and be given up unto all abominable lusts and practices.

We may therefore inquire by what ways and means God doth so punish and revenge the beginnings of wilful apostasy from the gospel, so that men shall complete them and prove obstinate in them unto their eternal destruction. And this he doth, --

First, By removing his candlestick from among them. This the Lord Jesus threatens his backsliding church withal, Rev. ii. 5. God will, by one means or another, deprive them of the light and means of the knowledge of the truth, so that ignorance and darkness shall cover them and irresistibly increase upon them. Some of the instruments of light, it may be, shall be taken away by death, and some shall lie under prejudices; the gifts of the Spirit shall be restrained or withheld from others, that they shall have darkness for vision, and "the sword of the Lord shall be upon their right eye, that it shall be quite dried up." In this condition of things, the minds of apostates, already bent upon backsliding, are, by their ignorance and darkness, more and more filled with prejudices against the truth, and alienated from it; for as they lose the knowledge and faith of any part of truth, their minds are possessed with what is opposite thereunto.

Secondly, In this condition God "sends them strong delusion, that they may believe a lie," 2 Thess. ii. 11. God is, as it were, now resolved on the end of these persons, -- what they have righteously deserved; and therefore he makes use of any means, as it is merely penal, to bring them thereunto. And as by the former act of his displeasure he took from them the knowledge of his truth, so by this he gives them up irrecoverably to adhere unto a lie. They shall not only profess it, but believe it; which is the cruellest slavery the mind of man is capable of. Now, God's sending on men "strong delusion, that they may believe a lie," consists in these things:--

1. Delivering them up to the power of Satan. He is the grand seducer, the deluder of the souls of men, the first author of lying, whose principal design it is to win over the faith and assent of men thereunto. This work he stands continually ready for, but that God is pleased to limit, bound, and restrain him, with respect unto those who are yet under his especial care. But as to these apostates, God breaks down all his fences about them, and by his efficacious permission suffers Satan to act his part to the utmost for their delusion. This was the state of things under the papal apostasy, wherein Satan had deluded men, as it should seem, to the satisfaction of his utmost malice; and to show how absolute he was in his success, he did, as it were, make sport with the deluded souls of men. There was nothing so foolish and sottish that he did not impose on their credulity. Many volumes will not

contain the stories of those ridiculous follies which he so imposed on the minds of poor deluded mortals, wherein he seemed to sport himself in the misery of blinded mankind. God grant that he never receive a commission to act the same part among us, whose sins seem to cry aloud for it, and men live as if they longed to be again given up to the power of the devil!

2. By suffering seducers and false teachers to come among a people with such advantageous outward circumstances as shall further their success. These seducers prepare themselves for their work by their own inclinations and the suggestions of Satan; but God, for the executing of his just displeasure, will, by his providence, put advantages into their hands of prevailing over the minds of men. So the chief seducers in the world at this day, -- namely, the pope and those acting with or under him, -- have possessed such place and obtained such reputation among men as gives them ofttimes an uncontrollable success in their work. Did men stand upon even ground with them who were in the profession of the truth, should any so come unto them to persuade them unto the errors, superstitions, and idolatry of the Papacy, they could not but despise their offer; but these men having once gotten the name of "The temple of God," and showing themselves to the people in the stead and place of God, what could they not draw and seduce them unto? Neither is their superstition or profession continued on any other grounds on the minds of the multitude, but only by that power over the consciences of men which names, titles, and the places they seem to possess in the church, do give unto them. Then, therefore, doth God give up men to delusions, when in his providence he affords such advantages unto them by whom they are to be deluded; for those who possess the places of outward veneration may lead a backsliding multitude unto what they please.

Lastly, God doth judicially smite such persons with blindness of mind and hardness of heart, that they shall not see, nor perceive, nor understand, even when the means of light and truth are proposed unto them. This effect of God's severity is declared, Isa. vi. 9, 10; and application is made of it unto the Jews under the ministry of our Saviour himself, John xii. 39-41, and that of the apostles, Acts xxviii. 25-27, and is expounded, Rom. xi. 7, 8.

When things are come to this issue; when God subducts the means of grace from men in whole or in part, or as unto their efficacy; when he permits Satan to deceive them by strong delusions; and, moreover, himself smites them with hardness of heart and blindness of mind, -- then is the state of such apostates miserable and irrecoverable. We are not, therefore, to think it strange that the light of the gospel diffuses itself no more in the world, -- that so eminent a stop is put unto its progress. God hath put an end unto his gracious dealings with some kinds of apostates, and they are reserved for another dispensation of his providence.

These are some of the general principles of that defection which is in the world from the mystery and truth of the gospel, with the reasons and causes of them; unto which more, I doubt not, of the like nature may be added.

But there is, moreover, a particular consideration to be had of those especial truths which any turn away from, and the imaginations they fall into; whereof the especial grounds and reasons, superadded unto those we have considered, as equally respecting every kind of defection from the gospel, are also to be inquired into; and it shall be done in one instance among ourselves.

Footnotes:

9. "Upsets," or "confounds." -- Ed.

Chapter VII – Instance of a peculiar defection from the truth of the gospel; with the reasons of it

Besides the reasons insisted on, which have a general influence into all apostasies from the doctrine or mystery of the gospel, each especial defection in every kind hath reasons and causes peculiarly suited unto its rise and furtherance. There are, indeed, not a few who forsake the truth which they have professed merely on the impressions of outward circumstances, in the encouraging examples of some who go before them in the same paths, from whom they expect advantage. And every age giveth us, in one place or another, renewed evidence, that, -- where either secular interest or weariness of the truth, through the love of the present world and hatred of holiness or strict evangelical obedience, doth give a propensity unto a declension from any doctrines of the gospel unto persons whose grandeur and outward advantages are sufficient to attract a compliance from the minds of men under the power of ambition, or any importunate desire of earthly things, -- multitudes of all sorts suppose there is nothing left for them but to crowd who shall come nearest the leaders in the apostasy. And it is not seldom that, meeting with new temptations, they outrun both them and themselves also into such extremes as at first they designed not; for hence it is that so many do even at present issue their recessions from the truth, under the conduct of those "ignes fatui" or erratic exhalations of countenance and favour, in the undesigned bogs of Popery on the one hand, or Socinianism on the other. But I shall not at present take them into farther consideration; nor, indeed, are they worthy of any at all whose minds are visibly biassed, in the profession of things spiritual and heavenly, with those that are earthly and carnal.

They are of another sort from whom we may take an instance of the especial reasons of a peculiar defection from the gospel; for it is manifest how some among ourselves are fallen off from the whole mystery of it, with respect unto the person and grace of Christ, the satisfaction for sin made by his death, the atonement by the blood of his sacrifice, justification by his righteousness, and sanctification by his Spirit. If any shall think themselves unduly charged herein, they may be pleased to know that none are intended but those who are really guilty. Whosoever owns the things mentioned, though he will causelessly make use of peculiar words of his own for their expression, neither scriptural nor proper, nor such as believers have in former ages been accustomed unto, yet whilst the things themselves are believed and received, at present we lay nothing to his charge. But unless, to secure a groundless, useless, irrational charity, we wilfully shut our eyes and stop our ears, we cannot avoid the evidence that these things are by many even totally renounced: yea, and this is done by them to the greatest disadvantage of themselves and dishonour of the truth that can be well imagined; for their profession is, that they have tried Christ and the gospel in these things, and find there is nothing in them for which they should abide in the faith of them or place their confidence in them.

I hope none of them have gone unto such length as to cast themselves under the dreadful doom in the apostolical, passage insisted on; but that their condition is dangerous cannot be denied. To prevent the like state in ourselves and others, we may do well to consider what are the true, real, next and immediate springs and reasons of such men's apostasy from the mystery of the gospel, as added unto the general reasons of all apostasy of this kind before mentioned; for so it is, that besides those general reasons and causes which have their efficacy and influence in all apostasies, and must always be considered in this matter, there are also reasons that are peculiar unto every especial instance of backsliding in any kind.

First, Ignorance of the necessity of Jesus Christ and the benefits of his mediation unto life and salvation hath betrayed them first into an indifferency about them, and then into a defection from them. They want a true, and in their own souls a full, conviction of their personal want of these things. Such apostates arise out of loose, notional professors, who never had any sound convictions of the want of Christ, like them [mentioned in] Acts ii. 37, or him, chap. xvi. 30. And although they lived, some of them, a long time in the outward profession that such a conviction of the worth and use of Christ and his grace was necessary unto them that would be saved, yet dare they not own that ever themselves had any such conviction; for if they had, why do they now forsake him as unto those ends for which they were convinced he was so to be desired? That faith alone will never forsake Christ which springs out of or is built on a conviction of the want of him. They who are well and in health will not always esteem the physician.

Unto this conviction of the want of Christ two things are required in all men, according to the measure of the light which they have received:--

1. The knowledge of the nature, guilt, filth, and desert of sin: for he came to save us from our sins; and no man will look after him to be delivered from he knows not what, or look to the brazen serpent who is not stung. Few have any knowledge hereof but what they cannot avoid, and fewer are sensible of these things in a due manner. The great design of Satan at this day in the world is, to extenuate sin in opinion, and so countenance it in practice Indeed, it ever was so; but it is in a peculiar manner at present visible and open, though the conspiracy be so strong that a public resistance unto it is scarcely maintainable. His aim in it is, and ever was, to take off from the necessity and usefulness of Christ and his grace, against which his malice is principally bent; and when once he can convey away the relief, he will be ready enough to aggravate the evil. Hence are those opinions so diligently advanced and greedily embraced against the guilt and power of original sin and the depravation of our nature, wherein men of all sorts conspire. Whatever some men may design, his end in them all is no other but to prevent a conviction of the want we have of Christ. So, also, are sins in practice extenuated; spiritual sins against the gospel are made nothing of, yea, laughed at, and immoralities against the law are lightly esteemed and easily passed over. To take off at present a sense of the want of Christ, and to make way for future apostasy, is the end of these and the like corrupt opinions. Accordingly it is come to pass in the world. Never was there less regard of the person and offices of Christ, of his grace, and benefits of his mediation, among them that are called Christians, than is found among many at this day. Unless God graciously relieve, the world is like to lose Christ out of the gospel, as to the true glory of his person and use of his mediation. Thus was it with the generality of them concerning whom we speak. They never had a thorough practical conviction of the want of Christ; for if they had had, they

would not so shamefully have left him as they have done. The general notions they had hereof serve only to entitle them unto a defection I know these things are despised by many, unto whom the want of Christ and the receiving of him, or an interest in him, are contemptible things. But that is all one. We must not forego the gospel, with our own experience, and ruin our souls, to escape their reproaches. Sin will be sin, and Christ will be Christ, and salvation by him will be what it is, when they have done what they can.

2. Hereunto is required a knowledge and sense of the weakness of the best of our duties, and their utter insuffciency to abide the trial in the sight of God. Without the former we cannot have, and without the latter we can never abide in, a sense of the want of Christ. A right consideration of the instability of our minds in them, the weak actings of grace for the most part, the weariness of the flesh that accompanies them, secret impressions from self, and inward oppositions from sin, that attend them, with the greatness and holiness of God with whom we have to do in them, is indispensably necessary to keep the Lord Christ and his grace always desirable unto us. Want hereof makes some dream of a perfection in themselves, and others of a justification by their own obedience; the first tending to the contempt, the latter unto the neglect, of Christ and his grace. This is the beginning of transgression unto many apostates. They never had a due sense of the want of Christ, either as to their deliverance from the guilt of sin, or as to the procuring of a righteousness wherewith they might appear in the presence of God. This are they to inquire after who shall endeavour their recovery. To contend with them about their own imaginations is, for the most part, endless and fruitless. Let it be inquired whether they ever had any conviction of the want of Christ for the pardon of sin, or for the obtaining of life and salvation. If they shall grant they had, it may be asked why they do not make use of him unto the ends with respect whereunto they were convinced of the want of him; and if they do so, we have no contest with them in this matter. If they acknowledge that they never had any such conviction, this is that which we are to confirm, that such a conviction of the want of Christ is indispensably necessary unto the salvation of all that are adult; and herein we have the testimony, upon the matter, of the whole Scripture, the law and the gospel, to confirm the truth we contend for. Want, therefore, hereof was one spring of this defection. For those who have owned the necessity of him, or an interest in him, for the ends mentioned, and afterward declare that there is nothing of goodness or truth in what they have found and discovered for which they should continue so to do, their profession is, that they have considered this matter, known it, and do condemn it; wherein the formal nature of apostasy doth consist. And all those disciples which they draw after them, they do it by hiding from them, or drawing them off from, any sense of a want of Christ or of his mediation. That which is the foundation of our profession, in opposition hereunto, which we lay the weight of all our eternal concerns upon, is, that without Christ, before we receive him as set forth by God to be a propitiation through faith in his blood, we are in a lost, undone, and accursed condition; that our closing with him, our believing in him, is upon a conviction of our want of him for life, righteousness, and acceptation with God, both before and after believing. And it is in vain for Satan himself to attempt the faith of God's elect herein. A concurrence of plain revelation and evident experience is invincible. But he who never knew, who never was made deeply sensible of, the want of an interest in Christ, will never persevere in the pin, suit of it, nor abide in what he hath attained, when attacked by any vigorous temptation.

Secondly, Want of a spiritual view of the excellency of Christ, both in his person and offices, is another spring and cause of this declension from the faith of the gospel. This view of him in types, shadows, and promises, was the life of the faith of the saints under the old testament. Herein "Abraham saw his day, and rejoiced," John viii. 56. So Cant. ii. 8, 17. And it is mentioned as their chiefest privilege, Isa. xxxiii. 17. These things they diligently inquired into, 1 Pet. i. 11, and longed after, desiring, if it were possible, to see them, Matt. xiii. 17; for the glory and life of all religion, of all intercourse with God, lay in them from the giving of the first promise. Christ was "all and in all" unto them, no less than unto us. Take a respect unto him and his offices out of the old administrations, and they are things of no value or signification. And it was better for them who were inquiring after Christ diligently under dark types and shadows, than it will be for those among us who shut their eyes at the glorious light of the gospel And the reason why he was rejected by the Jews at his coming (for "he came unto his own, and his own received him not," John i. 11), was, because they could "see neither form, nor comeliness, nor beauty in him, why he should be desired," Isa. liii. 2. None can or will abide constant in his doctrine who is not able spiritually to discern the glory of his person and offices. Hence the apostles lay it down as the foundation of their faith, that "they beheld his glory, the glory as of the only-begotten of the Father, full of grace and truth," John i. 14; and that which they had in themselves they endeavoured to communicate unto others, that they also might believe through their word, and have fellowship with him, 1 John i. 3. So he himself makes this the foundation of his church, the rock upon which he will build it; for on the confession of Peter that he was "the Christ, the Son of the living God" (which expresseth the glory both of his person as the Son of the living God, and of his offices as the Christ), he says, "On this rock will I build my church, and the gates of hell shall not prevail against it," Matt. xvi. 16-18. Whosoever builds not hereon builds on the sand, and will be prevailed against. So our apostle declares that those that hold him not as the Head will be beguiled, and vainly puffed up by their fleshly minds, falling into foolish errors and vain curiosities, Col. ii. 18, 19. And he rests the whole foundation of all gospel faith in this glory of his person and offices, Heb. i. 2, 3; Col. i. 15-19. It is this knowledge of him alone that will make us disesteem and despise all other things in comparison of him, Phil. iii. 8-10.

Wherefore, a spiritual view of him, an acquaintance with him, as "the brightness of the Father's glory, and the express image of his person," as him in whom all the perfections of the divine nature, as wisdom, goodness, and grace, do centre, as to their manifestation, even in the union of his natures, the glory of his offices, the suitableness of his person and grace unto all the wants and desires of the souls of men, is indispensably necessary unto our preservation from apostasy. And I could easily manifest by particular instances that a failing herein hath had a principal and prevalent influence into all the apostasies that have been in the Christian world, both as unto faith and worship. It is, though a new, yet a most wicked attempt that Satan is making by some against the whole of our religion; whilst allowing his person to be what it is (which for secular ends they dare not deny), they endeavour to render him of little or no use in our profession. This is to "fight neither against small nor great, but against the King of Israel;" and if such serpentine attempts be not prevented, the public profession of religion among us will issue in atheism, or somewhat of a near alliance thereunto.

Thus it seems to be with some of them of whom we speak. They had, among other notional professors, an historical knowledge of Christ, and thereof made profession, but they were never spiritually acquainted with the glorious excellencies of his person and offices; for if they had, they would not have forsaken the "great mystery of godliness, God manifested in the flesh," for other uncouth notions of their own. Who can think it possible that any one who hath known the Lord Jesus Christ, the Lord of glory, the Son of God incarnate, receiving our nature into a hypostatical union with himself and a blessed subsistence in his own person, as proposed unto us in the gospel, as evidently therein crucified before our eyes, as the apostle and high priest of our profession, as our advocate with the Father, as making peace for us and reconciliation through the blood of his cross, as made of God unto us wisdom, righteousness, sanctification, and redemption; -- who that ever had experience or benefit, in his temptations and trials, of his love, care, tenderness, compassion, readiness and ability to succour them that come to God by him, -- can renounce all these things, to betake himself to vain notions of a light and perfection of his own in their stead? I hope they are few who do so practically, but the expressions of many have a dangerous aspect that way; and it is certain there is nothing more necessary unto all that are called Christians than to have clear, distinct notions in themselves of the person of Christ, and plainly to declare how they place their whole faith, hope, and trust in him. And for such as really do so, though not able to express themselves in a due manner, yea, though unduly captivated unto some novel conceptions and expressions, the good Lord pardon them, and let mercy and peace be on them, and on the whole Israel of God! Whereas, therefore, some who have made a profession of these things do now relinquish them, I shall pray they may take heed that they do not thereby "crucify the Son of God afresh, and put him to an open shame." Neither is it a verbal acknowledgment, in owning that Christ which suffered at Jerusalem, which will free any from this charge and guilt. Unless the Lord Christ, that Christ which is God and man in one person, be owned, received, believed in, loved, trusted unto, and obeyed in all things, as he is proposed unto us in the Scripture, and with respect unto all the ends of righteousness, holiness, life, and salvation, for which he is so proposed, he is renounced and forsaken. Who can sufficiently express the cunning sleights of Satan? who can sufficiently bewail the foolishness of the hearts of men, that after they have, at least doctrinally, known and professed these things, they should be turned aside from the glory, truth, and holiness of them? Let Christians therefore know and beware, that if they find any decay in faith, love, delight, and trust in the person and mediation of Christ, they are in the way that leads to some cursed apostasy of one kind or another.

But where the divine person of Christ is denied, or all acquaintance with him is despised; where the communication of grace from him unto believers is scorned; where no use by faith of his love, care, compassion, and power, as our high priest and advocate with the Father, in our duties, sins, temptations, and sufferings, is allowed, -- we need not represent the danger of falling into apostasy; such persons are already in the depth of it. I speak this with the more earnestness, because, of all the evils which I have seen in the course of my pilgrimage (now hastening unto its period), there hath been none more grievous than the public contempt I have lived to see cast on the person of Christ, as to its concernment in our religion, and the benefits we receive from him. But God taketh care of these things.

Thirdly, Want of experience of the power and efficacy of the Spirit and grace of Christ, of his life and death, for the mortification of sin, hath been another spring of this apostasy. How it is wrought by these means, and can be no otherwise accomplished, I have showed elsewhere at large, and must not here assume the same argument again; only, two things may be observed concerning this work and duty: as, --

1. It is that wherein or whereunto the greatest wisdom and exercise of faith doth consist, or is required. It is a matter purely evangelical, to derive strength and ability from Christ for the mortification of sin, by virtue of his death, in a way of believing. Unenlightened reason can neither see nor understand any thing of this matter; yea, it is foolishness unto it, as are all other mysteries of the gospel. There is not any other way for the same end which it will not more willingly embrace.

2. It is a work and duty whereunto there is a great reluctancy in the flesh, in corrupted nature. There is nothing it had rather be freed from, and that whether we respect the inward nature of it or the constant continuance in it that is required of us. Yet is it such as that without it we can never attain life and salvation; for "if we by the Spirit do mortify the deeds of the flesh, we shall live," and not otherwise. Wherefore, when men once begin to be sensible of the powerful inward workings of sin, they will take one of these two ways, nor can they do otherwise: for either they will yield themselves up "servants unto sin," and make "provision for the flesh to fulfil the lusts thereof," according as they are able, and as far as consists with their secular interest, as do the most; or they will betake themselves to some way or other for its restraint and mortification, either in part or in whole. And here many things will present themselves unto such persons, some, it may be, of their own devising, and some of God's appointment, but for other ends than what they apply them unto. Hence multitudes faint in this work, and at length utterly give it over. They begin in the Spirit and end in the flesh; for, not striving lawfully nor in the right way, sin gets ground and strength against them, and they yield up themselves to the service of it. Hence have we so many who, having under their convictions contended against their lusts in their youth, do give up themselves unto them in their age. But so it is in this matter, that those who, through their unbelief, cannot rise or attain unto an experience of the power and efficacy of the grace of Christ for the mortification of sin will betake themselves to somewhat else for their relief; and this is that principally which hath brought forth that light within among some, which must do all this work for them, and much more. If any will betake themselves thereunto, they shall find that remedy against sin, and that perfection of holiness, in a few days, which they had been looking for from Christ a long season to no purpose. So would they have us to think who, it may be, never had experience what it is to derive spiritual strength from Christ, or to wait on him for it; only they have been wearied by the successlessness of their convictions, and the burdensomeness of lifeless duties. For some of them were for a season not only sober in their conversation (which I hope they yet continue to be), but diligent in duties of religion; but finding neither life, power, nor success in them, through their own uncured unbelief, they seem to have grown weary of them: for nothing is more grievous than the outward form of spiritual duties where there is no experience of inward power and sweetness. Wherefore, the corrupt minds of men will be ready to relinquish them for any thing that pretends a better relief.

What was the reason that so many in the Papacy betook themselves to penances, severe disciplines, and self-macerations, for the relief of their consciences with respect unto the mortification of sin? It all sprang from this root, or ignorance of the power and efficacy of the Spirit and grace of Christ for that end. Somewhat must be done unto this purpose, and not knowing the right way and gospel method of it, they betook themselves unto what they could invent, or what was imposed on them by the superstition of others, that pretended to afford them a relief. Somewhat hereof those among us seemed for a while to make an appearance of, in an outward gravity and seeming austerity of life; but the things themselves they had no mind unto, as not compliant with other interests they had to pursue. But the light within shall do all of this kind for them; wherefore, in comparison thereof, and as unto this end at least, they reject the Lord Christ, and do what in them lies to "put him to an open shame;" for what do they less who declare that that is done in a few days for them by another means which could not be effected by the faith which for so long a season they professed in him? But the cause of the whole lies solely in their own ignorance and want of experience of the things which themselves professed.

Fourthly, Ignorance of the righteousness of God hath been another spring of this apostasy. This the apostle expressly declares to be the reason why men go about to establish a righteousness of their own: Rom. x. 3, "Being ignorant of God's righteousness, and going about to establish their own righteousness, they have not submitted themselves unto the righteousness of God." And this he speaks of the Jews, and that the best of them, who "followed after the law of righteousness, but sought it as it were by the works of the law," Rom. ix. 31, 32. Of all men they thought themselves most knowing of the "righteousness of God;" for they "made their boast of God, and knew" (as they thought and professed) "his will, and approved the things that are more excellent, being instructed out of the law, and were confident that they themselves were guides of the blind, and the light of them which are in darkness, instructors of the foolish, and teachers of babes, having the form of knowledge and of the truth in the law," Rom. ii. 17-20. Yet these men submitted not unto the righteousness of God, but went about to establish their own righteousness, because they were ignorant of the righteousness of God. And wheresoever this ignorance is, men will do so.

Take the "righteousness of God" in any sense wherein it is mentioned in the Scripture, and this event will follow upon the ignorance thereof; for it must be either the righteousness that is in him, or the righteousness he requires of us in the law, or the righteousness he hath provided for us in the gospel. Consider it any of these ways, and the ignorance of it is that which countenanceth men in betaking themselves unto a righteousness of their own, yea, unavoidably casteth them upon it; for, --

1. A right understanding of the infinite purity, the glorious essential holiness, of the nature of God, of his absolute eternal righteousness as the Lord and judge of all, will teach men what apprehensions they ought to have of any thing done in them or by them. "Our God is a consuming fire," Heb. xii. 29; "a God of purer eyes than to behold evil," Hab. i. 13; "who will by no means clear the guilty," Exod. xxxiv. 7; "whose judgment it is, that they which commit sin are worthy of death," Rom. i. 32; "an holy God, a jealous God, who will not forgive transgressions and sins," Josh. xxiv. 19. Whilst the dread and terror of the excellency of his holiness and righteousness is before men, they will not easily betake themselves and their trust unto a righteousness of their own. There are two sorts of persons that the Scripture represents under an apprehension of this righteousness of God. The first are, convinced, guilty sinners; and the other, humble, holy believers. And what thoughts of themselves each sort is thereon filled withal it doth declare. For the former sort, we have an instance in Adam, Gen. iii. 10; in others, Isa. xxxiii. 14, as also Mic. vi. 6, 7. The sum is, they can think of nothing, have no other conceptions in their minds, but how either they may flee from him and hide themselves, or feign to themselves impossible ways of atonement, or be swallowed up in horror and despair. Send them in this condition unto a righteousness of their own, and

they will easily understand you do but reproach their misery. And for the other sort, or humble, holy believers, we may see also how on this occasion they express themselves in this matter, Job iv. 17-19, ix. 2; Ps. cxxx. 3, cxliii. 2. They all jointly acknowledge that, such is the glorious holiness and righteousness of God, such the imperfection of our righteousness and impurity of our works, there is no appearance or standing before him on their account. It is the want of a due meditation hereon that hath produced the many presumptuous opinions in the world concerning the justification of sinners. The Scripture, speaking of justification, directs us to conceive it "in God's sight," Ps. cxliii. 2, or "before him," Rom. iii. 20; teaching us that in this matter we should set ourselves as in the presence and under the eye of this holy God, and then consider on what ground we may stand before him. But when men are "ignorant of the righteousness of God," when they have secret thoughts that he is "altogether such an one as themselves," as the psalmist speaks, -- that is, one who is either not so holy in himself as is pretended, or one who doth not require a suitableness in us unto his holiness, but is little concerned in our duties, less in our sins, -- is it any wonder if men think they can of themselves do that which is satisfactory unto him, and so "go about to establish their own righteousness?" And this way even in teaching have some betaken themselves unto. They endeavour to satisfy their disciples that there is no such severity in God against sin as some pretend, no such holiness in his nature as necessarily to infer an indignation against every sin; that they are but vain frights and needless disquietments which either their own consciences or the preaching of some men do put them unto. And if they can prevail to be credited herein, there is no doubt but that those whom they so persuade will be pleased with their own righteousness: but whether God, in this matter of justification, will be pleased with it or no is not so easy to be determined.

And hence it is that all opinions of a self-righteousness, or justification by works, have always produced licentiousness of life, though they who assert it clamorously pretend to the contrary. So when a righteousness of works was absolutely enthroned in the Papacy, before the Reformation, the lives of the generality of men were flagitiously wicked, and most of the good works that were performed amongst them were but barterings with God and conscience for horrible vices and impieties. According, also, unto the growth of the same opinion, in its various degrees, among us, is the progress of all sorts of impiety and licentiousness of life. And if the masters of these opinions would but open their eyes, they would see that whereas they assert their justification by works under a pretence of a necessity so to do, for the maintenance of holiness and righteousness among men, unholiness, unrighteousness, intemperance of life, and all abominations, do grow upon them, such as were not heard of in former days among them who made any profession of religion. And the reason hereof is, because the very same notions of God which will allow men to suppose that they may be justified in his sight by their own duties, will also accommodate their lusts with several apprehensions that he will not be so severe against their sins as is supposed. However, this is plain in matter of fact, that the opinion of self-righteousness and looseness of conversation in the practice of sin have gone together generally, from the days of the Pharisees to this present season. And as this proud conceit receives daily advancement in several degrees, under various pretences, it is to be feared the world will be more and more filled with the bitter fruits thereof. It is grace, and the doctrine of it, as well as its power, that must put a stop to sin. He that drives men into a righteousness of their own at one door opens another unto their sins. And all that we have got hitherto by fierce disputations about justification as it were by works, is only that the faith of some hath been weakened, the peace of multitudes disquieted, differences increased, without the least evidence of holiness improved or the vices of men reformed by them. And it will not be granted that the strictest professors in these days (whether they have imbibed these opinions or no) do in real holiness and fruitfulness of life exceed those of the foregoing age, who firmly, and without hesitation, trusted unto the Lord Christ alone for life, righteousness, and salvation.

2. Suppose the righteousness God requires of us in the law to be intended; the ignorance thereof also is a great reason why men venture on a righteousness of their own, and go about to establish it. Were they indeed acquainted with the purity, spirituality, severity, and inexorableness of the law, they would never be possessed with imaginations that the perfection which they dream of in themselves would endure its trial. But when men shall suppose that the law respects only outward duties, and those also of the greatest notoriety, as to sin and obedience, and can relieve themselves in sundry things by pharisaical distinctions and expositions of it; when they consider not, or understand not, the extent of it, -- unto an exacting of the entire image of God in us, wherein we were created, unto the regulating of all the frames, figments, and first motions of the heart, and its application of the curse unto the least deviation from it, -- they may please or some way satisfy themselves by establishing a righteousness of their own, as it were by the works of the law.

3. But the "righteousness of God" in this place is taken principally for that righteousness which he hath provided for us in the gospel; and what this is the apostle declares in the next verse: "For," says he, "Christ is the end of the law for righteousness unto every one that believeth," Rom. x. 4. And this he calls "The righteousness which is of faith," chap. ix. 30. Wherefore, the "righteousness of God" is Christ as fulfilling the law and answering the end of it, received by faith. This is that righteousness of God, which whosoever are ignorant of and submit not unto, they will go about to establish a righteousness of their own, and trust unto it. And thus hath it openly and visibly fallen out with them concerning whom we treat. They will not deny but that, under their convictions, they were solicitous after a righteousness with which God might be well pleased; -- and if they should deny it, they were not to be believed, because it is impossible it should be otherwise with any in that condition; for conviction is principally a sense of the want of a righteousness. In this state, the gospel which they had, and which it may be they heard preached, presented unto them "Christ as the end of the law for righteousness unto every one that believeth," as it is fully declared, Rom. iii. 21-26, with chap. v. 18, 19. This divers of them for a season professed themselves to embrace and acquiesce in. But when things came to the trial, it generally appeared that they had all along been ignorant of this righteousness of God; for they have left it for a righteousness of their own, which, had they truly and really known it, they could not have done. He who hath ever truly and really made Christ the end of the law for righteousness unto himself, by believing, will not cast contempt and scorn upon his righteousness imputed unto us, as is the manner of some to do. But herein is the Son of God in some measure "crucified afresh, and put to an open shame." When men shall profess that they did look after righteousness by him, and would have received him as the end of the law for righteousness, but not finding that therein which they expected, they have betaken themselves to a righteousness wholly within them, and so wholly their own, they will not easily contrive a way whereby

they may reflect more dishonour upon him. Whatever pretences may be made to the contrary, whatever maze of words any may lead men into and tire them withal, whatever reviling and reproaching of others they may compass them with, they cannot but know in their own consciences that it is thus with them.

Notwithstanding any profession that they ever made, they never did come, nor ever could attain unto, a real knowledge of and acquaintance with this righteousness of God, so as to receive it by faith, and obtain thereby rest unto their souls. And hence it is that, as unto profession at least, they have betaken themselves unto an endeavour to establish their own righteousness; which, if it produce and effect a real holy conversation and righteousness in them of any long continuance, they are the first in whom it ever had that effect in this world, and will be the last in whom it shall find that success.

Fifthly, Want of submission unto the sovereignty of God hath contributed unto the furtherance of this evil. The sovereignty of God acting itself in infinite wisdom and grace is the sole foundation of the covenant of grace, and runs through the whole mystery of the gospel. Thence proceedeth the incarnation of the Son of God, and his being filled with all grace to be a Saviour, John iii. 16; Col. i. 19; John i. 16. Other account thereof none can be given. Thence was his substitution as the surety of the covenant in our stead, to undergo the punishment due to our sins, Isa. liii. 6, 10; 2 Cor. v. 21. Eternal election flows from thence, and is regulated thereby, Rom. ix. 11, 18; so doth effectual vocation, Matt. xi. 25, 26, and justification by faith, Rom. iii. 30. The like may be said of all other mysteries of the gospel. Love, grace, goodness, dispensed in a way of sovereign, unaccountable pleasure, are in them all proposed as the objects of our faith. The carnal mind is pleased with nothing of all this, but riseth up in opposition unto every instance of it. It will not bear that the will, wisdom, and pleasure of God should be submitted unto and adored in the paths which it cannot trace. Hence the incarnation and cross of the Son of God are foolishness unto it, 1 Cor. i. 23-25; the decrees of God as to election and reprobation unjust and unequal, overthrowing all religion, Rom. ix. 17-21; justification through the imputation of the righteousness of Christ that which everts the law, and renders all our own righteousness unnecessary. So in the whole mystery, in all the doctrines, precepts, or promises of the gospel, that spring from or are resolved into the sovereignty of God, -- the carnal mind riseth up in opposition unto them all; for whereas the formal nature of faith consisteth in giving glory to God by believing the things that are above reason as it is ours, and against it as it is carnal, Rom. iv. 18-21, this sets up an enmity unto it in all things. It is therefore always tumultuating against the mysteries of the gospel; and if it once come to make itself the judge of them, taking aid from sensual affections and the vain imaginations of the mind, it will make havoc of all the articles of faith. And thus it seems to have fallen out in this matter. Those concerning whom we treat seem to have cast off a due regard unto the sovereignty of God, because themselves were never bowed by faith savingly thereto. Wherefore, in an opposition unto it, they have set up their light within, as the rule, measure, and judge, of the truths and doctrines of the gospel. Instead of becoming fools, by a resignation of their reason and wisdom to the sovereignty of God, that so they might in the issue be really wise, they have become wise in their own conceit, and have waxed vain in their foolish imaginations. Neither, indeed, is there any broader way of apostasy from the gospel than a rejection of God's sovereignty in all things concerning the revelation of himself and our obedience, with a refusal to "bring into captivity every thought unto the obedience of faith;" which first brought forth Pelagianism, and of late Socinianism, as hath been showed, from which two the whole of the present defection is derived.

Sixthly, We may add hereunto, as another spring of this partial apostasy, want of an evidence in themselves of the divine authority of the Scriptures. It is not enough, to establish any man in the profession of the gospel, to own in general that the Scripture is the word of God, or a divine revelation of his will. He that hath not an experience of a divine authority in it upon his own soul and conscience will not be steadfast when his trial shall come. God looks with regard unto them alone who tremble at his word, as owning his present authority in it. Where this doth not abide upon them, "unlearned and unstable men," as the apostle speaks, will be bold to "wrest the Scriptures, to their destruction," or to prefer other things before them, or at least to equalize them with them. It is not, therefore, enough that we assent unto the truth of the word of God, unless also we are sensible of its power, and of that claim which it makes in the name of God to the absolute subjection of our whole souls and consciences unto it. Now, this evidence in themselves of this present; divine authority, differing it unconceivably from all other real or pretended conveyances of truth, these persons either never had or have insensibly lost, or cast off openly the yoke of God therein. Hereon every imagination of their own exalts itself into an equality of right and authority with it. The end of these things is, that God gives men up to "strong delusion, to believe a lie," because they "received not," or retained not, "the truth in the love thereof," 2 Thess. ii. 10, 11. And when once it comes unto this, it is the work of Satan (which, he easily accomplisheth) both to suggest unto them endless delusions, and to render them so obstinate therein as that they shall despise every thing that is tendered unto conviction.

This is the first way whereby men fall away from the gospel, -- namely, from the mystery and doctrine of it as it is the object of our faith; wherein they do what in them lies "to crucify the Son of God afresh, and to put him to an open shame."

Chapter VIII – Apostasy from the holiness of the gospel; the occasion and cause of it — Of that which is gradual, on the pretense of somewhat else in its room

There is, secondly, a falling away from the gospel with respect unto the holiness of its precepts, which are to be the matter, as they are the rule, of our obedience. And this also is of a nature no less perilous, and attended with consequents and effects no less dangerous, than the former, and doth no less than that expose the Son of God to open shame: yea, an apostasy from the holiness of the gospel is, on many accounts, more dreadful and dangerous than a partial apostasy from its truth; for as it is more spreading and catholic than that is, and of less observation or esteem, so it is usually more irrecoverable, most men under it being greatly hardened through the deceitfulness of sin. Besides, commonness hath taken off the sense of its evil and danger. If there be an error broached against the doctrine of the gospel, it is odds but some or other will take notice of it, confute it, and warn all men of the danger wherewith it is attended; but let the whole world, as it were, lie in evil, let the generality of mankind drown themselves in lusts and pleasures, let the lives and conversations of men be as contrary to the rule of the gospel as darkness is to light, so they make no disorder in this or that way of outward worship, and be either good Catholics or good Protestants, or any thing else of that kind, he shall scarcely escape the censure of peevishness and severity (it may be of self-conceitedness and hypocrisy) who shall reflect any great blame on these things. And yet, notwithstanding this partiality in judgment or practice with respect unto these evils, it is generally acknowledged that it is possible that men may please God and be accepted with him, notwithstanding many mistakes, errors, and misconceptions of their minds about spiritual things: but that any one should ever come unto the enjoyment of him who lives and dies impenitently in any sin, against the rule and tenor of that holiness which the gospel requireth, I know as yet none that pleadeth; for, once to pretend that men may live in, and habitually act any known sin, without striving against it, labouring for repentance, and endeavouring its mortification, is all one as avowedly to attempt the overthrow of Christian religion. Wherefore, on these and sundry other considerations, this latter sort of apostasy from the holiness of the gospel is at least as perilous, as much to be opposed and contended against, as that which is from the mystery and doctrine of it, and that whereof the generality of men are more earnestly to be warned, as the evil whereunto they are more obnoxious than to the other. And we do conjoin both these together, not only as those which are of the same tendency, and do alike both ruin the souls of men and put the Lord Christ to oven shame, but also as those concerning which we are forewarned that they shall enter and come into the world together in the "latter times." And whatever sense the "latter times" mentioned in the Scripture may be taken in, either those of the world and of religion in general, or of the particular churches whereunto men may belong, they are unquestionably come upon us; whose danger and duty, therefore, are declared in these pre-admonitions. Wherefore of the first our apostle speaketh, 1 Tim. iv. 1, "The Spirit speaketh expressly, that in the latter times some shall depart from the faith, giving heed to seducing spirits and doctrines of devils." I doubt not but this prediction had its signal accomplishment in the Papacy, and am well persuaded that the Holy Ghost had respect in particular unto those principles and practices which a learned person of this nation hath laid open, under the title of "The Apostasy of the Latter Times." [10] But we find also, by woful experience, and that renewed almost every day, that it hath respect unto us also and the times wherein we live.

The entrance and coming of that kind of apostasy which we have now designed to treat of is in like manner foretold, 2 Tim. iii. 1-5. The sum of what the apostle there instructeth us is, That in these "latter times," under an outward profession of the gospel, men should give up themselves unto the pursuit of the vilest lusts and the practice of the most abominable sins. And we fear this prediction is in like manner fulfilled.

Now, although these things are evil and dangerous, both in their own nature and tendency, especially as they come together and make their joint attempt against the honour of Christ and the salvation of the professors of the gospel, yet this prediction of them and pre-admonition concerning them may be of advantage unto them that are sincere and upright, if duly improved. For, --

1. If this twofold ruinous apostasy will and doth press upon us, on whom the ends of the world are come, we ought surely to stand upon our guard, that we be not surprised with it nor overcome by it. How ought we to "pass the time of our sojourning here in fear!" It was the advice of him whose confidence had like to have been his ruin. It is assuredly no time for any to be careless and secure who design, or so much as desire, to be preserved from this fatal evil. However, we cannot any of us plead that we were not warned of our danger, nor called on for that circumspection and watchfulness, that care and diligence, that earnestness for divine help and assistance, which our condition requireth, and which will be a means of deliverance and safety. And, --

2. Being found in the way of our own duty, we need not be greatly moved or "shaken in our minds" when we see these things come to pass. It may be a prospect of the state of religion at this day in the world is ready to terrify the minds of some, at least to fill them with amazement; for if things should always so proceed, they may be afraid lest Christian religion should at length lose all its beauty and glory. But these things are all of them punctually foretold, whereby the efficacy of the temptation from their coming to pass is prevented. Yea, considering that all our faith is resolved into the Scripture, and built on the infallibility of its prophecies and predictions, seeing they are foretold, the temptation would be accompanied with more vigour and efficacy if we saw them not come to pass than it is now we do, seeing it is evident from other circumstances that we are fallen into the "latter times," which the accomplishment of these predictions renders unquestionable. See Matt. xxiv. 9-13, 25; Acts xx. 29, 30; 2 Thess. ii. 3; 1 Tim. iv. 1-3; 2 Tim. iii. 1-5. And the truth is, there was never any persuasion more pernicious befell the minds of men, than that churches, this or that church, or any church, are not, or is not liable or obnoxious unto these decays, declensions, and apostasies, or that any in them or of them can be preserved from them without the utmost care and diligence in attending unto the means appointed for their preservation. When the Jews fell

into such a foolish confidence with respect unto their temple and worship, God was wont to bid them go to Shiloh and see what was become thereof, as assuring them that what fell out in one time and place might do so in another. And we know how it was in this matter with the first Christian churches, and how soon (as hath been declared), Rev. ii. 4, 5, iii. 1-3, 14-17. We may go to them and learn how vain are all the pretences of outward privileges and exemptions; for assuredly, "unless we repent, we shall all likewise perish."

That, therefore, which we shall now inquire into is, the nature, the causes, and occasions, of that apostasy or falling off from the holiness of the gospel, in churches and by particular persons, which is thus foretold to fall out in the "latter times," and hath done so accordingly. And we shall have respect herein Both unto that general apostasy of this kind which fell out in former ages under the conduct of the Roman church principally, and that also which, by various ways and means, is at present prevailing in the world. And some things must be premised unto our consideration hereof:--

1. The doctrine of the gospel is a doctrine of holiness. This it teacheth, requireth, and commandeth; this the mysteries and grace of it lead unto; this the precepts of it require; and this the great example of its Author, proposed in it unto us, doth enjoin. And it doth not this as that which is convenient for us, or some way or other necessary unto us, but as that without which we can have no interest in any of its promises. No unholy person hath any ground to expect the least advantage by the gospel, here or hereafter. When all things come to their issue, and shall fall under eternal judgment according to the gospel, all other pleas and pretences will utterly and for ever fail them who are "workers of iniquity," Matt. vii. 22, 23.

2. The holiness which the gospel requireth is an obedience of another nature and kind than what is required by any other doctrine or way of instruction. The law of nature continueth to suggest unto us many important duties towards God, ourselves, and other men; the written law is an exact representation of all those moral duties which were required of us in the state wherein we were created; -- but there is a holiness required by the gospel, which, although it include these things within the compass of its law and order, yet (on sundry considerations) is of another kind than what is required by those laws, in the manner wherein it is required in them; for it proceedeth from other principles, on another formal reason and motives, hath other essential properties, acts, duties, and ends, than the obedience by them required hath. This hath been so fully evinced in our discourse of the nature and necessity of gospel holiness [11] that it need not be here again insisted on.

3. Together with the light and doctrine of the gospel, or the preaching of it, there is an administration of the Spirit, to convince men of sin, righteousness, and judgment. This God hath promised, Isa. lix. 21, and this the Lord Christ doth effect wherever the word is orderly dispensed according unto his mind and will, John xvi. 7-11. Hereby are men wrought upon unto a profession of this holiness, and expression of it in outward duties; for all that religion which hath any thing of truth and reality in it in the world is an effect of the word and Spirit of Christ. Multitudes in all ages have hereby been made really holy, and many yet continue so to be. These (as we believe) shall never fall utterly from it, but shall be preserved by the power of God through faith unto salvation. But yet such as these also may decay as unto degrees in holiness and the fruitfulness of it; and in every such decay there is a partial apostasy and much dishonour unto Jesus Christ; nor doth any man know in that condition but that in the issue, as to his particular, it may be total, and

destructive to his soul. Thus was it with those churches and persons whom our Lord Jesus Christ chargeth to have lost their first faith and love, whom he admonisheth to remember whence they are fallen, and to repent. And it is principally for the sake of these, that Christ and the gospel be not dishonoured by them nor their eternal concernments hazarded, and those who, in the use of means, are in a thriving progress towards the same condition, that the ensuing cautions and warnings are prepared. And others there are who are brought only unto a profession of this holiness in inward convictions and outward duties; and although they are not yet arrived unto a full possession of its power and conformity unto its rule, yet are they in the way of attaining thereunto. Such as these may, on various occasions, first decay in their profession and duties, and afterward utterly fall from them into the open service of sin and the world.

Thus also it is with churches. At their first planting, they were set in a pure and holy state as to the doctrine, professed holiness, and worship of the gospel. They were all planted noble vines, wholly of a right seed, however they turn afterwards "into the degenerate plant of a strange vine." They may lose of this order and beauty, part with truth, decay in holiness, and the faithful city thereby become a harlot. How this hath come to pass; how thereby Christianity hath lost its glory, power, and efficacy in the world; how that blessing which it brought along with it unto the nations is lost and forfeited, and by what means, -- shall in some principal instances be declared.

4. Where this holiness is professed, and the power of it evidenced in its fruits, there, and then alone, is Christ glorified and honoured in the world. It is true, there are other things that belong unto that revenue of glory which our Lord and King requireth of us, -- such are the profession of the truth and observance of the worship of the gospel, -- but if these things are disjoined and separated (as they may be) from holy obedience, they no way advance the glory of Christ. But where churches and persons professing the gospel are changed and renewed into the image of God; where their hearts are purified within, and their lives made fruitful without; where they are universally under the conduct of a spirit of peace, love, meekness, benignity, self-denial, heavenly-mindedness, and are fruitful in good works, -- in which things and others of an alike nature this holiness doth consist, -- there do they make a due representation of the gospel and its Author in the world; then do they evidence the power, purity, and efficacy of his doctrine and grace, whereby he is glorified. Herein doth he "see of the travail of his soul and is satisfied;" this is "his portion and the lot of his inheritance" in this world. But where it is otherwise, where men, where churches, are called by his name, and, under a profession of his authority and expectation of mercy and eternal blessedness from him, do come short of this holiness, and walk in paths contrary unto it, there is the holy Son of God "crucified afresh, and put to an open shame."

These things being premised, way is made for the due consideration of what was before proposed; for whereas there is an open, shameful, manifest apostasy from the holiness of the gospel among the most who are called Christians at this day in the world, it is worth our while to inquire a little into the reasons or causes of it, and the means whereby a stop may be put unto it, or at least particular persons may be preserved from the guilt of it, and the judgments wherein it will issue. If any shall think that there is not such an apostasy in the world, but that the face of things in Europe and among ourselves doth make a due representation of the gospel, and that those things which we hear of and see continually amongst the generality of Christians are the true and genuine effects of the doctrine and principles of our religion, I shall no way contend with them, so as that they will but a little stand out of our way, and not hinder us in our progress.

Now, the apostasy that is in the world from gospel holiness, or evangelical obedience, is of two kinds; for some fall from it as formally such, and others as to the matter of it. Of the first sort are they who would advance another kind of obedience, a course of another sort of duties, or the same as to the substance of them, but as proceeding from other principles and carried on by other motives than what it requireth, in the stead thereof. Thus it is with many in the world. They pretend unto a strictness in some duties, and a multiplication of others, at least unto a great appearance thereof; but it is hard for any one to discover how that which they do belongeth to evangelical holiness, if its nature depend on evangelical principles and ends. Others fall from it openly and visibly, into a sinful, worldly, flagitious course of life. This is that apostasy which the Christian world groans under at this day, and which, as it is to be feared, will bring the judgments of God upon it. The very profession of piety is much lost, yea, much derided, amongst many. Duties of holiness, strictness of conversation, communication unto edification, are not only neglected, but scorned. It is in many places a lost labour to seek for Christianity among Christians; and the degeneracy seems to be increasing every day. It is the latter of these which I principally intend, as that which is of most universal concernment. But the former also, though under many specious pretences, being of no less pernicious event unto many, must not be wholly passed by. I shall therefore first give some instances of men's declension from the holy ways of gospel obedience into paths of pretended duties of their own finding out, and add those reasons of their dislike of the good old way which give them occasion so to do.

I. The first and most signal instance of this kind is given us by the Romanists. None boast more than they of holiness, -- that is, of their church, making its sanctity a note of its truth. But because the wicked and flagitious lives, not only of the body of the people among them, but of many of their chief rulers and guides, is openly manifest, in the defence of their confident claim, as that alone which will give countenance unto it, they betake themselves unto their votaries, or those who dedicate themselves by vow unto more strict exercises in religion than others attain or are obliged unto; and this sort of people have obtained alone the name and reputation of Religious among them. What is their way and manner of life, what the devotion wherein they spend their hours, what the duties they oblige themselves unto in great variety, and the manner wherein they perform them, I shall take for granted, and pass by as generally known. Many have already discovered the vanity, superstition, and hypocrisy, of the whole outward course wherein they are generally engaged; though they neither do nor ought to judge of the hearts, minds, and state of individuals, unless where by their deeds they manifest themselves. I shall only evince that what at best they pretend unto (though boasted of not only to be all, but more than God requireth of them) is not that holiness or obedience which is prescribed unto us in the gospel, but somewhat substituted in the room of it, and, consequently, in opposition unto it. And, --

1. It hath not that evidence of spiritual freedom and liberty which gospel holiness, in all the duties of it, is accompanied withal. The first effect of the truth upon our minds is to "make us free," John viii. 32. It is the principle of all holiness, and enlargeth the mind and spirit unto it, whence it is called "The holiness of truth," Eph. iv. 24. So, "Where the Spirit of the Lord is, there is liberty," 2 Cor. iii. 17. Men are naturally the "servants of sin," willingly giving up themselves unto the

fulfilling of its lusts and commands, and are only "free from righteousness." But where the Holy Spirit worketh with the word of truth, men are made "free from sin, and become servants to God, having their fruit unto holiness," Rom. vi. 20, 22. So it is said of all believers that they "have not received the spirit of bondage again to fear, but the Spirit of adoption, whereby they cry, Abba, Father," Rom. viii. 15; not "the spirit of fear, but of power, and of love, and of a sound mind," 2 Tim. i. 7. The meaning of all these and the like testimonies is, that God by his grace enlargeth, makes free and ready, the hearts of believers unto all gospel obedience, so as that they shall walk in it, and perform all the duties of it, willingly, cheerfully, freely, without that fear and dread which is an effect of the power of the law. They are not in a scrupulous bondage unto outward duties and the manner of their performance, but do all things with delight and freedom. They have by the Spirit of adoption, as the reverential fear of children, so their gracious inclination unto obedience. But in that exercise of devotion, and multiplied outward duties of religion, which the Romanists boast of as their especial sanctity, there are great evidences of a servile bondage or slavish frame of spirit; for they are forced to bind themselves, and to be bound unto it, by especial vows, in whose observation they no more act as their own guardians, or as those who are "sui juris," but are under the coercive discipline of others, and outward punishment in case of failure. And those who are so servants of men in religious duties are not God's freemen, nor have they Christ for their Lord in that cage who have another. The foundation of all these duties, and which alone obligeth them unto their performance, are vows nowhere required by God or our Lord Christ in the gospel; and the principal regard which any have in their strict attendance unto them is the obedience which they owe unto the superintendents of those vows It is easy to apprehend how inconsistent this way is with that spiritual freedom and liberty of mind which inseparably accompanieth true gospel holiness. Besides, the opinion of merit, which not only goeth along with them, but also animates them in all these services, makes them servile in all they do; for they cannot but know that every thing in merit must not only be tried by the touchstone of sincerity, but weighed in the balance to the utmost scruple, to find out what it amounts or comes unto. And this is perfectly destructive of that liberty in obedience which the gospel requireth. So also is that tormenting persuasion which they are under the power of, -- namely, That they have no grounds of confidence or assurance that either they are accepted with God here, or shall come to the blessed enjoyment of him hereafter. Hence, in all duties, they must of necessity be acted with a "spirit of fear," and not "of power and of a sound mind."

2. The rule of their duties and obedience, as to what is, in their own judgment, eminent therein, is not the gospel, but a system of peculiar laws and rules that they have framed for themselves. So some obey the rule of Benedict, some of Francis, some of Dominic, some of Ignatius, and the like. This utterly casts out their whole endeavour from any interest in gospel holiness; for the formal nature of that consists herein, that it is a conformity unto the rule of the gospel as such, or a compliance with the will of God as manifested therein. Hence do they multiply unrequited duties, yea, the principal parts of their devotion and sanctity consist in them which are of their own devising, for which they have no gospel precept or command; and such, in particular, are those vows which are the foundation of all that they do. In this case, our Saviour, reproving the Pharisees for their additional duties beyond the prescript of the word, shows them how they "made the commandment of God of none effect by their tradition," and that "in vain they

worshipped God, teaching for doctrines the commandments of men," Matt. xv. 6, 9. And when they were offended at his rejection of one of their new imposed duties, he replies that "every plant which his heavenly Father hath not planted should be rooted up," verse 13; so wholly rejecting all those religious duties which they had framed by rules of their own devising. Nor are these of the Roman devotionists of any better constitution; they are plants of men's own planting, and shall be rooted up accordingly and cast into the fire. Let the number of false invented duties of religion be never so great, let the manner of their performance be never so exact or severe, they serve to no other end but to divert the minds of men from the obedience which the gospel requireth.

3. There is nothing in all that is prescribed by the masters of this devotion, or practised by the disciples, but it may all be done and observed without either faith in Christ or a sense of his love unto our souls. The obedience of the gospel is the "obedience of faith;" on that and no other root will it grow; -- and the principal motive unto it is the "love of Christ," which "constraineth" unto it. But what is there in all their prescriptions that these things are necessary unto? May not men rise at midnight to repeat a number of prayers, or go barefoot, or wear sackcloth, or abstain from flesh at certain times or always, or submit to discipline from themselves or others, and (if they have bodily strength to enable them) undergo all the horrid, and indeed ridiculous, hardships of standing on a pillar continually, or bearing great logs of wood on their shoulders all the day long, that are told or fabled of the Egyptian monks, without the least dram of saving faith or love? All false religions have ever had some amongst them who have had an ambition to amuse others with these self-inflictions and macerations, wherein the devotions among the Banians do exceed at this day whatever the Romanists pretend unto.

4. The whole of what they do is so vitiated and corrupted with the proud opinion of merit and supererogation as renders it utterly foreign unto the gospel. It is not my present business to dispute against these opinions. It hath been already abundantly manifested (and may be yet so again where it is necessary) that they wholly enervate the covenant of grace, are injurious to the blood and mediation of Christ, and are utterly inconsistent with the fundamental principles of the gospel. Whereas, therefore, these proud imaginations do animate their whole course of duties, the gospel is not concerned in what they do.

And we may add unto what hath been remarked already, the consideration of that gross superstition, yea, and idolatry, which they give up themselves unto almost in most of their devotions. This is not the least of their transgressions in these things, but is sufficient to violate all they do besides.

Wherefore, notwithstanding their pretence unto sanctity and a more strict attendance unto duties of obedience than other men, yet it is manifest that the best of them are under a defection from the holiness of the gospel, substituting an obedience unto their own imaginations in the room thereof.

II. Again; others confine the whole of their obedience unto morality, and deride whatever is pleaded as above it and beyond it, under the name of evangelical grace, as "enthusiastical folly." And the truth is, if those persons who plead for the necessity of gospel grace and holiness, which is more than so, do understand each other, and if somewhat of the same things are not intended by them under different expressions and diverse methods of their management, they are not of the same religion. But if they mistake the meaning of each other, and differ only in the manner of teaching the same truth, I suppose they steer the safest course, and are freest from just offence, who follow and comply with the manner wherein the things intended are taught in the Scripture, rather than those who accommodate their discourses unto the phraseology of heathen philosophers. But the truth is, the difference seems to be real, and the principles men proceed upon in these things are contradictory to each other; for some do plainly affirm that the whole of gospel obedience consists in the observance of moral virtue, which they so describe as to render it exclusive of evangelical grace. This others judge to contain an open declension from and waiving of gospel holiness. It is granted freely, that the performance of all moral duties evangelically, -- that is, in the power of the grace of Christ, unto the glory of God by him, -- is an essential part of gospel obedience. And whoever they are who (under the pretence of grace or any thing else) do neglect the improvement of moral virtues, or the observance of the duties of morality, they are so far disobedient unto the gospel and the law thereof. And some men do not understand how contemptible they render themselves in the management of their cause, when they charge others with an opposition unto morality or moral virtue, and setting up they know not what imaginary holiness in the room thereof; for those whom they so calumniate are not only immediately discharged from any sense of guilt herein by the testimony of their own consciences, but all other men, so far as the rule of ingenuity is extended, do, from the knowledge of their doctrine and observation of their practice, avouch their innocence.

"But is it not so, then, that men do condemn morality, as that which is not to be trusted unto, but will deceive them that rest in or upon it?" I answer, They do so when it is made (as it is by some) the whole of religion, and as it is obtruded into the place of evangelical grace and holiness by others. They take moral virtue, as it always was taken until of late, for natural honesty, or such a conformity of life unto the light of nature as to be useful and approved among men. But this may be, -- men may do what is morally good, and yet never do any thing that is accepted with God; for they may do it, but not for the love of God above all, but for the love of self. And therefore they charge morality with an insufficiency unto the end of religion, or the saving of the souls of men, --

1. Where nothing is intended by it but that whereof the rule and measure is the light of nature: for that doth direct unto every duty that is properly moral; and what it doth not direct unto, what is not naturally by the law of our creation obligatory unto all mankind, cannot be called moral. Now, to confine all religion, as to the preceptive and obediential part of it, unto the light of nature, is to evacuate one half of the gospel.

2. Where it is in practice an effect of conviction only, and performed in the innate strength of the rational faculties of our souls, without the especial supernatural aid of the Spirit and grace of God, Whatever name any thing may be called by that is not wrought in us by the grace of God, as well as by us in a way of duty, is foreign unto evangelical obedience. And those who reject morality as insufficient unto acceptation with God and eternal salvation, intend only what is of that kind performed in the power of our natural faculties externally excited and directed, without any supernatural influence or operation of especial grace; and, indeed, so to place a confidence in such duties is open Pelagianism.

3. Where it proceedeth not from the spiritual, supernatural renovation of our souls. The rule and method of the gospel is, that the tree be first made good, and then the fruit will be so also. Unless a person be first regenerate, and his nature therein renewed into the image and likeness of God, -- unless he be endued with a new principle of spiritual life from above, enabling him to live unto God, he can do

nothing, of whatsoever sort it be, that is absolutely acceptable unto God. And it is especially under this consideration that any reject morality as not comprehensive of gospel obedience, yea, as that which is apt to draw off the mind from it, and which will deceive them that trust to it, -- namely, that it proceedeth not from the principle of grace in a renewed soul; for whatever doth so, though it may be originally of a moral nature in itself, yet from the manner of its performance it becomes gracious and evangelical And we need not fear to exclude the best works of unrenewed persons from being any part of gospel holiness or obedience.

4. Where those in whom it is, or who pretend unto it, are really destitute of the internal light of saving grace, enabling them to discern spiritual things in a spiritual manner, and to know the mysteries of the kingdom of God. That there is such a saving light wrought in the minds of believers by the Holy Ghost, that without it men cannot discern spiritual things, so as to favour, like, and approve of them, hath been elsewhere at large demonstrated. But this belongs not unto the morality contended about. It is not only independent of it, but is indeed set up in competition with it and opposition unto it. No man need fear to judge and censure that morality, as unto its interest in gospel obedience and sufficiency unto the salvation of the souls of men, which may be obtained, practised, and lived up unto, where God doth not "shine in the hearts of men, to give them the light of the knowledge of his glory in the face of Jesus Christ;" where no work of spiritual illumination hath been in their minds, enabling them to discern and know the mind of God, which none knoweth originally but the Spirit of God, by Whom it is made [known] unto us, 1 Cor. ii. 11, 12. Yet this is that which some men seem to take up withal and rest in, unto the rejection of evangelical obedience.

Lastly, The same censure is to be passed on it wherever it is separable from those fundamental gospel graces which, both in their nature, acts, and objects, are purely supernatural, having no principle, rule, or measure, but truth supernaturally revealed. Such, in particular, is the whole regard we have unto the mediation of Christ, as also unto the dispensation of the Spirit, promised to abide with the church for ever as its comforter, with all the duties of obedience which depend thereon. He is ignorant of the gospel that knows not that in these things do lie the fundamental principles of its doctrine and precepts, and that in the exercise of those graces in a way of duty which immediately concern them, consist the principal parts of the life of God, or of that obedience unto him by Jesus Christ which is indispensably required of all that shall be saved. Whereas, therefore, these things cannot be esteemed merely moral virtues, nor do at all belong unto, but are considered as separate from, all that morality which is judged insufficient unto life and salvation, it is evident that it is not in the least dealt withal too severely, nor censured more harshly than it doth deserve. If, therefore, any betake themselves hereunto as to the whole of their duty, it comes under the account of that partial defection from the gospel which we inquire into.

III. Some there are who, as unto themselves, pretend they have attained unto perfection already in this world; such a perfection in all degrees of holiness as the gospel is but an introduction towards. But this proud imagination, destructive of the covenant of grace, of all use of the mediation and blood of Christ, contrary to innumerable testimonies of Scripture and the experience of all that do believe, and concerning which their own consciences do reprove the pretenders unto it, needs not detain us in its examination. It is sufficient unto our present design to have given these instances how men may, in a pretended conscientious discharge of many duties of obedience, yet fall off and decline from that which the gospel requireth. The occasions and reasons hereof (supposing those more general before considered with respect unto the truth of the gospel, which all of them take place here, and have their influence upon their dislike of its holiness) may be briefly inquired into and represented; nor shall we confine ourselves unto the instances given, but take in the consideration of every declension from it which on any account befalls them who, having had a conviction of its necessity, yet refuse to come unto its universal practice. And to this end we may observe, --

1. That the holiness which the gospel requireth will not be kept up or maintained, either in the hearts or lives of men, without a continual conflict, warring, contending; and that with all care, diligence, watchfulness, and perseverance therein. It is our warfare, and the Scripture abounds in the discovery of the adversaries we have to conflict withal, their power and subtlety, as also in directions and encouragements unto their resistance. To suppose that gospel obedience will be maintained in our hearts and lives without a continual management of a vigorous warfare against its enemies, is to deny the Scripture and the experience of all that do believe and obey God in sincerity. Satan, sin, and the world, are continually assault-hag of it, and seeking to ruin its interest in us. The devil will not be resisted (which it is our duty to do, 1 Pet. v. 8, 9) without a sharp contest and conflict; in the management whereof we are commanded to "take unto ourselves the whole armour of God," Eph. vi. 12, 13. "Fleshly lusts" do continually "war against our souls," 1 Pet. ii. 11; and if we maintain not a warfare unto the end against them, they will be our ruin. Nor will the power of the world be any otherwise avoided than by a victory over it, 1 John v. 4; which will not be carried without contending. But I suppose it needs no great confirmation unto any who know what it is to serve and obey God in temptations, that the life of faith and race of holiness will not be preserved nor continued in without a severe striving, labouring, contending, warring with diligence, watchfulness, and perseverance; so that I shall at present take it as a principle, notionally at least, agreed upon by the generality of Christians. If we like not to be holy on these terms, we must let it alone; for on any other we shall never be so. If we faint in this course, if we give it over, if we think what we aim at herein not to be worth the obtaining or preserving by such a severe contention all our days, we must be content to be without it. Nothing doth so promote the interest of hell and destruction in the world as a presumption that a lazy, slothful performance of some duties and abstinence from some sins, is that which God will accept of as our obedience. Crucifying of sin, mortifying our inordinate affections, contesting against the whole interest of the flesh, Satan, and the world, and that in inward actings of grace and all instances of outward duties, and that always while we live in this world, are required of us hereunto.

Here lies the first spring of the apostasy of many in the world, of them especially who betake themselves unto and take up satisfaction in another way of duties than what the gospel requireth. They had, it is possible, by their light and convictions, made so near approaches unto it as to see what an incessant travail of soul is required unto its attainment and preservation.

They are like the Israelites travelling in the wilderness towards the land of Canaan. When they came near unto the borders and entrance of it, they sent some to spy it out, that they might know the nature and state of the land and country whither they were going. These, for their encouragement, and to evince the fruitfulness of the earth, bring unto them "a branch with one cluster of grapes," so great and fair that "they bare it between two upon a staff; and they brought also pomegranates and figs," Num. xiii. 23. But withal, they told them of the hideous difficulties they were to conflict withal, in that the people were strong, their cities walled, and the Anakims dwelling amongst them, verse 28. This utterly disheartens the carnal people, and, notwithstanding the prospect they had of the "land that flowed with milk and honey," back again they go into the wilderness, and there they perish.

So it is with these persons. Notwithstanding the near approach they have made, by light and convictions, unto the kingdom of God (as our Saviour told the young man, who was as one of them, Mark xii. 34), and the prospect they have of the beauty of holiness, yet they turn off from it again, and perish in the wilderness: for upon the view they have of the difficulties which lie in the conflict mentioned, they fall under many disadvantages, which at length utterly divert them from its pursuit; as, --

(1.) Weariness of the flesh, not enduring to comply with that constant course of duties continually returning upon it which is required thereunto. Various pleas will be made for an exemption from them, at least in some troublesome instances; and the carnal mind will not want pretences to countenance the flesh in its weariness. Hereon one duty after another is first omitted and then utterly foregone. Neglect of a vigorous constancy in subduing the body and bringing of it into subjection, commended by the apostle in his own example, 1 Cor. ix. 27, is with many the beginning of this kind of apostasy. These things, I say, will ofttimes fall out, that through the weariness and aversation of the flesh, countenanced by various pretences of the carnal mind, sundry duties will be omitted. But this is the faith and trial of the saints; here is the difference between sound believers and those who are acted only by convictions: Those of the first sort will, sooner or later (for the most part speedily), be humbled for such omissions, and recover their former diligence, according to the prayer of the psalmist, Ps. cxix. 176; but where this ground is won by the flesh, and men grow satisfied under the loss of any duty, it is an evidence of a hypocritical, backsliding heart.

(2.) When men are come unto the height of their convictions, and proceed no farther, indwelling sin, with its lusts and corrupt affections (which have for a while been checked and mated by light), will insensibly prevail, and weary the mind with solicitations for the exercise of its old dominion; for the spring of it being not dried, the bitter root of it being not digged up nor withered, it will not cease until it hath broke down all the bounds that were fixed unto it, and bear down convictions with force and violence.

(3.) Ignorance of the true way of making application unto the Lord Christ for grace and supplies of the Spirit, to bring them unto or preserve them in a state of gospel holiness, is of the same importance. Without this, to dream of being holy according unto the mind of God is to renounce the gospel. We need not look farther for men's apostasy than this, if they are satisfied with such a holiness, such an obedience, as is not derived unto us by the grace of Christ, nor wrought in us by the Spirit of Christ, nor preserved in us by the power of Christ. The way hereof such persons are always ignorant of, and at length do openly despise; yet may men as well see without the sun or light, or breathe without the air, or live without natural spirits, as engage into or abide in the practice of gospel holiness without continual applications unto Christ, the fountain of all grace, for spiritual strength enabling thereunto. The way and means hereof these persons being ignorant of and unacquainted withal, the holiness which the gospel requireth becomes unto them a thing strange and burdensome; which therefore they desert and refuse. If, therefore, it be true that without Christ we can do nothing, -- that in our life unto God he liveth in us, and efficiently is our life; if from him, as the head, nourishment is supplied unto every living member of the body; if the life which we lead be by the faith of the Son of God; and if the only way of deriving these things and all supplies of spiritual strength from him be by the exercise of faith in him, -- it follows unavoidably that all those who are unacquainted with this way, who know not how to make their application unto him for this end and purpose, can never persevere in a pursuit of gospel holiness. So hath it fallen out and no otherwise with them concerning whom we speak. As ignorance of the righteousness of God, or of Christ being the end of the law for righteousness unto them that do believe, is the reason why men go about to establish a righteousness of their own, and will not submit to the righteousness of God; so ignorance of the grace which is continually to be received from Christ in a way of believing, that we may be holy with gospel holiness, is the reason why so many turn off from it unto another kind of holiness of their own framing, which yet is not another, because it is none at all. But many are so far from endeavouring after or abiding in gospel holiness on this foundation of continual supplies of grace from Jesus Christ to that end, as that they avowedly despise all holiness and obedience springing from that fountain or growing on that root; in which case God will judge. In the meantime, I say (and the matter is evident) that one principal reason why men turn off from it upon the prospect of the difficulties that attend it, and the oppositions that are made unto it, is their unbelief and ignorance of the way of making application unto Christ by faith for supplies of spiritual strength and grace.

(4.) Unacquaintedness with the true nature of evangelical repentance is another cause hereof. This is that grace which comfortably carrieth the souls of believers through all their failings, infirmities, and sins; nor are they able to live to God one day without the constant exercise of it. They find it as necessary unto the continuance of spiritual life as faith itself. It is not only a means of our entrance into, but it belongs essentially unto, our gospel state and our continuance therein. Hereunto belongs that continual humble self-abasement, from a sense of the majesty and holiness of God, with the disproportion of the best of our duties unto his will, which believers live and walk in continually; and he that is not sensible of a gracious sweetness and usefulness therein knows not what it is to walk with God. Hereby doth God administer several encouragements unto our souls to abide in our way of obedience, notwithstanding the many discouragements and despondencies we meet withal. In brief, take it away, and you overthrow faith, and hope, and all other graces. Those, therefore, who are unacquainted with the nature and use of this grace and duty, who can taste no spiritual refreshment in all its sorrows, who know nothing of it but legal troubles, anguish, fear, and distraction, will not endure the thought of living in the practice of it all their days; which yet is as necessary unto gospel holiness as faith itself. Men, I say, falling into this condition, finding all these difficulties to conflict withal, and lying under these disadvantages, if any thing will offer itself in the room of this costly holiness, will readily embrace it. Hence, as some betake themselves unto a pretence of morality (which as unto many is a mere pretence, and made use of only to countenance themselves in a neglect of the whole of that obedience which the gospel openly requireth), so others do, under other expressions, retreat unto the mere duties of their own light, and these as only required therein, with some peculiar reliefs unto the flesh in what is burdensome unto it. As, for instance: There is nothing that the flesh more riseth up in a dislike of and opposition unto than constancy in the duty of prayer, in private, in families, on all occasions, especially if attended unto in a spiritual manner, as the gospel doth require; but in itself, and as to the substance of it, it is a duty which the light of nature exacteth of us; -- but whereas this may prove burdensome to the flesh, a relief is borrowed from a pretence of gospel light and liberty, that men need not pray at any time unless their own spirits or light do previously require it of them: which is to turn the grace of God into an occasion of sinning. By this means some have gotten a holiness, wherein, for the most part, it seems indifferent to them whether they pray at any time or no. And other instances of the like kind might be given. Upon the whole matter, to free themselves from this state, so uneasy to flesh and blood, so contrary unto all the imaginations of the carnal mind, some men have betaken themselves unto another, wherein they have, or pretend to have, no conflict against sin, nor to need any application unto the Lord Christ for supplies of spiritual strength; which belongs not unto that holiness which the gospel requires and which God accepts.

It may be said that in some of the instances before given, especially in that of the Papacy, there is an appearance of a greater conflict with and more hardships put on the flesh than in any other way of obedience that is pleaded for; and there is indeed such an appearance, but it is no more. The oppositions that arise against their austerities are from without, or from nature as it is weak, but not as it is carnal It is possible that sin may not be concerned in what they do, neither in its power nor reign; yea, so far as it is leavened by superstition, it acts itself therein no less than it doth in others by fleshly lusts. But it is an internal, spiritual, immediate opposition unto its being and all its actings, that it riseth up with such rage against as to weary those who have not that living principle of faith whereto the victory over it doth peculiarly appertain.

2. This evangelical holiness will not allow of nor will consist with the constant, habitual omission of any one duty, or the satisfaction of any one lust of the mind or of the flesh. As we are, in all instances of duty, to be "perfecting holiness in the fear of God," 2 Cor. vii. 1, so "no provision is to be made for the flesh, to fulfil the lusts thereof," Rom. xiii. 14. This is that which loseth it so many friends in the world. Would it barter with the flesh, would it give and take allowances in any kind, or grant indulgence unto any one sin, multitudes would have a kindness for it which now bid it defiance. Every one would have an exemption for that sin which he likes best, and which is most suited to his inclinations and carnal interests. And this would be virtually a dispensation for all unholiness whatever. But these are the terms of the gospel: No one duty is to be neglected, no one sin is to be indulged; and they are looked upon as intolerable. Naaman would not give himself up unto the worship of the God of Israel but with this reserve, that he might also bow in the house of Rimmon, whereon his power and preferment did depend. Many things the young man in the Gospel boasted himself to have done, and was doubtless willing to continue in the performance of them; but yet, through his whole course, the love of the world had the prevalency in him, and when he was tried in that instance, rather than relinquish it he gave up the whole. But this is the law of the gospel. Although it provide a merciful relief against those daily sins which we are overtaken withal by our frailty and weakness, or surprised into by the power of temptations, against the bent of our minds and habitual inclination of our wills, 1 Pet. iv. 1, 2, yet it alloweth not the cherishing or practice of any one sin whatever, internal or external. An habitual course in any sin is utterly inconsistent with evangelical obedience, 1 John iii. 6-9, yea, it requireth indispensably that we be engaged, in our minds and wills, in an opposition unto all

sin, and in a constant endeavour after its not-being in us, either in the root or in the fruit thereof. It will not connive at or comply with any inordinate affection, any habitual sinful distemper, nor the first motions of sin that are in the flesh. This is that perfection which is required in the new covenant, Gen. xvii. 1, that sincerity, integrity, freedom from guile, walking after the Spirit, and not after the flesh, and that newness of life, which the gospel everywhere prescribeth unto us. On no other terms but universality in obedience and opposition unto sin will it approve of us, 1 John iii. 7-10.

And this occasioneth the turning aside of many from the pursuit of an endeavour to be holy, according unto the rule of the gospel. When by light and convictions they come to take a view of what is required thereunto, it disliketh them, they cannot bear it; and therefore they either at once or gradually give over all ways of pursuing their first design. And men break with the gospel on this account by the means ensuing:--

(1.) They cannot make the same judgment of sin that the gospel doth, nor will judge all those things to be sin and evil which the gospel declares so to be; yea, we have some come unto that pharisaism, that they scarce think any thing to be sinful or worth taking notice of unless it be openly flagitious. Under this darkness and ignorance, all sorts of filthy, noisome lusts may be cherished in the hearts of men, keeping them at as great and real a distance from the holiness of truth as the most outrageous outward sins can do. And this neglect or refusal to comply with the rule of the gospel before laid down is grounded in and promoted by two occasions:--

[1.] They have a willing insensibility of the guilt of some unmortified lust. This they will abide in and cherish; for their minds being habituated unto it, they find no great evil in it, nor do see any cogent reason why they should forego it. So was it with the young man with respect unto the love of the world. He was sorry that he could not be evangelically obedient whilst he retained it; but seeing that could not be, he did not discern any such evil in, nor was sensible of any such guilt from it, nor could apprehend any such equality in or necessity of gospel holiness, that he should renounce the one for the embracing the other. So will it be when any lust is made familiar unto the mind; it will not be terrified with it, nor can see any great danger in it. It is between such a soul and sin as it is between the devil and the witch, or one that hath a familiar spirit, as we render the Hebrew "ob" [וֹן?] and "yideoni," [יִדְנִי?]. At the first appearance of the devil, be it in what shape it will, it cannot but bring a tremor and fear on human nature, but after a while he becomes a familiar; and when alone he is to be feared, he is not feared at all. The poor deceived wretch then thinks him in his power, so that he can use or command him as he sees good, whereas he himself is absolutely in the power of the devil. Men may be startled with sin in its first appearance, on their first convictions, or its first dangerous efforts; but when it is become their familiar, they suppose it a thing in their own power, which they can use or not use as they see occasion, though indeed themselves are the servants of corruption, being overcome thereby and brought into bondage. Hence it is inconceivable how little sense of guilt in some sins men find after they are habituated unto them. In some sins, I say, for with respect unto sins absolutely against the light of nature, conscience will not easily be bribed not to condemn them. It will not in such cases be speechless, until it be seared and made senseless. But there are sins not accompanied with so great an evidence, yet attended with no less guilt than those which directly militate against the light of nature. In this case, when the word of the gospel comes as it is "living and powerful, sharper than any two-edged sword, piercing even to the dividing asunder of the soul and spirit, and of the joints and marrow, as a discoverer and judge of the thoughts and intents of the heart;" when it comes and discovers the secret frames, figments, imaginations, and inclinations of the mind, and condemneth what is in the least measure or manner irregular; when it will not be put off, nor accept of any composition or compensation by the most strict and rigid profession in other things, -- men are ready to withdraw themselves to the rule of their own light and reason, which they find more gentle and tractable.

[2.] A dereliction of the gospel on this account, with respect unto the inwardness, spirituality, and extent of its commands, is much increased under the influence of corrupt opinions. And of this nature are all those which tend unto the extenuation of sin; for some there are who suppose that there is not such a provoking guilt, such a spiritual outrage in sin, as others pretend. Hence multitudes, as they judge, are needlessly troubled and perplexed about it. "A generous mind, free from superstitious fears and dark conceits imbibed in education, will deliver the mind of man from the trouble of such apprehensions; -- a great sense of the guilt of small sins is an engine to promote the interest of preachers, and those who pretend to the conduct of conscience; -- the filth and pollution of sin is a metaphor which few can understand, and none ought to be concerned in; -- that the power of the remainders of indwelling sin is a foolish notion; and that the disorderly frames of the heart and the mind, through darkness, deadness, spiritual indisposition, or other secret irregularities, are fancies, not sins, which we need not be troubled at ourselves, nor make any acknowledgment of unto God;" -- these and the like opinions are the pharisaical corban of our age, corrupting the whole law of our obedience. And it were easy to manifest how perilous and ruinous they are unto the souls of men; what powerful instruments in the hand of Satan to eclipse the glory of the grace of Christ on the one hand, and to promote apostasy from holiness in the hearts and lives of men on the other. I shall only say, set the corrupt heart of men by any means at liberty from an awe and reverence of the holiness of God and his law with respect unto the inward actings and frames of the soul, with a sense of guilt where they are irregular, and a necessity of constant humiliation before God thereon, and an equally constant application of itself unto the Lord Christ for grace and mercy, and it is wholly in vain to think of fixing any bounds unto the progress of sin. The ignorance hereof is that which hath produced in some the proud imagination of perfection, when they are far enough from bringing their consciences and lives to the rule of the gospel, but only aggravate their guilt by attempting to bend that inflexible rule unto their own perverse and crooked minds.

(2.) In this case, carnal interest, which takes in and compriseth all the circumstances of men, calls for an indulgence unto some one sin or other, which the gospel will not admit of. Pride or ambition, covetousness or love of this present evil world and the perishing things of it, uncleanness or sensuality in eating and drinking, self-exaltation and boasting, vain-glory, idleness, one or other must be spared. One thing or other, I say, on the account of carnal interest, -- either because small, or useful, or general, or suited unto a natural temper, or, as is supposed, made necessary by the occasions of life, -- must be reserved. Where this resolution prevails, as men are absolutely excluded from any real interest in gospel holiness, which will admit of no such reserves, so it will not fail to lead them into open apostasy of one kind or other; for, --

[1.] Such persons are unapproved of God in all that they do, and so have no ground for expectation of his blessing or assistance; for the allowance of the least sin is such an impeachment of sincerity as casteth a man out of covenant communion with God. This is that "offending in one point" which ruins a man's obedience, and renders him guilty against the whole law, James ii. 10. Any one actual sin makes a man guilty of the curse of the whole law as it contains the covenant of works; and the willing allowance of a man's self in any one sin habitually breaks the whole law as it contains the rule of our obedience in the covenant of grace. And if in this disapproved condition men meet with outward prosperity in the world, their danger will be increased as well as their guilt aggravated. And the utmost care of professors is required in this matter; for there seems to be among many an open indulgence unto habitual disorders, which hazards their whole covenant interest, and must fill them with uncertainty in their own minds. High time it is for all such persons to shake off "every weight, and the sin that doth so easily beset them, and to run with redoubled diligence" the remainder of "the race that is set before them."

[2.] This indulgence unto any one sin will make way in the minds, consciences, and affections of men, for the admission of other sins also. It will be like a thief that is hidden in a house, and only waits an opportunity to open the doors unto his other companions; to this end he watcheth for a season of sleep and darkness, when there is none to observe his actings. Let a person who thus alloweth himself to live in any sin fall into temptation whilst he is a little more than ordinary careless, his allowed corruption shall open his heart unto any other sin that offers for admission. "Look not," saith the wise man, "upon the wine when it is red, when it giveth his colour in the cup, when it moveth itself aright. Thine eyes shall behold strange women, and thine heart shall utter perverse things," Prov. xxiii. 31, 33. One sin liked and loved will make way for every other. There is a kindred and alliance between sins of all sorts, and they agree in the same end and design. Where any one is willingly entertained, others will intrude themselves beyond all our power of resistance.

[3.] It will divert the soul from the use of those means whereby all other sins should be resisted, and thereby apostasy prevented; for there is no means appointed or sanctified by God for the resistance or mortification of sin, but it opposeth sin as sin, and consequently every thing that is so, and that because it is so. Wherefore, whoever willingly reserves any one sin from the efficacy of the means God hath appointed for its mortification doth equally reserve all. And as those means do lose their power and efficacy towards such persons, so they will insensibly fall off from a conscientious attendance unto any of those ways and duties whereby sin should be opposed and ruined. 3. Many of the graces in whose exercise this evangelical holiness doth principally consist are such as are of no reputation in the world. The greatest moralists that ever were, whether Pharisees or philosophers, could never separate between their love and practice of virtue on the one hand, and their own honour, glory, and reputation on the other. There was in them, as the poet expresseth it in one instance, --

"Amor patriæ, laudumque immensa cupido."

Hence they always esteemed those virtues the most excellent which had the best acceptation and the greatest vogue of praise among men. And it seems to be ingrafted in the nature of man to have some kind of desire to be approved in what men judge themselves to do well and laudably. Neither is this desire so evil in itself but that it may be managed in subordination unto the glory of God; which nothing that is absolutely evil, or in its own nature or any considerations or circumstances, can be. But when at any time it swells into an excess, and the pharisaical leaven of being seen and praised of men puffeth it up, it is the worst poison that the mind can be infected withal. In what degree soever it be admitted, in the same it alienates the mind from gospel holiness; and it doth so effectually, -- I mean this self-love and love of the praise of others doth so, -- for the reason mentioned, namely, that the graces in whose exercise it doth principally consist are of no reputation in the world. Such are meekness, gentleness, self-denial, poverty of spirit, mourning for sin, hungering and thirsting after righteousness, mercy and compassion, purity of heart, openness and simplicity of spirit, readiness to undergo and forgive injuries, zeal for God, contempt of the world, fear of sin, dread of God's judgment for sin, and the like. These are those adornings of the inner man of the heart which with God are of great price. But as unto their reputation in the world, "weakness, softness of nature, superstitious folly, madness, hypocritical preciseness," is the best measure they meet withal. When men begin to discern that as unto this holiness of the gospel, its principal work lies within doors, in the heart and mind, in the things that no mortal eye seeth and few commend so much as in the notion of them, and which in their outward exercise meet with no good entertainment in the world, they betake themselves unto and rest in those duties which make a better appearance and meet with better acceptance; and many of them are such as, in their proper place, are diligently to be attended unto, provided they draw not off the mind from an attendance unto those despised graces and their exercise wherein the life of true holiness doth consist. And it is well if we are all sufficiently aware of the deceits of Satan in this matter. In the beginnings of the general apostasy from the power and purity of Christian religion, to countenance all sorts of persons in a neglect of the principal graces of the gospel, the necessity of regeneration, and a heavenly principle of spiritual life, they were put wholly on outward splendid works of piety and charity, as they were esteemed. Let their minds be defiled, their lusts unmortified, their hearts unhumbled, their whole souls unfurnished of spiritual and heavenly graces, yet (as they would have it) these outward works should assuredly bring them all unto a blessed immortality and glory! But this face of the covering, this veil that was spread over many nations, being now in many places (particularly among us) rent and destroyed, both wisdom and much circumspection are required, that, either under a pretence or under a real endeavour after the inward spiritual graces of Christ and their due exercise, we do not countenance ourselves in the neglect of those outward duties which are any way useful unto the glory of God and the good of mankind.

These are some of the causes, and others there are of an alike nature, from the powerful influence whereof upon their minds men have changed gospel holiness for other ways of obedience, which also they give other names unto.

Footnotes:

10. Owen refers to a work by the learned Joseph Mede, entitled, "The Apostasy of the Latter Times; or, the Gentiles' Theology of Demons Revived in the Invocation of Saints, Adoring of Relics," etc. It was published in 1642. An edition of it appeared so recently as 1836. -- Ed.

11. See vol. iii. books iv. and v. -- Ed.

Chapter IX – Apostasy into profaneness and sensuality of life — The causes and occasions of it — Defects in public teachers and guides in religion

That which yet remaineth to be considered under this head of backsliding from the commands of the gospel and the obedience required of them is of a worse kind and of a more pernicious consequence; and this is that open apostasy into profaneness and sensuality of life which the generality of them who are called Christians are in most places of the world visibly fallen into. If any be otherwise minded, if they suppose and judge that the ways and walkings of the generality of churches and individual Christians, of whole nations that profess themselves to be so, are such as the gospel requireth and approveth of, they seem either to be ignorant of the true state of these things in the world, or to be highly injurious unto the grace and truth which came by Jesus Christ. To suppose that he by his gospel giveth countenance unto or conniveth at that darkness, profaneness, sensuality, those bloody contentions and oppressions, in a word, all those filthy and noxious lusts, which at this day have overwhelmed the Christian world, is to do what we can to render and represent it not only useless, but extremely pernicious unto manind; for we do say therein that by him and his doctrine countenance is given unto that degeneracy in wickedness which heathenism would not allow, whereby the world is filled with confusion, and in danger to be precipitated into ruin. I shall therefore at present take it for granted (with the highest readiness to give up that concession when any tolerable evidence shall be given to the contrary) that there is, among and in the churches whereunto the generality of Christians do reckon themselves to belong, a visible apostasy from that piety, holiness, and righteousness, which the gospel indispensably requireth in all the disciples of Christ, and which the primitive Christians did earnestly follow and eminently abound in. An inquiry into the means and causes hereof is that which now lies before us. And that especial instance which I shall always regard is the church of Rome; which, as it hath given the most eminent example of apostasy in this kind of any church in the world, so whatever of the same nature befalleth others, it is sufficiently represented therein.

The immediate internal causes (which are, as the rise and original of all sins, so of those wherein this apostasy doth consist, because they are not peculiar hereunto, but equally respect all sins at all times) belong not unto our present inquiry. By these causes I intend, in general, the depravation of nature; the power and deceitfulness of sin; love of the world, the profits, honours, and pleasures of it; the rage of the flesh after the satisfaction of its sensual lusts; with the aversation of the minds of men from things spiritual and heavenly, as being "alienated from the life of God" through the darkness and ignorance that is in them: for these and the like depraved affections, being excited and acted by the crafty influences of Satan, and inflamed with temptations, do incline, induce, and carry men into all manner of wickedness with delight and greediness, James i. 14, 15. But whereas all these things in general respect equally all times, occasions, and sins; and whereas it is the constant work of the ministers of the gospel (those, I mean, who understand their employment, with the account they must give of the souls committed unto their charge) to discover the nature, detect the deceit, and warn men of the danger, of these principles and occasions of sin within them and without them, -- I shall not need particularly here to insist upon them. It is the more public external means and causes which have produced, furthered, and promoted the apostasy complained of, that we shall take under consideration.

I. The first occasion hereof, in all ages, hath been given by or taken from the public readers, guides, or leaders of the people in the matter of religion. I intend them of all sorts, however called, styled, or distinguished, into what forms or orders soever they are cast by themselves or others; and I name them so at large, because it is known how variously they are multiplied, especially in the church of Rome, where, as to these parts of the world, this apostasy began, and by which it is principally promoted, and that by all sorts of them. These at all times have, and must have, an especial influence into the holiness or unholiness of the people; yea, the purity or apostasy of the church, as to outward means, doth principally depend upon them, with the discharge of their office and duty. In many things they succeed into the room of the priests of old, and frequently fall under the command and rebuke given unto them, Mal. ii. 1-9, "O ye priests, this commandment is for you. If ye will not hear, and if ye will not lay it to heart, to give glory unto my name, saith the Lord of hosts, I will even send a curse upon you, and I will curse your blessings: yea, I have cursed them already, because ye do not lay it to heart. Behold, I will corrupt your seed, and spread dung upon your faces, even the dung of your solemn feasts; and one shall take you away with it. And ye shall know that I have sent this commandment unto you, that my covenant might be with Levi, saith the Lord of hosts. My covenant was with him of life and peace; and I gave them to him for the fear wherewith he feared me, and was afraid before my name. The law of truth was in his mouth, and iniquity was not found in his lips: he walked with me in peace and equity, and did turn many away from iniquity. For the priest's lips should keep knowledge, and they should seek the law at his mouth: for he is the messenger of the Lord of hosts. But ye are departed out of the way; ye have caused many to stumble at the law; ye have corrupted the covenant of Levi, saith the Lord of hosts. Therefore have I also made you contemptible and base before all the people, according as ye have not kept my ways, but have been partial in the law."

That holy, humble, laborious ministry, which Christ first instituted in the church, was the great means of converting men unto evangelical obedience and the preserving of them therein. This their doctrine, their spirit, their example, their manner and course of life, their prayers: preaching, and entire endeavours, tended unto, and were blessed and prospered of God unto that purpose. Then were the lives of Christians a transcript of the truth of the gospel. But through the degeneracy of the following ages, those who succeeded them became troubled fountains, polluting and corrupting all the streams of Christian religion It is no uneasy thing to observe, in the course of ecclesiastical records and stories, how, by various degrees, the leaders of the church became corrupt, and did corrupt the people, giving them in themselves an example of strifes, divisions, ambition, worldly-mindedness; and, by their negligence in discharge of their duty, depriving them of the means of being made better by the power of the doctrine and commands of the gospel. Under the old testament, the priests and prophets led the people into a double apostasy:-- First, Into that of superstition and idolatry, Jer. xxiii. 9-15; and this continued prevailing among them until their sin issued in a desolating calamity. This was the Babylonish captivity, wherein all their idols were buried in the land of Shinar, Zech. v. 11. Secondly, After the return of the people from thence, when they would no more be inveigled into idolatry, whereof God designed that captivity for an effectual cure, the same sort of persons, by negligence, ignorance, and their evil example in profaneness, turned them off from God and his law. This was begun in the days of Malachi, the last of the prophets, and ended in the total apostasy and destruction of that church and people. And when the whole came unto its last issue in the rejection of the Lord Christ, the Son of God, the same sort of persons, even the guides and teachers, led, and even forced, the body of the people into that great rebellion and impenitency therein, as is evidently declared in the gospel. And it is to be feared that something of the like nature hath fallen out among Christians also. The first apostasy the Christian world fell into was by superstition and idolatry, principally under the conduct of the church of Rome; and this, as it will always be, was accompanied with wickedness of life in all sorts of persons. Many churches and nations being delivered from this abomination, it is well if, by the same means, they are not falling into that of a worldly, sensual, profane conversation.

The Scripture is so full on this subject, and the nature of the thing itself is such, as seems to require a deep and thorough consideration of it; but the nature of my design will not admit of enlargement on any particular head, for I intend only to point at the chief springs and occasions of this evil, and accordingly this part of our subject must be only briefly (as that preceding) treated on.

What was before asserted in general, namely, that the well-being of the church depends on the right discharge of the office of the ministry, will, I suppose, be acknowledged by all; and it is plainly declared by the apostle, Eph. iv. 11-15. In proportion thereunto it will thrive or decay. The nature of this office, the ends of its institution, the works and duties of it, with the universal experience of all ages and places, do evince this observation beyond all contradiction. If, therefore, those who undertake the exercise of this office do eminently and notoriously fail in the performance and discharge of the duties thereof, especially if they do so generally, and in any long succession of time, it cannot be but that the people will be corrupt, and degenerate from the rule of the gospel. The flocks will not be preserved where the shepherds are negligent; and fields will be overrun with weeds, thorns, and briers, if they be not duly tilled. I shall therefore, in the first place, call over some of those things which are indispensably required in and of the ministers and teachers of the church, that it may be preserved in its purity, and kept up unto its duty in evangelical obedience; and I shall insist only on those which all men will acknowledge to be such duties, or which none who own the gospel can or dare deny so to be:--

First, It is required of them that they keep pure and uncorrupted the doctrine of the gospel, especially that concerning the holiness enjoined in it, both as to its nature, causes, motives, and ends. So of old, the "priest's lips were to keep knowledge," and "the people were to seek the law at his mouth." This was one main end for which the Lord Christ gave unto, and instituted the office of the ministry in the church: Eph. iv. 11-15, "He gave some, apostles; and some,

prophets; and some, evangelists; and some, pastors and teachers; for the perfecting
of the saints, for the work of the ministry, for the edifying of the body of Christ: till
we all come in the unity of the faith, and of the knowledge of the Son of God, unto
a perfect man, unto the measure of the stature of the fulness of Christ: that we
henceforth be no more children, tossed to and fro, and carried about with every
wind of doctrine, by the sleight of men, and cunning craftiness, whereby they lie in
wait to deceive; but speaking the truth in love, may grow up into him in all things,
which is the head, even Christ." The preservation of the truth, the declaration,
vindication, and defence of it, so as the members of the church, the disciples of
Christ, committed to their charge, be neither through weakness or ignorance as
children, nor through the delusions of seducers, turned off from it or unsettled in it,
was one great end why the Lord Christ instituted this office therein. And upon their
discharge of this duty depend the growth, the obedience, the edification, and
salvation, of the whole body. And therefore doth the apostle give this principally in
charge unto the elders of the church of Ephesus, in his solemn giving of it up unto
their care and inspection, when he himself was no more to come among them: Acts
xx. 28-30, "Take heed therefore unto yourselves, and to all the flock, over the
which the Holy Ghost hath made you overseers, to feed the church of God, which
he hath purchased with his own blood. For I know this, that after my departing
shall grievous wolves enter in among you, not sparing the flock. Also of your own
selves shall men arise, speaking perverse things, to draw away disciples after
them." As he hath a regard unto other things, so in an especial manner to the
introduction of perverse and corrupt opinions, contrary to the truth wherein they
had been instructed by him, which comprised "all the counsel of God" concerning
their faith and obedience, with his own worship, verse 27. This they were to do by
their careful, faithful, diligent declaration, vindication, and defence, of the doctrine
which they had received. Especially doth he press this upon his beloved Timothy.
He being for a season fixed in the ministry of the church, he was chosen out by the
wisdom of the Holy Ghost to be a pattern and example, in the instructions given
unto him, unto all ministers of the gospel in succeeding generations. This charge is
expressly committed unto him, 1 Tim. vi. 13, 14, "I give thee charge in the sight of
God, who quickeneth all things, and before Christ Jesus, who before Pontius Pilate
witnessed a good confession; that thou keep this commandment without spot,
unrebukable, until the appearing of our Lord Jesus Christ." Verse 20, "O Timothy,
keep that which is committed to thy trust, avoiding profane and vain babblings, and
oppositions of science falsely so called." 2 Tim. ii. 13, 14, "If we believe not, yet
he abideth faithful: he cannot deny himself. Of these things put them in
remembrance, charging them before the Lord that they strive not about words to no
profit, but to the subverting of the hearers." And what he was enjoined in his own
person, that also he was directed to commit unto others with the same charge, that
the truth of the gospel might be preserved incorrupt in succeeding generations, 2
Tim. ii. 1, 2, "Thou therefore, my son, be strong in the grace that is in Christ Jesus.
And the things that thou hast heard of me among many witnesses, the same commit
thou to faithful men, who shall be able to teach others also." The vehemency of the
apostle in this charge, and his pathetical exhortations, do sufficiently evince the
moment and necessity of this duty, as that without which the church would not be
continued to be "the pillar and ground of the truth."

There are three repositories of sacred truth, or of the truths of the mystery of
the gospel, -- the Scripture, the minds and hearts of believers, and the ministry of
the present age. In the first, God preserveth them by his providence; in the second,

by his Spirit and grace; in the last, by way of an ordinance or especial institution for that end.

In the first way they have been kept, and shall be kept, safe against all oppositions of hell and the world, unto the consummation of all things. And if this way might fail, we acknowledge that the others would do so also, whatever some pretend of their traditions, and others of their present inspirations. And whilst this doth abide (as it shall always do), the loss that may befall in the other ways may be retrieved; and so it hath been several times, when the faith of the church hath been recovered and its profession reformed by the light and knowledge derived afresh from the Scripture. This fountain, therefore, of truth shall never be dry, but men may always draw sufficiently, yea, abundantly from it, whilst they use the means appointed thereunto. But yet this alone will not secure the public interest of truth and holiness. There must be other means also of communicating what is contained therein unto the minds and consciences of men; and the Scripture itself doth both appoint and require a ministry unto this end. Secondly, There may be a preservation of the truth derived from the Scripture for a season in the minds of men and hearts of private believers. So was it in the days of Elijah, when, in a destitution of all outward ministry, seven thousand were preserved in faith and the fear of God, "not bowing the knee unto Baal," 1 Kings xix. 18. This the Holy Ghost is in an especial manner promised and given unto them to effect, John xiv. 16, 17, 26, xvi. 13, 1 John ii. 20, 21: for herein is the promise accomplished, that "they shall be all taught of God," John vi. 45; which though it be not wholly without means, yet it is such as doth not always and in all things indispensably depend thereon, Heb. viii. 11 And unto this work of the Spirit preserving the truth in the minds and hearts of true believers, the continuance of it in the world, as to its power and profession, under great and general apostasies, is to be ascribed. So I no way doubt but that during and under the papal defection, there were great numbers in whose hearts and minds the principal truths of the gospel were preserved inviolate, so as that by virtue of them they lived unto God and were accepted with him. But this way of the preservation of the truth is confined unto individual persons, and as such only are they concerned therein. [Thirdly], As unto public profession and the benefits thereof, all sacred truth is committed unto the ministry of the present age; and on the due discharge of their office and work it doth depend. The imagination of the church of Rome about keeping sacred truths in the hidden cells of tradition or invisible, fantastical treasures, which requires neither care, nor wisdom, nor honesty unto its custody, but a mere pretence of key to open it, was one engine whereby both truth and holiness were driven out of the world.

These things are inseparable. Gospel truth is the only root whereon gospel holiness will grow. If any worm corrode, or any other corrupting accident befall it, the fruit will quickly fade and decay. It is impossible to maintain the power of godliness where the doctrine from whence it springs is unknown, corrupted, or despised. And, on the other side, where men are weary of holiness, they will not long give entertainment to the truth; for as to their desires and affections, they will find it not only useless but troublesome. Hence the great opposition which is made at this day against many important truths of the gospel ariseth principally from the dislike men have of the holiness which they guide unto and require.

Secondly, It is required of the same persons that they diligently instruct the people in the knowledge of the whole counsel of God, in the mystery of the gospel, the doctrine of truth, that they may know and do the will of God; and this are they to do by all the means and ways that God hath appointed, pressing it instantly, together with instructions on their souls and consciences for its practice. The end why evangelical truth is committed unto their care is, not that they may keep it to themselves, so locking up the key of knowledge, but that they may communicate it unto others and instruct them therein. And he who doth not desire and endeavour to communicate unto his flock all things that are profitable for them can have no evidence in his own mind that God hath called him to the office of the ministry. The apostle, proposing his own example unto the elders of the church of Ephesus, affirms that he had "not shunned to declare unto them all the counsel of God," Acts xx. 27, and that he had "kept back nothing that was profitable unto them," verse 20. Men begin to talk or write about preaching on this or that subject: some, they say, preach all about Christ and grace, and justification by the imputation of Christ's righteousness, and the like; but they preach about God's attributes, moral duties, obedience to superiors, and things of that nature. But whether this fancy have more folly or malice in it is not easy to determine. It is like those who make this plea do speak truly as to their own concernment. They preach of the things they express, exclusively unto the others, which they meddle not with at all; for if they do teach them, then is the opposition they fancy between those ways of preaching altogether vain. But that others do preach the things ascribed unto them, with a neglect of those other doctrines, which such persons pretend to appropriate to themselves as their province, is a fond imagination. And, to increase the vanity of it, the distribution is made by some with a total silence on all hands, -- both on their own, which they extol, and on that of others, which they condemn, -- of that which certainly ought to be the principal subject of all preaching, namely, Jesus Christ and him crucified. But the truth is, he who knows not that it is his duty to declare unto the people, not this or that part of it, but the whole counsel of God, and who is not endowed with some measure of wisdom, so as to discern what is useful, profitable, and seasonable unto his hearers, according as their spiritual states and occasions do require, knows not what it is to be a minister of Christ or his gospel, a faithful steward of the mysteries of God, nor is meet to take that office upon him. And there are three things which ministers, teachers, leaders of the people, are to attend unto in the discharge of this principal part of their office, in the communication of the knowledge of the truth committed to them unto others:--

1. That they are to do it with all care, diligence, and sedulity. How vehement is our apostle in his charge to this purpose! 2 Tim. iv. 1, 2, "I charge thee therefore before God, and the Lord Jesus Christ, who shall judge the quick and the dead at his appearing and his kingdom; preach the word; be instant in season, out of season; reprove, rebuke, exhort with all long-suffering and doctrine." How ought these words to sound continually in the ears of all ministers who design to be faithful in the discharge of their duty! How ought the power of them to abide on their hearts! Are they spoken alone unto Timothy? or will the souls of men be preserved, edified, saved, now with less pains and at an easier rate than formerly? It will appear at the last day that others also have an eternal concernment herein.

2. That they labour with the utmost of their strength, even to fatigation and weariness. All the names whereby their office and their work are expressed in the New Testament do include this kind of labour. As they are to "give themselves continually to the ministry of the word," Acts vi. 4, -- that is, wholly and entirely, in their utmost endeavours, continually unto this work, -- so are they enjoined kopian, "to labour to the utmost of the strength" they have therein, 1 Tim. v. 17; 1 Cor. xvi. 16; 1 Thess. v. 12. It is not bodily labour alone in the dispensation of the word (wherein there may be much variety, according unto the various natural

dispositions or tempers of men, and of acquired gifts), but that earnestness and intension of spirit which will carry along with them the laborious pains of the whole person, that I intend. The cold, formal pronunciation or reading (as is the manner of some) of a well-composed oration doth not well express this labouring in the word and doctrine.

3. That their whole work and all their endeavours therein be accompanied with constant prayer, that the gospel in their ministry may run and be glorified, that the word may prosper in the hearts and lives of the people. So the apostles affirm that they would "give themselves continually to prayer and to the ministry of the word," Acts vi. 4. That ministration of the word which is not accompanied with continual prayer for its success is not like to have any great blessing go along with it. As our apostle calls God to witness of his frequent mention of them in his prayers unto whom the word was preached, Rom. i. 9, 10, so he desireth the prayers of others also, that his work and labour in the ministry might be prosperous and successful, Eph. vi. 18, 19. For a minister to preach the word without constant prayer for its success is a likely means to cherish and strengthen secret atheism in his own heart, and very unlikely to work holiness in the lives of others.

Thirdly, It is in like manner required of them (so far as human frailty will permit) that they do, in their persons, ways, and walkings or conversations, especially in the discharge of all their ministerial duties, give a true representation both of the doctrine which they preach and of Him in whose name they dispense it. What meekness, humility, and zeal for the glory of God; what moderation, self-denial, and readiness for the cross; what mortification of corrupt affections and inordinate desires of earthly things; what contempt of the world; what benignity, condescension, and patience towards all men; what evidences of heavenly-mindedness, -- are required hereunto, both the Scripture declares and the nature of the thing itself makes apparent What can any men rationally believe, but that they who preach Christ and the gospel unto them do declare that they have no other effect or tendency but what in themselves they express and represent unto them? There is a secret language in the ministry of men, that what they are and do is that which the doctrine they preach doth require, which their hearers do understand and are apt to believe. The very philosophers saw that so it would be with respect unto them who publicly taught philosophy; to which purpose the words of Themistius are remarkable: Orat. 1, Aneleutherous te de oun houtos heuriskontes kai philochrematous te kai harpages, loidorous te kai philapechthemonas kai alazonas, dolerous te kai epiboulous, ouk hoiesontai ek phuseos e tes proteras banausias echein tas keras, all' aitiasontai ek philosophias prosginesthai. Whatever vices most men observe in such persons, they will not attribute them unto their depraved natures or inward corruptions, but unto the philosophy they profess Hence it is enjoined them that in "all things they show themselves patterns of good works," Tit. ii. 7; 2 Thess. iii. 9. "Be thou," saith our apostle unto his Timothy, "an example unto believers, in word, in conversation, in charity, in spirit, in faith, in purity," 1 Tim. iv. 12. This is the dignity, honour, and preferment, that the Lord Christ calls his ministers unto, namely, that they should in their own persons represent his graces and the holiness of his doctrine unto others. Those who are otherwise minded, whose designs and affections look another way, will find themselves to fall under the effects of a great mistake. I do not reflect any thing upon what outward, secular, circumstantial advantages men may have in this world, but I do say, whatever they have of that kind which doth not enable them the more effectually in their course and work to express the meekness, humility, self-denial, and zeal of Christ, with the holiness of the doctrine they teach, or should so do, it will not redound unto any great account in the kingdom of God.

Fourthly, It is also incumbent on them to attend with diligence unto that rule and holy discipline which the Lord Christ hath appointed for the edification of the church, and the preservation of it in purity, holiness, and obedience. This, indeed, most pretend a readiness to comply withal, as that which is condited unto their appetite by an appearance of authority and power, which seldom are unaccompanied with other desirable advantages, I shall only say, it will be well for them by whom they are administered according to the mind of Christ; but that more belongeth thereunto than is usually apprehended so to do, I suppose few sober and intelligent persons will deny.

That these things, yea, and many others of the like kind, with all those duties which are subservient or any way necessary unto them, are required of all ministers of the gospel, teachers, guides, rulers of the church, and that constantly to be attended unto with zeal for the glory of God and compassion for the souls of men, none, I suppose, who profess themselves Christians will in general deny. And if in these things the life and power of the ministry (whereon the purity and holiness of the church depend) do consist, where they are wanting, it is morally impossible but that the generality of the people will gradually degenerate into ignorance, profaneness, immorality, and unholiness of every kind.

There is nothing I could more desire than that the present defection from evangelical holiness, which is so visible in the world, might neither in whole nor in part be charged on a defect in these thing among this sort of men, yea, that it might not be so unto qualifications, principles, and actings directly contrary unto what is thus required; for if it be not so, there will be yet hopes of a stay to be put unto its progress, yea, of a healing and recovery from it. But I shall a little inquire into that which offers itself unto the view of all, premising these two things:-- 1. That I do not intend the ministry of any one place or nation, or age or time, more than another, but shall speak indefinitely unto what hath been and is in the Christian world. 2. That if indeed, upon trial, none be found blameworthy, none defective in these things, there is no harm done in that any are warned what to avoid. And, --

1. Have they all kept the truth, and doctrine, and mysteries of the gospel, committed to the ministers thereof? Are there not many of this sort who are themselves woefully ignorant of the counsel of God revealed therein? nay, are there not many who have neither will nor ability to search into the mysteries of the doctrine of Christ, and do therefore despise them? Can men keep in a way of duty what they never had, nor ever used those means for the attaining of it without which it will not be so done? And is it not manifest what must needs be, and what really are, the effects and fruits hereof? Do not hereon multitudes perish for want of knowledge and continue in the ways of sin because they have none to teach them better, at least none to teach them on such principles as are alone effectual unto their conversion and holiness? They must die, they shall die in their sins, but the blood of their souls will be required at other hands; for all the causes of gospel holiness, all proper motives unto it, all effectual ways and means of attaining it, are hid from them.

It is known how brutishly ignorant the generality of their priests are in the Papacy; neither, for the most part, do the rulers of that church require any more of them than that they have skill enough to read and manage their public offices of devotion. Neither is it much otherwise in the Greek church, in any of the branches of it, whereby whole nations, under a public profession of Christianity, are through stupid ignorance degenerated into a profane course of life, no less vile than that of the heathens. It is well if it be not so in some measure in other places also. But the truth is, the ignorance of many who take upon them the office of the ministry, and their unconscionable idleness when they have so done, is the great occasion of the continuance of profaneness and ungodliness among the people. And if the preaching of the gospel be the only sovereign, effectual means appointed by God for the change of men's natures and the reformation of their lives (a denial whereof includes a renunciation of Christianity), it is a vain expectation that either of them will be wrought in such a way as to restore the beauty and glory of religion in the world, unless provision be made for an able ministry to instruct the body of the people, through all their distributions, in knowledge and understanding.

2. It is the duty of this sort of persons, unto the same end, to preserve the truth pure and uncorrupted. Unless this be done carefully and effectually, holiness will not be maintained or preserved in the world. And it is evident how many of them have acquitted themselves herein, as hath been in part declared in the foregoing account of apostasy from the doctrine and truth of the gospel By them principally it hath been debased, corrupted, perverted, and continueth yet so to be; neither is there at this day scarce any one doctrine that should really promote evangelical obedience which is free from being despised or depraved by some of them. But this is not that which we now speak unto; it hath been done already. Our present inquiry is after that love and care of, that zeal for the truth, which are eminently required of them. Do they pray, and labour, and plead with God and man for its preservation, as that wherein their principal interest doth lie? or do many esteem of it any farther but as their outward advantages are secured by it? A fault there is in this matter, and it is not without the especial guilt of some that the world is come to such an indifferency about the principal truths of the gospel that from thence men slip into atheism every day.

3. Neither are these defects supplied by diligence in their work; yea, the want thereof is of all other evils in this kind most evident. No words are sufficient to express the sloth and negligence, the coldness and carelessness, that are found amongst many in the discharge of their duty, as to the instruction of others, and the application of the word of God to the hearts and consciences of men. I shall not mention particular instances, that none may be offended. The matter itself is evident, and the effects of it manifest. It may seem to some desirable that such things should be concealed, but whilst by reason hereof the souls of multitudes are in danger of eternal ruin every day, those who are sensible of their misery may be allowed to complain. How few, therefore, do diligently and industriously lay out themselves and their strength in the ministry, with zeal for the glory of God and compassion unto the souls of men! How few do take heed to themselves and to the flocks, do watch and pray, and press their message on the consciences of their hearers! Alas! it is but little of saving truth that many know in the notions of it, less they care to communicate unto others, because they know it not in its power. Will the souls of men be brought into the obedience of faith, will the power and interest of sin and the world in them be cast down and destroyed, will gospel obedience be preserved in the lives of men, by such weak and languid endeavours as many satisfy themselves withal! If it be so, conversion unto God and the fruits of holiness must be looked on as most easy things, and the ministry itself to be of little use in the world. Certainly, there is another representation of these things in the Scripture; and notwithstanding the growth of some opinions that would render the whole work of Christianity so easy and facile as to be accommodated unto a negligent

ministry, yet the event thereof is openly pernicious. Wherefore we need not fear to say, that coldness, lukewarmness, sloth, and negligence, especially when accompanied with ignorance and spiritual darkness about the principal mysteries of the gospel, with an unconcernment of mind and affections in the importance, end, and design of their work, among them who are looked on as the public teachers of the church, at any time or in any place, keeps open a wide door for the lusts of men to pour forth themselves into that deluge of apostasy from the power of godliness which the world is even overwhelmed withal.

So was it with the church under the old testament, as God by the prophets complains in a hundred places. Can any man be so stupid as to imagine that the ordinary discharge of the priestly office in the church of Rome, in saying their offices at canonical hours, hearing of confessions and giving absolutions, without the least dram of labouring in word and doctrine, is a means to keep up the power of Christian religion, or is not an effectual means to drench mankind in sin and security? Neither doth the calling of things by other names change their natures. Wherever there is the same neglect of the true work of the ministry, in the matter of it or manner of its performance, the same event will ensue thereon. And it will be nowhere more fatal than where men love to have it so, and despise whatever is spoken to the contrary, so as that it shall be esteemed a crime for any one to be dissatisfied with the soul-ruining sloth and negligence of this sort of men.

4. Moreover, whereas great relief in all these cases might be taken from a holy, exemplary conversation and walking among them in whom it is required as an ordinance of God for the direction and encouragement of the people, it is manifest in the world, and sufficiently taken notice of, that many of them in their own persons are openly ambitious, insatiably covetous, proud, sensual, haters of them that are good, companions of the worst of men, evidencing the depraved habits of their minds in all signal instances of vice and folly. He that shall consider what was the state, what were the lives, of the apostles and first preachers of the gospel, with those who succeeded them for some ages following, not merely as to their outward condition of straits and poverty (which, as it will be pleaded, was occasioned by the state of things then in the world), but as to that humility, lowliness of mind, self-denial, contempt of the world, zeal for God, purity of life, which they prescribed unto others and gave an exemplification of in themselves; and then take a view of that universal contradiction unto them and their ways which the lives and course of very many in the world do at this day openly express; he must conclude that either all those things were needless in them, as to the public interests of Christianity, or that they are unspeakably endamaged by those of some at present.

Wherefore, it cannot with any modesty be denied but that by reason of these and the like miscarriages in the spiritual guides of the people, the generality of Christians have been either led or suffered insensibly to fall into the present apostasy. When God shall be pleased to give unto the people who are called by his name, in a more abundant manner, "pastors after his own heart, to feed them with knowledge and understanding;" when he shall revive and increase a holy, humble, zealous, self-denying, powerful ministry, by a more plentiful effusion of his Spirit from above; then, and not until then, may we hope to see the pristine glory and beauty of our religion restored unto its primitive state and condition.

Those who do yet judge that matters among the common professors of Christianity, as to the obedience of faith, are in as good a posture as they were at any time formerly, or as they need to be, who have no other desire or interest in them but only that they should not be better, may abide in their security without troubling themselves with these things. But for such as cannot but see that a revolt or defection from gospel obedience is not only begun in the world, but carried unto that height that it is ready to issue in idolatry or atheism, it is time for them to consider under whose hand this hath fallen out, and be stirred up to put a stop unto its progress before it be too late. Nor is it to be expected or fancied that there will be a recovery of the people from ungodliness and profaneness, or unto the holy obedience the gospel requireth, until there be such a change wrought in the ministry that the word may be so dispensed and such examples given as may be effectual unto that end. It is to cast the highest contempt on the office itself to imagine that this breach can be otherwise healed; for whereas this declension is fallen out under the conduct of the present ministry and that of the foregoing ages, it is not to be thought that it will be retrieved under the same conduct. And to suppose that it can be done any other way, that the world of professed Christians shall be recovered unto holy obedience by any other means but the ministerial dispensation of the word, is to render it a thing altogether useless. Here, then, must begin the cure of that lethargy in sin that the world is fallen into, -- namely, in the renovation of a powerful evangelical ministry, or the due discharge of that office by them that are called thereunto or possess the place of it, if ever it be effected unto any purpose in this world.

Chapter X - Other causes and occasions of the decay of holiness

II. Multitudes are led into and countenanced in the ways of sin and profaneness, freely indulging unto their lusts and corrupt affections, by a false appropriation of justifying names and titles unto them, in ways of sin and wickedness. This was one principal means of old whereby the Jews were hardened in their impieties and flagitious lives; for when the prophets told them of their sins, and warned them of God's approaching judgments, they opposed that outcry unto their whole ministry, "The temple of the Lord, The temple of the Lord, The temple of the Lord, are these;" -- "Say what you please, we are the only posterity of Abraham, the only church of God in the world." This contest they managed with the prophet Jeremiah in an especial manner. Chap. vii., he saith unto them in the name of the Lord, "Amend your ways and your doings, and I will cause you to dwell in this place," verse 3. Their reply and defence is, "The temple of the Lord," etc., verse 4. Whereunto the prophet makes that severe return, verses 9, 10, "Will ye steal, murder, and commit adultery, and swear falsely, and burn incense unto Baal, and walk after other gods whom ye know not, and come and stand before me in this house, which is called by my name?" -- "Will ye give up yourselves unto all manner of wickedness, and countenance yourselves therein by being a people unto whom the temple and the worship of it are appropriated?" And this, in like manner, was the great prejudice which the Baptist had to contend withal when he came to call them to repentance. Abraham's children they were, and by virtue of that relation had right unto all the privileges of the covenant made with him, whatever they were in themselves, Matt. iii. 9. And it is evident in these examples that the nearer churches or persons are unto an utter forfeiture of all their privileges, and to destruction itself, for their sins, the more ready they are to boast of and support themselves with their outward state, as having nothing else to trust unto. But if men were able to countenance themselves in their sins on this pretence against that extraordinary prophetical ministry which endeavoured to discard them of it, and called them unto the necessity of personal holiness, how much more will they be able to shelter themselves under its shades when they shall be taught so to do!

When men who have given up themselves unto a vicious, sensual, worldly course of life, having either fallen into it by the power of their lusts and temptations, or were never brought into a better course by any means of correcting the vices of nature, shall find that notwithstanding what they are, what they know themselves to be, and what judgment others must needs pass of them, yet they are esteemed to belong to the church of Christ, and are made partakers of all the outward privileges of it, it cannot but greatly heighten their security in sin, and weaken the efficacy of all means of their reformation. And when others, not so engaged in the ways of sin and profaneness, shall see that they may have all the external pledges of divine love and favour communicated unto them, although they should run into the same compass of riot and excess with others, it cannot but insensibly weaken their diligence in duty, and render them more pliable subjects of temptations unto sin; for they are but few who care to be better than they judge they must be of necessity. When the church of Sardis was really dead, the principal means of keeping it in that condition was the name it had to be alive.

Let us, therefore, consider how it hath been in the world in this matter. Whilst these things have been communicated promiscuously unto all sorts of men, yea, to the worst that live on the earth, is it not evident that the name of the church and the administration of its ordinances would be made use of to countenance men in a neglect of holiness, yea, a contempt and hatred of it? Whilst these sacred names, titles, and privileges, these pledges of the love of God, and of all the benefits of the mediation of Christ, are forced to lackey after men into the most provoking courses of flagitious sins, what can put a stay to the lusts of men? If the church be that society in the world which is alone the object of God's especial love and grace, if the principal end of the administration of its ordinances be to confirm unto men their interest in the benefits of the mediation of Christ, how can the lusts of men be more accommodated than by the application of these things unto them, whilst they are flagrant in their pursuit? It may, indeed, be supposed that the Lord Jesus Christ hath made evangelical obedience to be the immovable rule of an interest in his church; indeed, whether obedience unto the precepts of the gospel be not the only and indispensable condition of a participation of the privileges of the gospel, ought to be out of dispute with them that own the truth of its doctrine. And whereas all that is required of us that we may be eternally saved is contained in the precepts of the gospel, men can have no other outward security of their souls' welfare than what doth accompany the church and its rights. When, therefore, they do find on what easy terms they may hold an indefeasible interest in them, so as that, by a compliance with some outward forms or constitutions, they may secure their right from any impeachment or forfeiture by the most profligate course of life which, for the satisfaction of their lusts, they can betake themselves unto, what remains of outward means that can put a restraint upon them.

This was the engine whereby Satan promoted that general apostasy from evangelical obedience which befell the church of Rome, in all its branches, members and adherents. For after that innumerable multitudes were brought unto the profession of Christianity, not through a conviction and experience of its truth, power, holiness, and necessity unto the present peace and eternal welfare of the souls of men, but in compliance with the rulers of the nations and their own secular interest, being once safely lodged (on most easy and gentle terms) in the church, they were quickly secured from all apprehensions of the necessity of that holiness which the gospel doth require: for being assured that although their lives were worse than those of the heathen; were they never so lewd, filthy, and wicked; did all manner of sins that may be named, or ought [not] to be named, abound among them; yet that they, and they alone, were the church of Christ, and could not be otherwise, -- to what purpose should they trouble themselves with mortification, self-denial, purity of heart and hands, and such other ungrateful duties? What ground is there to expect the same course of obedience from them who engage into a profession of Christianity on these terms, with those who in the primitive times embraced the truth in the love of it, for its own sake, with a deliberate resolution to forego all things rather than forsake its profession or decline from its commands?

Especially were men confirmed in their security when they saw others condemned body and soul unto hell, and consumed with fire and sword in this world, for not being what they were, -- that is, the church! They could not choose but applaud their own happiness, who on such easy terms were certainly freed from present and eternal flames. When hereunto, for the necessary satisfaction of some convictions, the reliefs of confession, penances, commutation, and redemption of sins by outward works of supposed piety or charity, were found out, with the great reserve of purgatory in all dubious cases, the generality of men bade an open farewell unto the holiness of the gospel, as that wherein they were not concerned and wherewith they would not be troubled.

In these things consisted the mystery of iniquity, the springs and occasions of that great apostasy which was in the world under the Papacy.

1. The doctrine of the gospel (as to its peculiar nature, the causes, motives, and ends of it) was generally lost, partly through the horrible ignorance of some, and partly through the pernicious errors of others, whose duty it was to have preserved it. And how impossible it is to maintain the life and power of obedience when this spring of it is dried up or corrupted, when this root is withered and decayed, is not hard to apprehend. Sometimes truth is lost first in a church, and then holiness, and sometimes the decay or hatred of holiness is the cause of the loss of truth; but where either is rejected, the other win not abide, as we have declared. And so it fell out in that fatal apostasy; these evils promoted and furthered each other.

2. The ground got by the loss of truth was secured by the application of the name, title, privileges, and promises of the church unto all sorts of men, though living impenitently in their sins; for there was and is virtually contained therein an assurance given unto them that they are in that condition wherein the Lord Christ requires they should be, which he accepts, approves, and hath annexed the promises of the gospel unto. When men are declared to be in this estate, what need they be at any pains or charge to have it changed or bettered? Certainly, in general, they are too much in love with their lusts, sins, and pleasures, to part with them, unless they see a greater necessity for it than such a condition would admit. And for their farther security herein, they were informed that the sacraments of the church did, by virtue of their administration alone, confer unto them all the grace which they do signify. Particularly, they were taught to believe that every one who had a mouth, whatever villainies his heart and life were filled withal, might eat the flesh and drink the blood of Jesus Christ (at least by concomitancy); which himself hath assured us that "whoso doeth hath eternal life," John vi. 53, 54. And other ways almost innumerable there were whereby, through their pretended interest in the church and its privileges, even flagitious sinners were secured of immortality and glory.

3. For the increase of their satisfaction, for the confirming of their security, they found that hell and destruction were denounced only against them who were not of the church. For besides one great maxim of truth which passed current amongst them, but [was] falsely applied unto their advantage, namely, that out of the church there was no salvation, which church they were; and one also of no less use to them, though of less truth in itself, that the church was like Noah's ark, all were saved that were in it, and all drowned that were out of it, with others of an alike encouraging nature; they saw the truth of them exemplified before their eyes: for if it so fell out that there were any who did not belong unto the church as they did, nor would comply with it, although they were evidently in their ways and lives more righteous than themselves, they saw them, by the authority of the church, cursed, condemned unto hell, cast into dungeons, and consumed with flames. And herewith they could not but be fully satisfied that there was no fear of danger and trouble, in this world or another, but only in not being of the church; which sin they

were resolved not to be guilty of, seeing they could avoid it on so easy terms. And it will be found always true, that as persecutions, with the sufferings of the saints of God, do tend to the brightening of the grace of some, and the confirmation of the faith of others who really believe, so they do greatly unto the obdurateness and impenitency of wicked men in their sins. Never was there a more pernicious engine against the glory of the gospel invented, than for professed Christians to persecute, hurt; and destroy others, in like manner professing Christian religion with themselves, who visibly excel them in a holy, fruitful conversation, because in some things they dissent from them; for what can more secure men in their impieties than to persuade them that they are justified in them by the rule of the gospel, above those who in all duties of morality do really excel them? Certainly, for swearers and drunkards, profane persons and unclean, to persecute such for religion as are visibly pious, sober, temperate, given unto prayer and good works, is no useful representation of Christianity. But, --

4. These privileges and these attestations were not absolutely and always such armour of proof unto sinners, but that some arrows of conviction would ever and anon pierce into their minds and consciences, giving them no small disquietment and trouble. One thing or other, either in some beam of truth from the gospel or from conscience itself, on the occasions of new surprisals into actual sin, or from fear, or an apprehension of some public judgments, would ever and anon befall them, and that unto an inward disturbance beyond what the advantages mentioned could reduce them from; and this was the most likely way of awaking them out of their security, and causing them to inquire what God yet required of them. In this case were the other helps and supplies mentioned found out and proposed unto them. "If it be so that you are not absolutely satisfied with your interest in the advantages of the church in general, if sin will yet give you any disquietment, then you must to confession, and penances, and works of redemption, with the like approved medicines and remedies for troubled minds. But if the conscience of any prove so stubborn or inflexible after all these mollifying and suppling medicines, that the wound will not be skinned over, all that is yet wanting shall be well issued and secured in purgatory, wherein it is most certain that never any soul did miscarry."

By these and the like means, the generality of mankind were brought into an utter unconcernment with gospel holiness. They neither understood it, nor found any need of it, nor did like what by any means they might hear of it, until at length a blind devotion, deformed with various superstitions, obtained the reputation of it, the world in the meantime being drenched in ignorance, profaneness, and all manner of wicked conversation. So, under the name of the church and its privileges, were Christ and the gospel almost utterly lost amongst men.

It will not be otherwise where the same principles are entertained, according unto the degrees of their prevalency. And were it not that the minds of men are powerfully influenced with reserves from these things, it were impossible that so many called Christians should in their lives and conversations exceed heathens and Mohammedans in wickedness. The commands of the gospel are most holy, its promises great, and its threatenings most severe; and yet, under a profession of owning them all, men lead lives worse than the heathens, who know nothing of that holy rule, or of those promises and threats of eternal things wherein the highest blessedness and utmost misery of our nature do consist, which these profess to be regulated by.

To suppose really the least countenance to be given hereunto by any thing that belongs unto the gospel, is to exercise against it the highest despite imaginable. This event, therefore, must and doth principally follow on the undue application of the outward tokens of God's favour and pledges of eternal blessedness unto men in their sins, by those unto whom the administration of them is supposed to be committed by Jesus Christ. And let none expect a return of a conversation becoming the gospel among Christians until things are so ordered in the church as that none may flatter themselves with a supposed interest in the promises and privileges of the gospel, who live not in a visible subjection unto and compliance with all the precepts of it. But whilst all things are huddled together promiscuously, and there is no more required to make a Christian than for him to be born in such a place or nation, and not to oppose the customs and usages in religion which are there established, we must be content to bear the evils of that defection which the world groans under.

III. Great examples of persons exalted in places of eminency giving up themselves unto boldness in a course of sinning, -- which have fallen out in all the latter ages of the church, -- have had a signal influence into the increase and furtherance of this apostasy; especially they have had so where the persons giving such examples have been such as pretended unto the conduct of religion. See Jer. xxiii. 15. It cannot with any modesty be denied but that the flagitious, scandalous lives of many popes and other great prelates of the court of Rome have hurried many into the very depths of atheism, and countenanced multitudes in a careless, voluptuous, sensual course of life. And if at any time a man whose ways are made conspicuous by the eminency of his employment, -- being, as it were, at the head of all the religion that is publicly professed, and having the chief conduct of it in his hand, as it is in the Papacy in many places, -- be vain in his communication, profane in his principles, sensual in his course of life, negligent in the duties of his office, no way rebuking open sins, but taking pleasure in them that do them, it is incredible how soon a whole age or generation of professed Christians will be influenced, corrupted, and debauched thereby; for what is the family like to be, when the stewards are such as the evil servant described Matt. xxiv. 48-51? As men are warned every day not to be wiser than their teachers, but duly to obey their guides; so they either cannot or will not, for the most part, see any reason why they should be better than they, or walk in any other paths than what they tread before them. When the sons of Eli, the sons and successors of the high priest, actually exercising the priests' office in their own persons, gave the people an open example of profaneness and lewdness of life, the body of the nation was quickly so far corrupted as that the judgments of God in the first captivity of the land ensued thereon. The world at present is so precipitate and headstrong in a course of sin, that the best examples are not able in any measure to stem the torrents of it. But if in any place, at any time, encouragements are given unto men by any eminent examples in sinning, helping to remove the remaining curbs of fear, shame, and reputation, impudence in sinning will rise unto an exorbitant and uncontrollable outrage. Hereby, then, hath the defection from holiness complained of been greatly promoted in all ages, for few or none of them have wanted plenty of these examples. Indeed, the first visible degeneracies of Christianity, as they accompanied, so they were occasioned by the open pride, ambition, strife, contentions, and conformity unto the world, that possessed the minds and stained the lives of far the greatest part of the prelates and principal leaders of the church, after it came under the protection of the Roman empire, and men thought to purchase an interest in the good things of religion, or at least a representation of them, by giving power, wealth, and honour, unto persons no way better than themselves, who had got the name and title of the "clergy," or "guides of the church;" for about these things they contended endlessly, to the shame of Christian religion, and the utter loss in the most of the true real power and virtue of it. And in following ages, as things grew worse and worse, the lewd and wicked lives of popes, prelates, and others, signalized unto the world by their power and dignity, did by their examples insensibly bring about a public conformity unto their vices, according as the concurrence of opportunity and ability did enable men thereunto. Wherever, therefore, persons fall within the compass of the ministry of the church, or, as guides thereof, are on that account (on what principles soever) exalted into places of eminence or dignity, whereby they are made conspicuous and observable, if they do not proportionably excel others in visible exemplary holiness, at least if they be not unblamable in such a godly conversation as truly expresseth the grace of the gospel, in humility, meekness, contempt of the world, of sensual pleasures, and of the pride of life, zeal and diligence in the dispensation of the word, it cannot be but that apostasy from the gospel, as to its power and holiness, will be kept up and promoted.

IV. This apostasy hath been very much promoted by persecution. I mean not that persecution which hath befallen the sincere, constant professors of Christianity from the avowed enemies thereof, upon the account of their profession of it. This is so far from being any cause or occasion of a defection from the holiness of the gospel as that it hath been the peculiar glory of our religion, and a notable outward means of the increase of it. So hath it been with respect unto the whole doctrine of the gospel in general, and so it is with respect unto any especial branch or part of it. It was the primitive glory of Christian religion that it set out in the face of a universal opposition from the whole world, and not only made good its station, but increased under the fiercest persecutions, until it had finished that glorious conquest which it was designed unto. And not only did it preserve its being and enlarge its extent under them, but they were means also to preserve its purity, and to exert its power in the hearts and lives of its professors. The church never lost finally either truth or holiness by the violent persecutions of its avowed enemies. But I speak not of the outrages committed on the flock of Christ by wolves in their own skins, but by such as have got on sheep's clothing; for these things, in whomsoever they are, proceed from the uncured, wolfish nature in persons on whom the gospel hath not obtained its promised efficacy, Isa. xi. 6-9. It is professing Christians persecuting one another, about some differences among themselves concerning their apprehensions of spiritual things and practice of divine worship, that I intend. And this hath been so great, especially in the latter ages of the church, that it is questionable whether there hath not greater effusion of the blood of Christians, ruin of families, and devastation of nations, been made by them who have professed the same religion in general, than by all the Pagans in the world since the first promulgation of it. He that shall impartially read the Gospel will not be able to discern how it was possible that any such things should ever fall out among those who pretend to avow it as their rule and guide in any measure; for the whole design and all the rules of it are so expressly contradictory unto any such practice, as that no man who had not learned the contrary from the event could possibly conjecture that any persons could ever fall into it without an antecedent renunciation of the gospel itself. But thus in process of time it did fall out, unto the irreparable scandal and detriment of Christian religion. And that so it would do was foretold; for the principal design of the book of the Revelation is, to foretell and delineate such an apostate state of the church as wherein the external power prevailing in it should persecute, destroy, and kill those who would not comply in the apostasy; for which reason, together with idolatry, that state is called Babylon. And we all know how it came to pass under the power and prevalency of the Roman church. And we may observe, that upon the destruction of Babylon, it is said that "in her was found the blood of prophets, and of saints, and of all that were slain upon the earth," Rev. xviii. 24, -- that is, for the gospel and the profession thereof. Whoever, therefore, offereth violence unto the life of any on the account of their profession of the gospel and religion of Christ, be it under what pretence it will, he doth therein and so far join himself unto that apostate state which shall be destroyed. Our Lord Jesus Christ came to restore that love of God which was departed from our nature, and thereon that love unto and among mankind which the law of creation originally required, and that advanced unto a higher degree of worth and excellency by an addition of new motives, duties, and ends, unto it. He came to save the lives of men, and not to destroy them, -- to deliver them out of a state of enmity and mutual hatred into that of peace and love; and can any sober man imagine that the hurting, imprisoning, fining, banishing, killing, and destroying of men, for no other reason or cause in the world but for believing in Christ, and worshipping of him according, as they are invincibly convinced they ought to do, is a good and due representation of this design of Christ? nay, is it not evident that this practice draws a veil over the glory of it, obscuring the principal attractive beauties of the gospel, and teaching the world a Christian religion, fierce, cruel, oppressive, vindictive, bloody, to the utter exclusion of that which is so indeed? There is therefore no more expedient course to draw off the minds of men from the due consideration of one principal end of the mediation of Christ (which is to turn them from the gospel, and to substitute another gospel in the room thereof, which yet is not another, because it is none, whatever it pretends), than for those who profess Christian religion to persecute others of the same profession for their profession, pleading this to be a duty of that religion. Wherefore, when the generality of mankind, by what they heard and saw, were persuaded that this was the true religion, -- namely, variously to persecute, and at length to destroy others, who professing it did yet in some things dissent from them in power, -- they had lost the true gospel and the benefits of it.

Besides, that religion is alien from the gospel, at least includes a notable defection from it, whose avowed profession doth not represent the spirit, graces, and virtues of Him who was its author; yea, conformity unto him in all things is the sum and substance of that obedience which it doth require. But in this way of external force and persecution, there seems to be an appearance of the spirit of Mohammed and Antichrist rather than of our Lord Jesus Christ. And hereby are the minds of men infected with false notions and apprehensions of the nature of Christian religion; which whilst they conform themselves unto, they depart from the glory and power of it. It hath been sufficiently elsewhere evinced how contrary also this practice is to the most plain rules and principal ends of the gospel. And when at any time there is this kind of persecution prevailing among Christians, there is not so much as the form, face, or appearance, of Christianity left amongst men. All that love, charity, peace, meekness, quietness, condescension, mercy, compassion, benignity, towards mankind, which belong essentially unto Christian religion, are forced to give way to wrath, strife, revenge, evil surmises, false accusations, tumults, disorder, force, rapine, and every thing that is evil. Whereas, therefore, this course hath been steered in many places of the world, and yet continueth so to be, the generality of men must needs be much untaught the truth of religion thereby; for that kind of profession thereof which is consistent with such practices is not directed in the least by the gospel. And when the minds of men are hereby unframed, they are unsuited unto all other evangelical duties Whatever advantages may shall pretend to have by this means accrued unto the truth (as they suppose) in some few instances, yet as none can be so immodest as to deny but that it hath been a thousand times more subservient unto the interests of error, so no pretended advantage of truth can countervail that corruption of Christian morality which hath been introduced and countenanced by it.

V. Want of watchfulness against the insinuation of national vices and the prevailing sins of any present age, hath effectually promoted an apostasy from evangelical holiness among the generality of Christians. There are some vices, crimes, or sins, that particular nations (on what grounds I shall not now inquire) are peculiarly inclined unto, which therefore abound in them; for it is evident what great advantages those vices must have on the minds of men, and how easy it is to have their practice imposed on them. All men are continually encompassed with them in their occasions, and commonness takes off the sense of their guilt, That which would be looked on in one nation as the greatest debauchery of human nature, is, through custom, in another passed by without any animadversion. Hence the prevalency of the gospel in any nation may be measured by the success it hath against known national sins. If these are not in some good measure subdued by it, if the minds of men be not alienated from them and made watchful against them, if their guilt appear not naked, without the varnish or veil put upon it by commonness or custom, whatever profession is made of the gospel, it is vain and useless. Thus the apostle allows that there were national sins prevalent among the Cretians, Tit. i. 12, 13, "One of themselves, a prophet of their own, said, The Cretians are alway liars, evil beasts, slow bellies. This witness is true. Wherefore rebuke them sharply, that they may be sound in the faith." Whatever their profession were, if they were not delivered by the gospel from the power and practice of these national sins which they were so prone unto, they would not long be sound in the faith nor fruitful in obedience. So among the Jews there was a peculiar kind of stubbornness and obstinacy, above any other nation under heaven, which God complaineth of in their successive generations from first to last, and which continueth to be their characteristical evil unto this day. Hence Josiah was eminently commended, "because his heart was tender," 2 Chron. xxxiv. 27. He was not under the power of the common sin of that people, which indeed includes all other evils whatever. It was a rare thing to find one of a tender heart among them.

And we may observe (it being easily demonstrable), that the great apostasy which is at this day among the nations which have received the Christian religion consists in a degeneracy into those customs, manners, humours, and courses of conversation, which were common among them and national before the entrance of Christianity. Set aside an outward profession and formality of worship, and the generality of men in most nations live as they did formerly, and are given up greatly unto those vices which were prevalent among them in their heathenism. A full evidence this is that the power of evangelical truth is lost among them, the efficacy thereof consisting in curing the vices of nature and those evils which men have been most habituated unto, as the prophet at large declares, Isa. xi. 6-9.

Thus the sin of this nation hath been always esteemed sensuality of life, in an excess of eating and drinking, with the consequents thereof. Hereunto of late have been added vanity in apparel, with foolish, light, lascivious modes and dressings therein, and an immodest boldness in conversation among men and women. These are corruptions, which, being borrowed from the neighbour nation, and grafted on crab-stocks of our own, have brought forth the fruit of vanity and pride in abundance. And it is the most manifest evidence of a degenerate people, when they are prone to naturalize the vices of other nations among them, but care not to imitate their virtues, if in any kind they do excel. But thus the lust of the eyes and the pride of life are joined unto the lust of the flesh, to give the world, as opposite unto God, a complete interest among us. It may be these things are restrained in some by contrary vices, as covetousness, and an earnest desire or ambition to enrich a family, and leave a name amongst men; -- a vanity infused amongst mankind from the great design of the builders of Babel; which was, to "make unto themselves a name," Gen. xi. 4. This is but another way of the exercise of the same sin.

Now, where sins are thus national and common, it is easier for men to preserve themselves from the most raging epidemical disease than from being, in one degree or other, tainted with the infection of them. It is almost inexpressible how efficaciously they will insinuate themselves into the minds and lives of men. They are so beset on every side with the occasions of them and temptations unto them, they offer themselves continually with so many specious pretences, as that there is no security against them but by being encompassed with "the whole armour of God;" a matter that few understand or apply themselves unto. But it is not [possible] on any other grounds or by any other means for single persons to hold out and prevail against a national confederacy in sin; for they who will not say "A confederacy" to them, or in those things wherein a whole people shall say "A confederacy," must be content to be for "signs and wonders," to be despised, and even hooted at, Isa. viii. 11, 12, 18. However, it is apparent that by them the general apostasy we treat of is visibly and openly promoted. Some are engaged in them by a corrupt course of education, and some are betrayed into the entrances of them by sloth, negligence, and security; some lose a sense of their guilt by their commonness; some yield to the arguments that are pleaded, if not in their justification, yet in their excuse or for their extenuation. One way or other, multitudes of all sorts are by them turned away from gospel obedience. Hence it is come to pass that Christianity is, as unto customs, manners, vanities, vices, and way of conversation, sunk down into heathenism; or prevalent national sins have drowned the power and left little but the outward form of it in the world. And where it is so, the life, substance, and all the real benefits of the gospel, are renounced; for it doth not design only to turn men in their outward profession from "dumb idols to serve the living God," to change the form and outward state of religion, -- as the Roman missionaries have made conversions of the Indians, giving them new images instead of their old idols, and new saints for their former Zemes, -- but to turn men also from "all ungodliness and worldly lusts, to live soberly, righteously, and godly, in this present world." Where this is not effected, either the gospel never really prevailed among men, or they are fallen away from it. And where men do engage into a profession of religion, disallowing and condemning such national vanities, vices, and customs, if they are publicly countenanced they occasion particular apostasies every day. This is that which, on the one side and the other, hath almost lost the protestant religion in some neighbour nations; for, not being able to hold out against those national vanities and vices which are publicly countenanced, they find no relief unto their minds but in a renunciation of that religion by which they are condemned. And this I look upon as the principal means of that general defection from evangelical holiness which prevails in most nations The gospel comes upon a nation as on a wilderness or forest that is full of such wood, thorns and briers, as the soil of itself is peculiarly disposed to produce. These it cuts down to the ground, planting good and noble plants in their room, whereby the barren wilderness becomes for a season a fruitful field. But in process of time, if continual care and culture be not used about it, the earth pours out of its own accord the weeds and briers which are natural unto it. These springing up abundantly choke the other plants and useful herbs, whereby the fruitful field is turned again into a wilderness There needs no more unto this apostasy but that national vices, for a time suppressed by the power of the word, should overgrow the generality of any people, whereby the graces of the gospel will be certainly stifled and choked.

VI. Mistakes about the beauty and glory of Christian religion have been no small cause of apostasy from its power and holiness. That it should have a glory, somewhat that might render it honourable in the eyes and esteem of men, was always thought unquestionable; and it is certainly true, provided that we suppose those with whom we have to do have eyes to see that glory, and minds enlightened to make a true judgment of it. In compliance here-withal was religion outwardly figured and represented among the Jews. And as the apostle declares that the worship of God in the administration of the gospel is truly glorious, and eminently so above what was to be found in the administration of the law; so Christian religion is in itself truly honourable, and contains in it every thing that is so, in the judgment of God and the rectified reason of mankind. But about the true notion and apprehension of that glory and honour which is proper unto religion and suited unto its nature, men have fallen into many woful mistakes; for whereas it principally consists in the glorious internal operations of the Holy Spirit, renewing our nature, transforming us into the image and likeness of God, with the fruits of his grace in righteousness and, true holiness, in a meek, humble, gracious conversation, and the performance of all duties according to the rule, few are able to discern beauty or glory or honour in these things. But yet where there is not an eye to discern them, the gospel must of necessity be despised and abandoned, and somewhat else substituted in the room thereof. This therefore also proved a great furtherance of the general apostasy, and continues an efficacious means of keeping multitudes under the power of it unto this day; for, --

1. Through the loss of spiritual light and neglect of the grace of God, things were come to that pass in the world, that those who had the conduct of religion saw no real glory themselves in the things wherein all the glory of the religion taught and appointed in the gospel doth consist. And they are but few that do so at this day. Therefore the profession that is made of them by any is generally looked on as hypocrisy, mixed with a certain kind of superstition, and is accordingly despised; yea, nothing is more contemptible in the world than the possession and profession of those ways which are truly, if not only, noble. Their view, therefore, being lost in the eyes of the leaders of the church, it could not be expected that they should be instrumental to open the eyes of others, or careful to instruct them how to look after what themselves did not discern.

2. They were fully satisfied that there was in these things no evidence of glory unto the eyes of the generality of mankind, whereunto they thought it wisdom to accommodate themselves and the notions of religion. Men naturally can see no more beauty in the spiritual power of Christianity than the Jews could see in the person of Christ when they rejected him, because unto them he made no

appearance thereof, Isa. liii. 2. That religion should be set off and represented as truly glorious and honourable in the eyes of men, they thought it incumbent on them to take care; but leaving herein the judgment of God, of Jesus Christ, and the Holy Spirit, as declared in the Scripture, they accommodated themselves unto the carnal apprehensions of them with whom they had to do, which were also suited unto their own. Wherefore, that this glory of religion consisted in a ministry in the church humble, holy, laborious, eminent in the graces and gifts of the Spirit, looking for no honour or respect but for their work's sake; in a worship plain, unadorned, spiritual, whose life and excellency consist in the invisible, effectual administrations of the Spirit of God; in meekness, self-denial, mortification of sin, and the fruits of righteousness, proceeding from the grace of the Holy Ghost, -- they neither did apprehend themselves nor could imagine that others would be of that mind: for the world generally supposeth the direct contrary unto all these to be honourable and glorious. Things which have a pretence of height and gallantry of spirit, a religions worship set off with such ornaments and modes as to affect the outward senses, with somewhat that may give satisfaction unto lust and conscience at the same time, are the things which unto the most are alone desirable. Wherefore, all pretence unto the power of religion dwindling away into an empty, jejune form and appearance of it in monkery, the supposed glory of Christianity in the world issued in these three things:--

(1.) The secular pomp and grandeur of the rulers of the church, This was designed to beget a reverence unto their persons and offices, without which religion itself would be despised. And it is easily conceivable how by this means their minds were drawn off from a due consideration of all those things which are truly honourable in them, and the neglect whereof will be the loss of the power of religion in the most at any time; for when they had secured unto themselves that honour, respect, and reverence which they esteemed needful unto the glory of religion, and found very suitable unto their own desires and ends, to what purpose should they trouble or perplex themselves with those hard duties of exemplary mortification, self-denial, and painful labour in the work of the ministry, when the whole of what they aimed at or needed was prepared for them? And how corrupt a spring of apostasy brake forth hereon hath been before declared.

(2.) A pompous, ceremonious worship, which began to be introduced by a pretence of outward solemnity, and ended in plain superstition and idolatry. And hereby were the minds of men diverted and taken off from inquiring after that spiritual exercise of the graces and gifts of the Spirit, wherein alone the beauty of evangelical holiness doth consist.

(3.) In works of magnificence and bounty, wherewith the clergy were enriched, and the consciences of men pacified in a course of sin or an unholy lithe. When the world was once persuaded that in these things consisted the glory and beauty of religion, and found them all readily compliant with their lusts and darkness, that real holiness and obedience which is required in the gospel was every day more and more neglected and despised. Besides, it is not expressible what wicked, scandalous practices, in pride, ambition, divisions, and contentions among the leaders of the church, did spring from and ensue on these principles. Henceforward no small part of ecclesiastical story is taken up with fierce contentions and quarrels about the pre-eminence, dignities, privileges, and jurisdiction of the prelates. Those who were wise and sober among the heathen observed this evil among Christians, reporting it as that whereby their religion was debased and corrupted. Such is the account given by Ammianus Marcellinus of that bloody and scandalous conflict between Damasus and Ursicinus whether of them should be bishop of Rome, lib. xxvii. cap. 6.

VII. During these seasons, Satan (as he will never be) was not wanting unto his own occasions and advantages; and they are altogether ignorant of his devices who discern him not at work even at present unto the same end and purpose. Nor is it possible that in any age, time, or place, the glory of the gospel should be abated, and the principal endeavour therein not belong to him. He is the head and leader of every apostasy from God. Therein he began his work in this world, and in the promotion of it he will finish it. And as he engaged all his power and art against the Head of the church, so by his total defeat in that attempt, wherein he made the clearest discovery of his pride and malice against God that it is possible for him to do, he is not discouraged from pursuing the same design against the whole church itself. And the way now insisted on hath been the chiefest path that he hath beaten in his course; for from the very entrance of Christianity, he Began to immix himself with all those lusts of men whereby a defection from its power and purity might be set on foot and effected. And he engaged against it in both his capacities, as a lion and as a serpent. As a lion he stirred up, acted, and animated all those bloody persecutions whereby the Jews and Pagan world attempted for three hundred years to exterminate the Christian profession. But herein his success was answerable to that of his attempt against the Head of the church, and ever will be so, by virtue of the victory the Lord Christ had over him in the same kind of conflict. The force of the devil and the world having been once fully broken and subdued by Christ, it shall never prevail in the issue against his followers. Satan, in a confederacy with the world, may as a lion, through rage and blood, make a great bluster, and scatter the churches of Christ for a season, but prevail unto the ruin of the church in this way he never did, nor shall. And if at any time, by national devastations, he do so far succeed as to expel the gospel from any place or country for a season, it shall be evident unto all that it shall turn greatly unto its advantage in general and in other places. Let not, then, any fear his bloody fury as to the interest of Christ and the gospel in the world. As sure as he was conquered and triumphed over in the cross of Christ, he shall finally be so in all such attempts. Happy and blessed are they, and shall they be, by whose blood and temporal ruin his power at any time is or shall be broken. So I say it fell out in his first attempt in this way against Christian religion; for through the efficacy of the grace of Christ, and by virtue of the victory obtained against him in his own person, he was overcome by the blood and constancy of innumerable holy souls, until he was cast out of the havens of the world, and an end was put unto his rage. But, in the meantime, whilst this sworn enemy of the church made all this bluster as a lion, and raised all these storms of persecution, which the minds of all the professors of Christianity were intent upon, and generally much fortified against, he was secretly at work as a serpent also. Herein he secretly and gradually infected the minds of many with ambition, worldliness, superstition, and a neglect of the power and simplicity of the gospel That this is his work as a serpent our apostle declares, 2 Cor. xi. 2, 3. And herein sometimes "he transformed himself into an angel of light," as he speaks in that place, verses 14, 15; for he not only poisoned and inflamed the lusts of men, but drew them aside from the gospel by suggestions and pretences of more piety and devotion, or at least of other outward modes and means of their expression, than it did require. So did the "mystery of iniquity" work in the days of the apostles themselves, 2 Thess. ii. 7. He was at work secretly, by ways and means not easy to be discovered, to draw off the minds of men from evangelical truth and holiness, by sowing the seeds of that ambition and superstition which afterward spread themselves over the face of the whole visible church. So was he the spirit which animated the apostasy which by various and insensible degrees prevailed in the following ages. Those who acted in it and promoted it never knew any thing of the design, but added one thing unto another, as occasion was offered, which gave it increase; but in him the projection was designed, and regularly carried on from the beginning. Hence had it the name of "The mystery of iniquity," as being insinuated and promoted by such unsearchable methods or depths of Satan, that those, for the most part, who were subservient to his design, knew not what they did, though sufficiently warned in the Scripture of what he would do and what should come to pass. Wherefore, being disappointed, as was said, in his endeavours by outward force and persecution (as he will ever be), leaving the name, power, and advantage of the church unto them that professed Christianity, he made use of all the darkness, ignorance, errors, ambition, and lusts of men, gradually to draw them from the truth and holiness of the gospel. And he ceased not until he had brought Christian religion to be looked on as made up principally, if not only, of those things which by his craft and the lusts of men were introduced into it. So did he pursue his work, almost undiscovered, until the generality of those who professed Christian religion were given up to the power of sensual lusts on the one hand, or brought under the power of superstition on the other. All this he attempted, and in a great measure effected, of his own accord. But after that men had voluntarily given up themselves unto his delusions, rejecting the truth and holiness of the gospel, as unto their love to them and delight in them, God in his righteous judgment gave them up unto his power, to be infatuated by him, and hardened to their eternal ruin. So the apostle expresseth it, 2 Thess. ii. 11, 12, "For this cause God shall send them strong delusion, that they should believe a lie; that they all might be damned who believed not the truth, but had pleasure in unrighteousness." Thus was the apostasy completed under the Papacy; and by the same artifices is Satan still at work among us unto the same ends and purposes.

VIII. Moreover, among the occasions of the present decay of holiness and the power of Christianity in the world, we may reckon the scandal that hath been given by or is justly taken at those who have professed the most strict obedience unto the rules of the gospel. There is nothing difficult herein but only to choose out the most pregnant instances in the multitudes which offer themselves to evidence this occasion. Nor do I intend such offences as some men will enviously seek after, and sometimes causelessly create, but such as are really given, and offer themselves unto the consideration of all sorts of men. Of these I shall mention two only, which are the most obvious and extensive; and, --

1. Offence hath been taken at the divisions that have been among them, and continue so to be, with the management of them in an evil, contentious frame of spirit. The Lord Christ hath declared and appointed that the mutual love of his disciples should be the great testimony of the truth of his doctrine and the sincerity of their obedience. He hath also commanded them to be one in heart, mind, and affection, praying for them also that so they might be. His commands and directions unto this purpose are known unto all who know the gospel, and so need not here to be repeated or insisted on. The blessed effects and fruits of them were eminent for a season among the professors of the gospel, and their mutual love was a convincing argument of the truth, efficacy, and holiness, of the doctrine which they did profess: for where there is oneness and love thereon, there is peace, order, usefulness to mankind, and every good work; whereas the want of them is attended

with strife, envy, confusion, disorder, and every evil work whatever. Some divisions, indeed, happened among the primitive Christians, but were quickly healed by the spirit of apostolical authority, and that love which was yet prevalent among them. But afterward all things grew worse, and the first visible degeneracy of Christianity consisted in the strifes, divisions, and contentions of its professors, especially of their leaders. And these in no long process of time proceeded unto that excess, and were acted with such an evil spirit of pride, ambition, envy, and malice, that the very heathens made themselves sport with their contentions, and observed that there were no sort of men in the world so ready for them and implacable in them as the Christians of those days were. But when once one or other party of them got into power, and, snatching that sword of force and violence out of the hands of Pagans which had been imbrued in the blood of the holy martyrs, began, in the pursuit of their divisions, to persecute one another (which way carnal men having tasted the sweetness and advantage of, as that which, gratifying their envy, malice, and ambition, doth also, as they suppose, secure all their earthly concerns, they would not forego, nor have so done until it is become the top-stone of many men's religion), it was merely from the unspeakable care and mercy of God that they made not the gospel an abhorrence unto all flesh; for who, not yet endued with that light and grace which might secure him from the power of such temptation, could look on the fierce, devouring, bloody contentions of its professors, and that solely on its own account, and not suppose that itself proceeded from a spirit of malice, strife, and disorder? But the truth and faithfulness of God preserved it against all the oppositions of its adversaries, and in the midst of the treacheries of its avowed friends. Thus was it in the primitive times; which as it was the first considerable stop unto the progress of the gospel, so it was one principal cause of corrupting the conversation of many, filling them with a frame of spirit in all things directly opposite unto that of the gospel. The differences, with their untoward management, which fell out among the first reformers, was the chief means that hindered their work from a universal success.

Is it much otherwise among the strictest sorts of professors at this day? Do not some seem to aim at nothing more than to multiply and increase divisions, and to delight in nothing more than to live and dispute in the flames of them? There is not the least different apprehension of men's minds about any thing in religion, but such persons suppose it a sufficient ground to quarrel and contend about it forever. By such ways and means scandals are given unto the world in its proneness unto apostasy, and seeking occasions for it or countenance unto it, which is its present posture; for these things are not done in a corner. Men who know nothing of the inward power and virtue of that religion which is in such professors, as it is hoped, seeing and observing those other distempers among them, are really alienated from all the good they do profess; and not only so, but do from thence justify and approve themselves in their immorality and profaneness, as those which allow them a better condition than such wranglers can afford them. By this means hath religion lost much of that awful authority in the world whereby it ofttimes put a restraint on the minds and consciences of men who were never acted by its power. What are the rules whereby we ought to walk under the continuance of these differences, and what are the best means to put an issue unto them, I have inquired in a treatise unto that purpose. [12] But it must be acknowledged that for the most part attempts for the rebuking of these distempers, the reconciliation of dissenters, and the uniting of professors, have been managed from such principles and in such a frame of spirit as have heightened and increased rather than allayed or diminished them.

2. Great offence is given to the world by the uselessness of professors, and in that they are not, what they ought to be, the common good and blessing of mankind. There is a selfish spirit on many of them, whence, contenting themselves with abstinence from known sins, and the performance of the religious duties of divine worship, they are of little or no use unto others. Some will be kind, benign, helpful, good, in some measure unto other men, but yet will and do give undue bounds and limits unto their actings in this kind. Their own household, and the household of faith, according unto that measure which from opinion or prejudice they take of it, they will alone regard. As for love, condescension, benignity, kindness, readiness to help, assist, and relieve all mankind, yea, the worst of men, as they have opportunity, they understand them not, yea, have many pretences that they are not required of them. But if we are Christians, it is required of us to "abound in love toward all men," 1 Thess. iii. 12; and our doing good unto all, being useful unto all, exercising loving-kindness in the earth towards all, is the principal way whereby we may express our sincere obedience unto the gospel. One professor that is kind, benign, condescending, charitable, useful, ready to become all things unto all men for their good, brings more glory to the gospel than a hundred who are looked on as those who live too much unto themselves. When the old saying was, "Bonus vir Caius Sejus, sed malus quia Christianus," -- "Such an one is a good man, evil only in this, that he is a Christian," religion did by such convictions insensibly get ground amongst men. If the world cannot see that it hath any advantage by professors, but hath trouble on the other hand by the hatred which it cannot but have of their profession, it is no wonder if it desire to have no more to do with them. Did men find that so soon as any gave themselves unto the strictest ways of profession, therewithal they became benign, kind, merciful, charitable, useful, and helpful unto all men, it could not but give an honourable reputation in their minds unto that religion which they do profess; but an observation of a contrary frame and temper in such persons, and of how little use they are in the world, must needs produce contrary effects. By reason of such miscarriages as these, and others of an alike nature, whereby some professors are so far from adorning the gospel of our Lord and Saviour Jesus Christ as that they cast, what lies in them, a blemish and reproach upon it, others are every day hardened in their alienation from all its concerns.

These few instances have I given of the means and ways whereby a general apostasy from the holy precepts of the gospel, as the rule of our obedience, hath been begun and carried on. Many others of an alike nature might be added unto them; but it is to no purpose to insist long on the nature of a disease when we find it to despise all possible remedies. Sovereign grace yet remaineth, whereunto this state of things is referred.

And this apostasy, in its measure and proportion, partakes of the guilt of that described in the text, which we made the foundation of this discourse: for therein also is Christ "crucified afresh, and put to an open shame;" for, --

1. All persons who profess the Christian religion, and yet are thus fallen off or alienated from its holiness, do really renounce and forego the commands of Christ, and those as enlivened by his promises, for the pleasure and wages of sin. And herein do they openly declare and avow, as the judgment and resolution of their minds, that there is not that excellency in his precepts, nor that goodness, beauty, desirableness, or satisfaction in obedience unto them, or not that assurance in his promises, or worth in the things promised, as that they ought to be preferred before

the course of the world and the pleasures of sin. Hence some commands of the gospel (and those of no small importance unto the furtherance of holy obedience) are neglected and cast from among the generality of Christians. Such are the commands for mutual love, whereof there is scarce any shadow left in the world: for that pretence of it which some seem to rest in and plead for as satisfactory, in the peaceable, and, as they say, loving converse of persons in their civil and ecclesiastical distributions, is no other than what is found among Mohammedans and Pagans on the like occasion; which, as it is good and commendable so far as it proceeds from and is suited unto the light of nature, so it no way answers, either in the kind of it or in its acts and fruits, unto that evangelical love which the Lord Christ requires among his disciples. That watchfulness over one another with love, care, and tenderness, those mutual admonitions, exhortations, and consolations, which the gospel so frequently and diligently prescribes unto us, are not only neglected, but so far despised that the very naming of such duties is made a matter of scorn, as a pretence of hypocritical preciseness; and no better entertainment have many other of the commands of Christ among the generality of them that are called Christians. So do many, on all accounts, openly profess in their walkings and conversation that they see no cogent reason why they should comply with him in his commands; and it is not easily to be conceived how they can cast a greater dishonour or contempt upon him.

2. By continuing in the outward profession of Christianity, they do most falsely represent Christ and the gospel unto the world, and thereby, what lies in them, "put him to an open shame;" for, pretending to yield obedience unto him, and to place their hope for life and blessedness in him by the gospel, they profess withal that he is a person that will approve of such ways as they walk in, and his gospel a doctrine that gives countenance unto all manner of licentiousness in sin. Who would judge otherwise who had no knowledge of him or it but by the representation that is made of them in the profligate conversation of such apostates? But this argument I have elsewhere insisted on.

Footnotes:

12. See vol. xv., in his treatise on Evangelical Love, Peace, and Unity. -- Ed.

Chapter XI – Apostasy from evangelical worship

Thirdly, That which was proposed to be considered in the last place is that apostasy which is in the world from the purity of the worship of the gospel as appointed by Jesus Christ; and herein principally did consist that great defection foretold by our apostle, 2 Thess. ii. 3-12, which is also prophesied of in the Revelation, and did accordingly come to pass. But because I have insisted on this subject on many other occasions, and some things relating thereunto are under difference and debate among such as are capable of the warning given concerning the apostasy that is in the world, I shall wholly waive the consideration of particulars about which any such differences may be, and only mention such things as the generality of Christians, at least of Protestants, cannot but acknowledge.

I shall take it for granted at present, that our Lord Jesus Christ did institute and appoint a solemn worship of God, to be continued inviolably and unalterably unto the end of the world. And the principal end of his appointing, continuing, or preserving any church on the earth, is the celebration of this worship; for herein alone consisteth that public revenue of glory which God requires from believers in this world. All other duties of the gospel may be performed by men in their single capacities, if there were no such thing as a church on the earth. And those churches do exceedingly mistake their duty, and every end of their being, which make it not their principal business to take care of the due celebration of that worship which the Lord Christ hath appointed. He was faithful in the whole house of God, as was Moses, Heb. iii. 5, 6; and if the life, being, happiness, and welfare, of the church of Israel, consisted in and depended on their remembrance of the law of Moses, which "God commanded unto him in Horeb, with the statutes and judgments," Mal. iv. 4, because he was faithful in the house of God as a servant, certainly the being and well-being of the Christian church consist in and depend upon that observing and doing of all whatsoever He hath commanded in the worship of God (as Matt. xxviii. 20) who is faithful as a son in and over the whole house of God.

Besides, it is acknowledged by all, -- and we shall, God willing, show the manner of it in our exposition of the seventh chapter of the Epistle to the Hebrews, -- that the Lord Christ, in and by the gospel, hath altered and abolished all that solemn worship, all those ordinances and institutions, which God himself had set up under the old testament, to continue unto the time of reformation; and hereby he rendered it absolutely unlawful for any one to serve God according unto those institutions. Hereunto God signally set his public seal of approbation in the sight of the world; for no sooner had the Lord Christ, by the promulgation of the gospel, taken away all their authority and obligatory power, so as that his disciples ought not to make use of them any longer, but God immediately, by severe and unparalleled judgments, destroyed the seat and place of them, so that those who would yet never could regularly make use of them unto this day. And shall we think that the Lord Jesus Christ thus took away and abolished the old solemn worship of the church, and substituted none in the room of it? or that he took away that which was erected by the wisdom of God, though but for a season, and left the church, as to its main duty and principal end in this world, unto the inventions and imaginations of men? One of these must be supposed, if it be denied that he hath established a solemn worship of God, to continue unalterably unto the end of the world; and both of them are highly blasphemous. Again, let any, in faith and obedience unto him, practice and attend unto all those parts of divine worship which he hath appointed, and I am persuaded no man will have the confidence to say that there is this or that wanting to render it a solemn and acceptable service, however they may contend for the conveniency of some circumstantial additionals. Wherefore I take it for granted at present, that the Lord Jesus Christ hath appointed such a solemn worship under the gospel, which all his disciples are obliged constantly and invariably to observe, as he declares, Matt. xxviii. 20. And with respect hereunto men may fall away and apostatize from the gospel, no less sinfully and fatally than they may fall from the mystery of its doctrine or the holiness of its precepts. And there are two ways whereby this may be done:-- 1. By neglecting and refusing to observe and do what he hath appointed; 2. By adding appointments of our own thereunto, inconsistent with and destructive of that which he hath ordained:--

I. In the first way we have some among ourselves who are fallen off from the worship of the gospel It is true, they will do some things which have an appearance of being what Christ hath commanded; such are their first-day's meeting, and their prayers, with speaking in them; -- but they neither observe the Lord's day, nor pray or speak in obedience unto any institution of his. Conveniency and the light within are all the reason and guide which they plead for them. And for the sacraments, or baptism and the supper of the Lord, which are so great a part of the mystical worship of the church, on I know not what fond pretences, they utterly reject them. In like manner they deal with a stated ministry as of Christ's appointment, although they have found out means to set up one of their own.

And because herein also Christ is "put to an open shame," we shall briefly inquire into the grounds and reasons of this defection from the obedience due to his commands:--

1. Now the principal reason, and which compriseth all others, why some men have forsaken the gospel, as unto the administration of its ordinances, is because they are no way suited unto, nor indeed consistent with, that faith and obedience which they have betaken themselves unto; for the ordinances of the gospel are representations of the things which we believe, and means of the conveyance of their efficacy unto us. Unto the confirmation of that faith and our edification therein are they suited, and to nothing else. Now, these persons having fallen, as we have showed, from the faith of the gospel in the mystery of it and the spiritual obedience which it doth require, of what use can the ordinances of worship be unto them? For instance, the ordinance of the Lord's supper is instituted in the remembrance of the death of Christ, of his suffering in our stead, of the sacrifice he made of himself therein, of the atonement or reconciliation with God that he wrought, and of the sealing of the new covenant with his blood. To what end should, any man solemnly worship God in and by this ordinance who upon the matter believeth none of these things, at least doth not believe them as proposed in the gospel, namely, as the principal causes and springs of life, righteousness, and salvation? Those who believe in God through these things, who find the effects of them upon their souls in righteousness and peace, cannot but delight to be found in

the exercise of faith through this ordinance, as they know it to be their duty so to do. But it is apparent that neither this nor the other ordinance of baptism doth contribute any thing to the furtherance, increase, or establishment, of that light within men which upon the matter they resolve their faith and obedience into; yea, they are, in their true and proper notion, as both directing unto the sanctifying and justifying blood of Christ, diametrically opposite thereunto and unto what is ascribed unto it. It is, therefore, so far from being strange that these men should forsake these ordinances of gospel worship, that the admission of them in their true and proper use and signification is destructive of the whole scheme of religion which they have formed unto themselves. Where the faith of the gospel is forsaken, the ordinances of worship must be so too, and so all instituted divine service be neglected, or other things found out that may suit unto the imaginations whereunto men are turned aside.

2. Another reason hereof hath been want of spiritual light to see through the veils of outward institutions, and of the wisdom of faith, to obtain communion with God in Christ by them. Our worship under the gospel is either absolutely spiritual, or that which comes immediately unto what is so. But in these institutions there is somewhat that is outward and sensible, and it is to be feared that many do rest in these outward things, and proceed no farther in the worship of God by them than the actions and words that are used will carry them; but they are, as appointed by Christ, "animæ vehicula," means of leading and conveying the soul unto an intimate communion with God. That they may be so unto us, three things are required:--

(1.) That we submit our souls and consciences unto the authority of Christ in these institutions. Unless this be the foundation which we build upon, the whole service will be lost unto us.

(2.) That we rest on the veracity of Christ for the working of the grace and accomplishment of the mercy represented in them and sacramentally exhibited by them; for they will not profit them by whom the promises of Christ, virtually contained in them and accompanying of them, are not mixed with faith, and we cannot believe the promise unless we submit to the authority of Christ in the appointment of that whereunto it is annexed.

(3.) That we understand in some measure the mystical relation that is between the outward symbols of the ordinance and the Lord Christ himself, with his grace represented thereby, wherein the nature, use, and end of the institutions are contained.

And all these are necessary to keep up any delight in them, or a conscientious use of them. Where, therefore, all these are wanting, -- as apparently they are in those concerning whom we treat, being none of them either understood, owned, or acknowledged by them, -- whereas they have neither spiritual light into the internal nature of these things, nor spiritual gifts for their administration unto edification, following the conduct of their own principles, they could do no otherwise but reject them, and therein fell off from the worship of the gospel, and thereby do reflect dishonour upon the Son of God, the author and Lord of all these institutions.

II. There is another way whereby men may, and many men do fall away, and have for many ages fallen away, from the gospel with respect unto its worship, and that is, by rejecting its simplicity and pure institutions, substituting a superstitious, yea, idolatrous worship of their own in the room thereof, 2 Cor. xi. 3: for whereas there are various degrees of declension from the purity of gospel worship, according as men forsake any part of it, or make any additions of their own unto it, yet at present I shall mention them only by whom it is wholly perverted, -- that is, those of the church of Rome; for as they have added unto it rites and institutions of their own in great number, partly superstitious and partly idolatrous, so there is no one ordinance or institution of Christ which they have not corrupted, the most of them so far as utterly to destroy their nature and use. Whereas, therefore, the Lord Jesus Christ doth in the ordinances of gospel worship and the due celebration of them represent his own religion and authority unto the church, to remove them out of the way, and to introduce another fabric of them of another constitution, is to represent Antichrist unto the church, and not Christ, and thereby to "put Christ to an open shame." The ways and means whereby this apostasy was effected, by the craft of Satan and the carnal interest of men, in a long tract of time, I shall not here declare; it shall suffice at present to observe, that as men grew carnal, having lost the spirit, life, and power of the gospel, and so far as they did so, they found it necessary to introduce a carnal, visible, pompous worship, suited unto that inward principle and light whereby they were acted. And as the people in the wilderness, being carnal in their hearts, and accustomed unto carnal ways of worship, upon the absence of Moses in the mount, cried out unto Aaron, "Make us gods, which shall go before us" (that is, gods visibly present), "for as for this Moses, we wot not what is become of him," whereupon they made a calf; so these men, finding the whole fabric of Mosaical institutions, consisting in outward images and representations of things, taken away, and themselves left as it were without any present gods to guide them, -- that is, such visible representations of the presence of God as their carnal hearts and minds might delight in, -- they provided all those calves whereof their present worship doth consist. And because there were many in those days when this design was first set on foot who were truly spiritual and holy, worshipping God in spirit and in truth, this idolatrous worship could not be introduced and preserved but by insensible degrees and in a long tract of time, throughout the whole whereof the "mystery of iniquity" wrought effectually unto the same certain end. Those, in the meantime, who worshipped God in truth, were either imposed on by a show of humility and devotion in the degrees of apostasy which were added in their days, or else complained of what they could not remedy.

And if these brief considerations of the nature of the present apostasy that is in the world from the power of Christian religion, in all the principal concerns of it, with the causes and occasions thereof, do excite or provoke any one who hath more leisure and ability for this work unto a more diligent and useful inquiry into them, it will be an ample reward unto my endeavours.

Chapter XII — Inferences from the foregoing discourses — The present danger of all sorts of persons, in the prevalency of apostasy from the truth and decays in the practice of evangelical holiness

The last part of this discourse is designed for cautions unto those who yet stand, or think they stand, with respect unto that general defection from the gospel whose causes and occasions we have thus far inquired into. And thereunto some directions may be added, to be used as preventives of its contagion.

This method are we guided unto by the apostle, who, having declared the apostasy and ruin which ensued thereon of the generality of the church of the Jews, improves the consideration of it unto the caution of others, under a present profession of the truth. "Thou wilt say then," saith he to the Gentile believers, "The branches were broken off, that I might be grafted in. Well; because of unbelief they were broken off, and thou standest by faith. Be not high-minded, but fear: for if God spared not the natural branches, take heed lest he also spare not thee. Behold therefore the goodness and severity of God: on them which fell, severity; but toward thee, goodness, if thou continue in his goodness: otherwise thou also shalt be cut off," Rom. xi. 19-22. And in another place, on an alike occasion, he speaks unto the same purpose: "Let him that thinketh he standeth, take heed lest he fall," 1 Cor. x. 12.

Most men are apt to suppose that the continuance of the true religion in any place depends solely on the prudence and industry of those unto whom the conduct of its outward concerns are committed. The interest of some and the duty of others, in the management of human laws and constitutions, are generally looked on as a sufficient and the only means of its preservation. And those of this persuasion think they have personally no concernment herein, but only to herd themselves in the multitude, and to take their fate, whatever it be. Such as these will despise our cautions, as those from which the reasons of their confidences and fears are most remote. But whereas the profession of religion in the community of Christians will not be preserved but by the power of it in individuals, the only root whereon it will long thrive or grow, we shall not at all concern ourselves in them by whom the directions of their duty are thought needless or useless; for after the utmost exercise of human policy, it is the wisdom that is from above which must be our stability. And if the power of truth and holiness be not preserved in the hearts and lives of particular persons, the profession of them in churches, or the pretence of them in nations (which are all that will remain), are neither acceptable unto God nor useful unto the souls of men.

Some think themselves, as for their own part, little concerned in these things. That there is such a defection from the gospel as hath been complained of they cannot deny, and they will also grant that it is desperately pernicious unto them that are overtaken thereby; therefore they suppose it not amiss that men should be warned of its danger and directed to avoid it. But this they think necessary for others, not for themselves; for as for their part, they have not the like occasions, nor are exposed unto the same temptations, with them who formerly apostatized from the gospel or are in danger now so to do. Besides, they know well enough what are their own resolutions, and that though all men should forsake either the doctrine taught in or the obedience required by the gospel, yet should their constancy be immovable! But I do not think these apprehensions sufficient to render our warnings needless. Occasions and temptations are not in our power; our greatest present freedom from them will not secure us from the assaults of the next hour. Peter foresaw not his dangers and fears when he so confidently engaged unto constancy in the profession of his Master, which yet within a few hours came upon him. And such is the subtlety of our spiritual adversaries, that sometimes we are under the power of temptation when we think ourselves most remote from it. It is beyond the compass of human reason to take at once a prospect of all the causes and means thereof, with the ways of its efficacy and prevalency. And if at any time we judge ourselves free from an hour of temptation, which comes upon the world to try them that dwell therein, which most are exercised with and many are prevailed on by, so as to be secure and regardless of the means of our preservation, of all men we are in the most danger to be ruined by it. Neither will the best of our resolutions be of any avail without the utmost of our endeavours. The great apostle thought and resolved with respect unto the person of Christ that he would neither deny him nor forsake him, and it this confidence did not betray him into his fall, yet to be sure it did not preserve him from it; and it was upon his own experience that he gave afterward that holy advice, that we should "give a reason of the hope that is in us with meekness and fear," 1 Pet. iii. 14, 15, and "pass the time of our sojourning here in fear," chap. i. 17. The highest present confidences have ever proved the most deceiving presages of future stability. Wherefore, the utmost I design in the ensuing cautions is but to excite men unto a due apprehension of their danger, that they be not surprised into that pernicious security which is the mire wherein this rush doth grow.

1. The consideration of the extent and almost universality of this apostasy may be of use unto this purpose. Ignorance, profaneness, worldly-mindedness, with sensuality of life, have obtained the most eminent catholicism in Christendom. The complaint of the prophet is not unsuited to the present state thereof: Isa. i. 4-6, "Ah sinful nation, a people laden with iniquity, a seed of evildoers, children that are corrupters: they have forsaken the Lord, they have provoked the Holy One of Israel unto anger, they are gone away backward. The whole head is sick, and the whole heart faint. From the sole of the foot even unto the head there is no soundness in it; but wounds, and bruises, and putrifying sores." Do we hear but of this or that individual person who hath apostatized from a profession of holiness, into a sensual, wicked, worldly course of life, or is turned from the faith into pernicious errors? there is no man that is wise and careful of his eternal concerns, but he will take it as a warning to examine, try, and be careful of himself; and this counsel is laid before us by the apostle, 2 Tim. ii. 17-19. What, then, is required of us when we see nations, churches, multitudes of people, by one means or other, degenerated from that power of godliness which once they professed? If we hear that one or

other in a city is visited with the plague, we are not altogether insensible of our own concern and danger, because we know how usual it is for the infection of that disease to spread and diffuse itself; but if the whole city be infected, and thousands fall under it every week, there is none so sottish as to need much warning of their danger. And shall we be less concerned for our immortal souls and their eternal condition than we are for these frail carcasses and their continuance for a few days in the world, which, if they escape one distemper, may yet in a few moments fall under the power of another? This spiritual "pestilence," that hath formerly "walked in darkness," is now a "destruction wasting at noonday." Nations are depopulated by it and cities left desolate, as unto their interest in God and the gospel; and is it not high time to "look diligently" lest the infection reach unto us also, lest we also should "fail" and come short "of the grace of God," and be "hardened through the deceitfulness of sin?" As, then, our bodies are of the same natural frame and constitution, as they have in them the same burnouts, the same kind of animal spirits, as are in those who are infected with the plague, whereby we are obnoxious unto the same infection with them; so there are in our souls and minds the same principles of sin and love of the world as are infected, drawn away, enticed, excited, and enraged, by outward occasions and temptations, until they have issued in apostasy. Do we think that we shall be always easily preserved, and that whilst we are careless and secure, from that torrent which hath carried away such multitudes before it? Are we in ourselves better than they, or any of them? Have we a patent for our preservation, whilst we neglect any ways, means, or diligence that the rule requireth thereunto? Doth not God show unto us, not one, but many churches and nations, saying, "Go unto those Shilohs where I some time placed my name, and see what is become of them, and what I have done unto them? Will ye go after them? have yea mind to be made like unto them? Think not to say within yourselves, We have Abraham to our father; we have those outward privileges and advantages which they had not:' for they also enjoyed the same until they had forfeited them by their apostasy." Certainly the general prevalency of this evil proclaims such a danger as no wise man, no man that takes care of his own salvation, ought or indeed can neglect. Wherefore, as it is always with Christians, if ever it be, a time to watch, to stand on our guard, to take unto ourselves the whole armour of God, to be jealous of ourselves, to be constant and diligent in the use of all means, both private and public, for our preservation, it is now a time so to be. And if professors will not be awakened; if they will not stir up themselves with the gifts and graces which they have received; if they will please themselves that all is well with them, and is likely so to be; if they will yet immix themselves with boldness and confidence in the ways of the world; -- oh that my head were a fountain of tears! oh that my soul could mourn in secret for them! seeing assuredly they will not be able to stand in that day of temptation which is come upon the face of the earth, to try them that dwell therein. The outward court is long since given to be trodden down by the Gentiles, and how soon the enemies may roar in the very sanctuaries, and set up their banners for tokens, we know not; for, --

2. The present state of this defection hath a dangerous aspect. Physicians say, "Nemo moritur in declinatione morbi," -- "No man dies in the declension of his disease;" and when a public pestilential distemper is in its wane or decay, the danger is esteemed in a great measure over. But whilst a disease is yet growing and daily spreading its contagion, whilst the bills of mortality are every week increased, they are only hardened and profligate persons whom the commonness of the judgment renders regardless and senseless of it. And it is no otherwise with the

evil complained of at this day. There is almost nothing in the world that all sober men do generally agree in but this alone, that the whole world doth daily wax worse and worse. Who can give an instance of the decrease or abatement of any one sin in its love or practice? but that some are advanced to higher degrees of confidence in their perpetration than former days or ages afford us any precedent of, every one can declare. What instances have we of a spiritual recovery from any of our decays? What attempts unto that purpose are made by any, unless by such as are not of consideration, as have not advantages to enable them to effect any thing therein? The world is highly at variance about religion, managing its differences with great animosities and industry, how one way, party, and profession, may draw persons from other ways and professions. The sole business of the church of Rome is, by all manner of artifices to win over men unto their communion; that is, a subjection of their souls, consciences, and entire interests here and for eternity, to the authority of the pope. Others bestir themselves as well as they are able to keep what they have, and to rescue men from their seductions; -- and although they have the advantage of the truth on their side, and for the most part the advantage of abilities in the management of their cause, yet they visibly lose ground every day; and where one is recovered from the Roman interest, many are added unto it. And there can be no reason assigned hereof, but only that the apostasy is upon its increase, this being one way of it. Half that pains would have formerly turned a whole city from Popery which will not now succeed unto the preservation of one person. But, in the meantime, both in one profession and another, all sorts of men continue regardless of gospel holiness and obedience; and whilst they quarrel about the outward form, the inward power of godliness lies neglected. Do we see things anywhere in the world upon a recovery, or any thriving design for the retrieval of holiness? The name and thing are growing more and more into contempt. What instance can be given wherein this apostasy from the gospel doth or may exert itself, -- be it in atheism, be it in Popery, in hatred of and scoffing at the mysteries of evangelical truth, in worldliness, profaneness, vanity, and sensuality of life, in the coldness of love and barrenness among professors, -- that is not openly in its progress? And is this a time to be secure, careless, or negligent? Are we sure that this epidemical infection shall not enter our habitations? Do we not find how it hath, one way or other, attempted us already? Can we find no decay in zeal or love among ourselves, no adherence unto the world unsuited unto our present state and condition in it, no neglect of duties, no rareness in divine visitations, no want of life and delight in spiritual communion with Christ, no hurtful growth of carnal wisdom, with all its attendants? or have we not found ourselves, one way or other, sensibly attacked by these evils? It is to be feared that those who can make no observation of any thing of this nature among themselves are somewhat sick of the Laodicean distemper. And if we will not be awakened and stilted up to a more than ordinary diligence, care, and watchfulness, at such a season as this is, it is to be feared that ere long the generality of professors will come to be in the condition of the church of Sardis, -- to have a name to live, but indeed and in the sight of Christ to be dead.

3. As this apostasy is yet in its progress, so what will be its event, what it will rise unto, is altogether uncertain. God can put a stop unto it when he pleaseth, as he hath in his holy purposes fixed bounds unto it which it shall not pass; but in the meantime, being greatly provoked by the ingratitude of a wicked world, no man knows how long he may suspend those more powerful influences and more extraordinary effects of his word and Spirit which are needful unto the healing of

the nations, and without which they will not be cured. I hope for better things and pray for better things; but I have no certain ground of assurance that this apostasy shall not grow until, in one instance or other of it, it swallow up all visible profession. The whole world, so far as I know (I mean these parts of it), may become papal again, or be so corrupted in their principles and profane in their lives as that it is no great matter what their profession in religion be. Two things I do know or believe, -- namely, (1.) That "the foundation of God standeth sure, having this seal, The Lord knoweth them that are his." His elect, that truly fear him and diligently serve him, shall be preserved from perishing eternally, and from every thing that necessarily leads thereunto. (2.) That God hath appointed a time and season wherein he will not only put a stop unto this defection from the gospel, but an end also. He will one day execute the vengeance that he hath written and recorded on the throne, power, and kingdom of the antichristian apostasy, and in one day shall the plagues of Babylon come upon her; and he will again "turn to the people a pure language, that they may all call on the name of the Lord, to serve him with one consent," Zeph. iii. 9. He will again revive the beauty of his worship, and the glory of holiness in the earth; but, in the meantime, what things may come unto I know not. Those who pretend to a clearer inspection into future things may not do amiss strictly to examine the grounds whereon they proceed; for many have been made ashamed of their predictions, that within such or such a time the yoke of Babylon should be broken. This is all I say (and I say it only for myself), I know no assurance that can be given on infallible grounds that the apostasy which we are treating of shall not one way or other, in one instance or other, become again to be catholic, and prevail against all open, visible profession of the purity and power of gospel worship and holiness. Now, if this be not so unto others, yet unto myself it ought to be a warning how I may be thought worthy to escape, and to stand before the Son of man. And I am sure there is so much danger of it at least as to deserve the consideration of all who take care of their eternal salvation; for if things should come to such a pass, they are not many, they are but very few, who will be entirely preserved. The most will, one way or other, suffer loss; and it is not an easy thing to be found among the number of the few in such a season. Can we think that men careless in holy duties, cold in zeal, lukewarm in love, barren in good works, cleaving to the world and conformable unto it, low in their light, dubious in their state, useless in the world, fearful of trials, will be of this number? They are woefully deceived who are pleased with such apprehensions Other principles, other ways, courses, and practices, will be required in them who shall be hidden and safeguarded in that day.

4. The various ways whereby this defection prevails in the world should also warn us to stand upon our guard. Were it of one sort only, did it work only one way, or make use of one engine alone for its progress, the evil and danger of it might be the more easily either withstood or avoided; but as we have before referred it unto three general heads, -- with respect unto the doctrine, the holiness, and the worship of the gospel, -- so under each of them there are various ways and means whereby it is promoted. The infection from this plague is taken innumerable ways, Heb. xii. 1. Some take it in their shops or especial vocations; some in their societies, civil and ecclesiastical; some from the vanities and pleasures, some from the profits and advantages, of the world. Unbelief, the deceitfulness of sin, corrupt lusts and affections, spiritual sloth, cares about and love of riches, lie all in a readiness to give entertainment to and to embrace any opportunity, advantage, or means, whatever it be, whereby this apostasy may be admitted and take place in

them. See Heb. iii. 12, 13, xii. 15-17. Satan, in the meantime, labours by his insinuations to corrupt our minds, to poison our lusts, and to supply them with all inveigling or provoking objects, 2 Cor. xi. 3; 1 Pet. v. 8. In this state of things, look how many public temptations there are in the world, so many general ways and means are there whereby this apostasy doth prevail; and who can reckon up these temptations? Hence it is that men fall under this evil in such various ways, and unto such various degrees. Some do so by errors and "damnable heresies, denying the Lord that bought them;" some by superstition and idolatry; some by a contempt of gospel mysteries, and preferring another way of duty before evangelical obedience; some by ambition and pride of life; some by love of the world, and a neglect of duties spiritual and moral, under a deceiving profession; some by suffering carnal wisdom and some sensual lusts to devour their convictions and their efficacy; some by the uncertainty of their minds, brought to an indifferency in all things supernatural and divine; some by vain-glory and shame to be found among the scorned society of those who are truly religious; and multitudes are initiated into an irrecoverable profaneness by the vain pomps and spectacles of the age. And other ways there are, more than can be recounted, whereby this evil is propagated, and men fall under the power of it. By this means the very common air we breathe in is infected, 1 Cor. xv. 33. Snakes are in all grass whereon we tread, and scorpions under every stone. Snares are laid for us on every hand, and those (some of them) so gilded and set off, that multitudes of loose professors have taken them up and wear them as their ornaments. Those who escape one evil do every day fall into others. And how shall they escape who are encompassed with so many dangers, if they live in the neglect of any one duty or means of their preservation that God hath appointed and made useful thereunto?

5. Consider that there is an apostasy which is irrecoverable, and it will end in eternal ruin. This is that which we are taught in this context, according unto the exposition before given of it. No man in this world can be, by the rule of the gospel, in an unsalvable condition, -- that is, be concluded under an unavoidable destruction by any known rule of the revealed will of God, -- unless it be an apostate. There are also several sorts and degrees of apostasy that may have several causes and effects, and so various events. Great surprisals, strong temptations, negligence in watching against the deceitfulness of sin, may produce temporary abnegations of Christ and the gospel, woful declensions from the due observation of his commands, with wandering into foolish opinions, and yet persons may be recovered from them all, and brought by repentance unto salvation. Signal instances of this grace and patience in God might be given. And this is sufficient to render the despair of them causeless who are ever awakened in this world [in] time enough to endeavour a deliverance from any sin, or course of sinning, provoking and destructive; for when any man is by any means called to have any thing to do with God about his eternal concernments, God doth not allow him to be the absolutely sovereign judge of himself, which would usurp his prerogative and put the sinner in the place of God. He that despairs says, "I am in the stead of God to myself in this matter. There is neither goodness, nor grace, nor mercy in him, but what I can comprehend." And this evil God hath obviated in signal instances of the recovery of great apostates. But yet withal there is, as we have showed, an apostasy that is irrecoverable; and hereof God permits many examples in this world, to put an awe not only on bold and presumptuous, but also on careless and negligent sinners: for whereas our apostle doth expressly twice mind the Hebrews of this severity of God against apostates, in this place and in chap. x. 26, 27, in the one he

doth it with respect unto unprofitableness under the means of grace, and in the other with respect unto a negligence in attending unto the administration of gospel ordinances. Now, whereas any men may be overtaken with the beginning of decays and declensions from the holiness and worship of the gospel, all which have a tendency in their own nature unto this irrecoverable apostasy, ought they not to be continually jealous over themselves, lest they should pass the bounds God hath fixed unto his patience and grace? Ought we not to be careful about every sin or omission of duty that hath a tendency unto this doleful issue? For this very end, that we may be warned to take heed of the beginning of apostasy, doth the apostle in this place declare the end of it. The reader may, if he please (to help him herein), consult our discourses on chap. iv. 3. [13] It is not an easy task to stop a course in backsliding when once it is entered into. And I shall close this warning with naming two directions unto this purpose:-- (1.) Take heed of a course in any sin. Though every sin cloth not immediately tend unto final apostasy, yet a course in any sin continued doth so. (2.) Take heed of touching on such especial sins as have a peculiar tendency thereunto; and of what nature they are hath been declared.

6. Our last consideration of this kind shall be taken from the nature and guilt of this sin, wherever it be found, with the severity of God against it; and we may look upon it as it is total, such as that supposed by the apostle, Heb. vi. 4-6. The exposition we have given of the words will warrant us to conclude that total apostasy from the gospel once professed is a greater sin, and of a more heinous nature, than that of the Jews in crucifying the Lord Christ in the days of his flesh. This was sufficiently proved in the exposition of the words. It remains only that we do briefly inquire what doth concur unto such a total apostasy, whereby the truth of the exposition and the necessity of the warnings given will be made yet more evident. And though I shall speak with especial respect unto total apostasy from all profession, yet are the things that shall be spoken to be found, in their degree and measure, in all those who are guilty of that partial defection which we have described. There are, therefore, always found in this great offence the things ensuing:--

(1.) The loss of all taste of any goodness or excellency in the gospel, in the truth or state of its profession and worship. There is no man who hath ever made a profession of the gospel in earnest, beyond pretence and custom, but he hath found some kind of taste, relish, or sweetness, in the things of it. They "taste of the good word of God, and the powers of the world to come." Either in the things themselves, or in the manner of their dispensation, or of the duties of worship enjoined therein, they have found somewhat that hath given their minds and consciences some satisfaction. A man cannot go into a pleasant garden in the spring but he will smell some savour from the flowers, though he gather not one of them. A man cannot take meat savoury and well condited into his mouth but he will taste the relish of it, though he have no mind nor appetite to eat it; nor can any man walk in the sun but he will have some impressions from its heat. It is so, it can be no otherwise, with them who live under the preaching of the gospel and make profession of its doctrine. More or less it will insinuate itself into their minds with a taste of its excellency and goodness. This in the case considered is lost in the first place; and generally it comes to pass by a love of sin and the pleasures of the world. When this hath filled and possessed the soul, all its senses grow dead unto spiritual things, it hath no faculty or ability to taste any relish in them, yea, it loathes and abhors them as contrary to what it hath immersed itself in or given up itself unto. This usually is lost in the first place. Such persons find nothing any longer in Christ or the gospel for which they should either delight in them or desire them. And it seems to be thus with so many in the world who once gave hopes of better things, that the consideration of it is dreadful.

(2.) This is quickly followed with a loss of all prevailing evidence and conviction of the truth of the very doctrine of the gospel. This conviction all are supposed to have who profess it, and all really have it who profess it in any sincerity. Why else do they make profession of it, if they assent not unto its truth upon its conviction and evidence? for we speak not at all of them whose profession hath no other principle or foundation but custom or education. Others build their persuasion upon grounds and evidences prevalent to obtain their assent unto the truth against temptations and objections. This apostates lose in the next place. The truth remains what it was, and so do the arguments and evidences of it; but they have no longer any force upon or authority in their minds. It may be they do not presently renounce the gospel as a lie or "a cunningly-devised fable;" they may let the notions of it lie loose in their minds for a season neglected and unregarded, but give them no part of that entertainment which is due unto acknowledged truths of that nature, nor do they receive any impressions from its authority. And when men have lost these, they have lost their assent to the truth of the gospel upon its proper evidence, and are directly unbelievers; and this on every occasion will issue in a formal renunciation of the truth of the whole. And when men arrive unto this posture in their minds, they will discover themselves, as by a conversation wholly regardless of the precepts of Christ, so also by light, irreverent expressions concerning the Scripture; which, where they have freedom, will be poured out from the abundance of their hearts. This step towards total apostasy will follow that foregoing. When once men have lost all taste and relish of the goodness and excellency of the word of God on their hearts and affections, they will not long retain any prevalent evidence of its truth in their minds. Hence, --

(3.) A contempt of the things promised in the gospel doth ensue. The promises of the gospel do indeed contain those things wherein the evident blessedness and happiness of our nature doth consist. Such are serenity of mind in this world, and eternal felicity in the enjoyment of God. These, for the substance of them, mankind cannot despise until they grow atheistically brutish; but they may, and many do so, in the manner and on the terms of their proposal and declaration by the promises of the gospel. That this enjoyment of God, wherein everlasting happiness consisteth, must be in and through Jesus Christ alone; that the way of attaining thereunto, and the only means of present peace and serenity of mind, is by faith and obedience in and unto him, -- this they despise and contemn. This naturally follows on the former; for all expectation of good by and from the promises of the gospel depends on the evidence that we have of the truth thereof, and when that is lost, these will be despised. Now, herein consisteth one of the greatest aggravations of this sin; for whereas men cannot but desire the things (for the substance of them) which are promised in the gospel, as those wherein their blessedness doth consist, they will, out of hatred to Jesus Christ, reject and despise them, and eternally deprive their souls of them, rather than accept of them in and through him. They will rather never have any interest in God than have it by Christ. This rejection, therefore, of the promises of the gospel, as those which either as to the matter of them are not to be desired, or as to the truth of them not to be trusted, is the most provoking sin. No greater reproach can possibly be cast on Jesus Christ, as that which leaveth him the honour neither of his truth nor power, neither of which the Jews could in the least impeach when they took away his life. And, --

(4.) They choose some other way or means in the place and stead of Christ and the gospel, for the ends which they once sought after by them. So did those persons who fell off to Judaism. They looked for that in the law and ceremonies which they could not find in the gospel. And of these there are two sorts:-- [1.] Such as retain their first end in general, but reject the gospel from being a sufficient means for attaining it; [2.] Some that renounce the whole end itself, and seek for satisfaction other ways. The former are such as preserve an aim in general to worship God, to do that in religion which may be accepted by him, and to believe that of him which is right; but they reject the gospel as an insufficient and deceitful guide in and about these things. And this is done either totally, by such as apostatize to Judaism or Mohammedanism; or partially, by such as turn off from the purity, truth, spirituality, and mystery of the gospel unto Popery, or the like. I say not this with an intention to charge the guilt of this whole sin on this latter sort; only I say, they share in a very considerable part of it, and without repentance will do so in the punishment due unto it. And this casts the scorn of folly on Christ and the gospel; both absolutely, as having neither truth nor efficacy sufficient for the end proposed by them; and comparatively, that a falsehood or lie, a diabolical invention or delusion, is to be preferred before them; -- which is the highest provocation unto the eyes of God's glory. The latter sort quite cast off the general end of pleasing God and living unto him. For a while they thought that this would have brought them in some considerable satisfaction, and used the gospel to that end and purpose; but now being fallen under the power of the former degrees of apostasy, in contempt of the gospel, as that which will not afford any tolerable answer unto their expectations, they take up in the lusts and pleasures of the world, preferring them before all the promises of Christ, and despising all the threatenings denounced against those that pursue them. And of this sort of apostates we have numberless examples in the world.

(5.) Hereunto is added a perfect hatred and contempt of such as abide constant in, their adherence unto and profession of the gospel. Constant observation hath approved the saying, "Apostata est osor sui ordinis;" great apostates have been always great persecutors, in word or deed, according to their power. As those who love Christ do love all that are his, because they are his, so they that hate him do hate all that are his, because they are his; and their hatred, because it is against the whole kind, acts itself every way possible. They despise them as weak and foolish for adhering and trusting to the things which they have relinquished, trusting to themselves, their reason, and gallantry of spirit. They are filled with revenge against them, as those who censure, judge, and condemn them as guilty of the highest villainy and most desperate wickedness. They know in their hearts that they have reserves against them, as persons whom their Lord will one day judge and destroy; which makes them design, if it were possible, their utter extirpation from the face of the earth. Those who crucified Christ in his own person did it but once, and could do so no more. These do so every day; for what is done unto any of his, for his sake, he esteemeth as done unto himself: "Why persecutest thou me?"

(6.) Those persons who proceed thus far do always fall into a peculiar contempt of the Spirit of God, and his whole work in the dispensation of the gospel. The promise of the dispensation of the Spirit is the especial privilege and glory of the gospel. He is sent and given in an especial manner by Jesus Christ as exalted. His whole work is to glorify and exalt Jesus Christ, and to make his mediation effectual unto the souls of men; and in the things which concern him and his work lies the life and soul of the gospel. Hence those who apostatize from it have a peculiar enmity against him and his work; and this usually is one of the first things wherein the fatal backslidings of men do manifest themselves. When once men "tread under foot the Son of God, and count the blood of the covenant, wherewith he was sanctified, an unholy thing," as they do in the former instances, they will assuredly "do despite unto the Spirit of grace," Heb. x. 29. How this is done in particular shall be considered on that place, if God will, and we live thereunto. Under this head and degree the sin of apostasy becomes formally irremissible.

(7.) An open profession of a detestation of the gospel, so far as it is consistent with their worldly interests and advantages, completes the soul-ruining sin we treat of. It may be they may live in such times and places as that it would be to their secular disadvantage openly to avow their renunciation of Christ; but when that is the only curb from the declaration of themselves, the frame of their minds is esteemed for a full profession of their apostasy.

Now, whereas all these things, and it may be sundry others, do concur unto this sin of apostasy, I shall conclude two things concerning it:-- 1. That it is a far greater sin than that of the generality of the Jews who crucified Jesus Christ in the days of his flesh, as was before asserted. 2. That it is inconsistent with the holiness, righteousness, honour, and faithfulness of God, to renew such persons as are fully and openly guilty hereof unto repentance. Repentance may be given unto them in hell with as much advantage unto the glory of God; for when men, after trial and experiment, with some convictions of its truth and excellency, do obstinately reject the only remedy and relief that God hath provided for sinners, and therein do despite unto the whole blessed Trinity, and each person thereof in his peculiar interest in the dispensation and application of grace, God neither in his faithfulness will, nor in his holiness can, have any thing more to do with such presumptuous sinners in a way of mercy. He may and doth endure them for a while in this world, and that without any visible tokens of his indignation, satisfying his justice in the spiritual judgments that are upon them; but it is only as "vessels of wrath fitted to destruction," and such "whose damnation slumbereth not." And these things may suffice to warn men of the danger of this evil; and they will be warnings unto all who shall consider them, who are not hardened through the deceitfulness of sin; and all the judgments of God, which are either impendent over or already inflicted on a wicked, apostatizing world, are calls from heaven unto a consideration of them.

Now, although the generality of men seem to be secure enough from any trouble or discomposure in their minds from the consideration of things of this nature, yet some there are who may by their own misapprehensions fall under such discouragements as may hinder them in that course of obedience which they would pursue. I shall therefore divert a little, to prevent or remove the objections which such persons make against themselves, and from whence their discouragement doth arise, adding some directions suited unto their state or condition; for, --

First, Some may suppose themselves so far interested in the backsliding and apostasy described, as that the threatening denounced in the text doth belong unto them also, and that they are now judicially shut up under impenitency; for they say that they had attained unto a greater measure or degree of holiness, unto more readiness, evenness, and constancy in the duties of obedience, than they do now retain. They have fearfully and woefully fallen off from a better frame, into deadness, barrenness, neglect of duties, and it may be in some instance into a sinful course, and that for many days. Hence now they fear, lest as they are sensible that they have forsaken God and gone off from him, so he should forsake them utterly, and they should be sealed up under impenitency.

Ans. As this case too often falls out, so it is often answered, and I shall not therefore much insist upon it, nor any otherwise but as our present design and discourse is concerned therein. And I say, --

1. It is to be granted that all such backslidings are not only evil and sinful, but dangerous also, as to the issue and event. Whoever, therefore, find themselves under the power of them, or any way overtaken by them, ought not only to consider the guilt of all the particular sins and omissions of duties which they contract, but principally the whole state of their souls, and the danger they are in of being "hardened through the deceitfulness of sin:" for no man in such a state can have the least spiritual assurance or security that he shall not fall totally and finally from God; and whatever persuasion he hath of that nature, it is but a deceiving presumption that will effectually promote his apostasy and ruin, for there is no word of truth, no promise of God, to assure any of his love and favour whilst they are in such a state. It is therefore unquestionably the duty of every one who is sensible of any evil of this nature, in the frame of his heart or course of his life, to give himself no rest therein, seeing the eternal welfare of his soul is highly in question. But, --

2. There is a decay, a falling away from the degrees of holiness and obedience that men may have attained, and that, it may be, for a long season, and possibly with respect unto some especial sin, which is recoverable, and which doth not cast persons under the power of it absolutely into the threatening here recorded. What circumstances are required hereunto and what aggravations of sin have been showed in the opening of the words. Now, there may be a falling away, and that great and dangerous, which yet riseth not up unto the provocation of the evil here in an especial manner intended. And I judge it may be given as a safe rule in general, that he who is spiritually sensible of the evil of his backsliding is unquestionably in a recoverable condition; and some may be so who are not yet sensible thereof, so long as they are capable of being made so by convictions. No man is past hopes of salvation until he is past all possibility of repentance; and no man is past all possibility of repentance until he be absolutely hardened against all gospel convictions. Wherefore there is a recoverable backsliding: for, -- (1.) Christ calleth men unto such a recovery, which, therefore, he approves of, and will assist them therein who conscientiously apply themselves unto their duty, Rev. ii. 5, iii. 1-3; which latter instance is great in this kind. (2.) God hath promised to recover and heal such backslidings in believers, Hos. xiv. 4. And unto whom this is not encouragement sufficient to endeavour a recovery of themselves, it is to be feared they will wax worse and worse through the power of sin, until it hath full dominion over them; yea, what pretences soever they make to keep themselves off from such endeavours, it is either unbelief or the love of sin that is the sole proper cause thereof. Wherefore, --

(3.) If the backsliding whereof men complain from the ways of holiness and obedience have not proceeded out of dislike unto Christ and the gospel; if they have not, by the power and deceit wherewith they are accompanied, chosen any other way of duty or sin in his stead, -- as there is all necessity imaginable that they should, so there is all encouragement necessary to put them upon the diligent use of all means of a blessed recovery. Suppose their decays have befallen them, or that they have fallen into them, through the power of temptations, the deceitfulness of sin joining with their own sloth and negligence, -- which is the highest supposition that can be made in this kind, -- yet if they shall say in their hearts that they "will return to their former husband, for then it was better with them than now," they had peace and much refreshment in their first ways of faith and obedience, which they will therefore return unto; as the Lord Christ calls upon them so to do, so he is ready in all the promises of the gospel to receive them upon their so doing. Only let such persons remember that the command is urgent on them, as on Lot when he was to flee out of Sodom, and the angel said unto him, "Escape for thy life; look not behind thee, neither stay thou in all the plain; escape to the mountain, lest thou be consumed." There is no time of deliberation, much less of delay in this matter. It is for their souls, and the present moment wherein they are warned is the only season for their escape; and if any shall yet linger as Lot did, the Lord lay hold upon them, and bring them forth by the power of his grace, that they may be delivered! What are the ways whereby this may be done, what duties such persons are with diligence to attend unto, what means they are to use, are not things which at present fall under our consideration. All that I design is, to show that those who thus complain are not cast under any discouragement by this context and its exposition from an endeavour of a recovery, wherein they will find acceptance with God.

Secondly, It may be alleged that, as to the issue of things, it will be all one whether we fall from gospel holiness or can never attain unto it; -- "And this," say some, "is our condition; for whatever we have thought of ourselves, or whatever others have thought of us upon our profession, yet we now find by experience that we have not attained the holiness which the gospel requires." For their corruptions (they say, this or that, it may be, in particular) are too strong for their convictions; and after they thought themselves above them, they have again been prevailed on and overcome. They find the power of one or other lust grown so habitual unto them that they fall again and again under the power of it, until, it may be, they have lost much of the sense of its guilt and more of their power to resist it. And it must be acknowledged, also, that this condition is spiritually dangerous, and such as, if deliverance be not obtained from [it], will probably end in total apostasy. To state things aright in this case, we may observe:--

1. That there are three degrees in the power and prevalency of sin, and it must be inquired under which of them they are supposed to be concerning whom this complaint is made. The first is that mentioned Rom. vii. 23, "I see a law in my members warring against the law of my mind, and bringing me into captivity to the law of sin." Where this is only, or the captivating power of sin, there are two things to be considered:-- (1.) That the will, in its dispositions and inclinations, is constantly fixed against the power and interest of sin, so that in all its prevalency it suffers hardship, and is sensible of its captivity. (2.) That this captivity unto the law of sin doth not reach unto the outward perpetration of sin, but only the conflict that is in the mind and affections about it. And this is a condition which no man in this world is absolutely freed from, but is in some measure or other exercised with it, even as the apostle himself was, and thereon groaned for deliverance, verse 24. Another degree of the prevalence of sin is expressed chap. vi. 16, 19, "Know ye not, that to whom ye yield yourselves servants to obey, his servants ye are to whom ye obey; whether of sin unto death, or of obedience unto righteousness?" There is a state and prevalence of sin wherein men, being wholly under its dominion, do give up themselves unto its service willingly, notwithstanding any checks from light or conscience they meet withal. And such as these, the willing servants of sin, that yield up themselves in their affections and members of their bodies unto the

obedience and service of it, we do not at present consider. Between these there is a degree of the prevalence of sin, beyond the first, yet falling short of the latter, expressed 2 Pet. ii. 19. Men are therein in some sense "servants of corruption," in that they are "overcome" by it and "brought into bondage." They are not such as willingly, without any contest or conflict, give up themselves unto the service of sin, but they are overcome by it, which manifests that they do in some measure strive against it. And, on the other hand, they go beyond them who complain they are led captives to the law of sin; for they are said to become "servants of corruption," which the others are not in any sense. These, therefore, seem to be such (and such I do intend) who, notwithstanding all their light and convictions, with all the endeavours that they use, are so far under the power of some prevalent habitual lust as to serve it in a frequent reiteration of actual sins.

2. If this be the case complained of, it is acknowledged to be a condition of no small hazard and danger. And he who is not deeply sensible hereof is "as he that lieth down in the midst of the sea, or as he that lieth upon the top of a mast;" as this state is at large described with respect unto them who are given to wine, Prov. xxiii. 29-35. Wherefore, unless some remedy be found out in this case, it must be acknowledged that it will deprive men of or keep them from any assured interest in gospel holiness.

I must not here divert to consider in general the nature and means of the mortification of sin; I have done it already in other discourses, with the best directions for that end which I am able to propose. Unto them I do refer the persons concerned for guidance and counsel, where better is not at hand. Unto what hath been so treated already I shall only add, that those who would secure an interest in gospel holiness, by a deliverance from the power of inveterate habitual corruptions, may take the ensuing directions:--

First, If they have in vain attempted their own deliverance, let them not delay to acquaint some able spiritual guide with their state and condition. This sometimes hath broken, defeated, and scattered at once the forces of sin in the soul, where in its own wisdom and strength it was no way able to conflict with it. And it is the ordinance of God to this purpose: James v. 16, "Confess your faults one to another," etc. It was no small effect of the craft of Satan so to abuse this ordinance of God by turning it into a necessary confession of all sin unto a priest, invested with power of absolution, which was attended with innumerable evils, and proved an effectual engine for the ruin of the souls of men, to keep them off from that benefit which the due use of it was designed to administer unto sinners. If, therefore, any have found that sin hath been and yet is too strong for them, and that that is come upon them which the wise man mentions, "Woe to him that is alone," let them address themselves for advice unto such as have "the tongue of the learned," to speak a word in season unto them that are weary and ready to faint, and they will find relief. God will discover that evil of this kind which men will hide to their own disadvantage, tie will lay open those festered wounds which men would cover until rottenness enter into their bones.

Secondly, The effect aimed at will never be accomplished without violence offered unto ourselves as unto all occasions of sin, -- namely, as to the particular corruption supposed prevalent. In this case, when known occasions of the excitation or acting of the evil complained of do occur, no deliberations, or inclinations, or civil compliances are once to be admitted. Violence and sudden execution of foretaken resolves, without any parley or debate, are to be pursued. This is the condition wherein our Saviour's advice must take place, if we intend to escape, namely, of "plucking out a right eye, and cutting off a right hand," Matt. v. 29, 30; which cannot be done without offering violence unto our affections and inclinations. This is the meaning of the counsel given, Prov. iv. 14, 15, "Enter not into the path of the wicked, and go not in the way of evil men. Avoid it, pass not by it, turn from it, and pass away." The multiplication of the expressions wherein the duty charged doth consist doth intimate that, in the obedience required in this particular, a resolution acted with a holy violence is required. And there are three things in this holy violence with respect unto the occasions of a prevalent corruption:--

1. The mind's rejection of their first solicitations. When such seasons do befall or are befalling any man as wherein his lust or sin hath wonted to act itself, they smile on one another and are ready to shake hands in folly, Ps. l. 18; Prov. xxiii. 31; and sundry things will present themselves unto the mind to render the occasion necessary, or at least not dangerous. But if all insinuations of that kind be not immediately rejected without parley or delay, the soul probably will be again entangled and overcome.

2. A stated satisfaction concerning the folly of reserves, although the occasion should be complied withal or embraced, so as that the mind will hear no more of them, under any pretence whatever. Such reserves will offer themselves, as that although a man proceed so far or so far in the gratification of his present inclinations, yet he will put a stop unto or avoid what they may lead unto. When the mind is fully possessed [aware] of the deceitfulness of the heart in this matter, it will see its own folly in listening after such false promises or reserves, and reject the first thought of them with indignation.

3. Local mutation, or avoiding the place itself, or society and company, with a holy force put upon the affections, where such occasions are offered. This is that which is so expressed and pressed on us in the place before mentioned, Prov. iv. 14, 15.

These things belong unto that holy violence which men are to use unto themselves, and must use, if ever they intend to be freed from the power of an habitually prevalent corruption; and those who judge their deliverance not to be worth this watchfulness and care will live and die under the power of sin.

Thirdly, Constancy in private prayer against the power of such a corruption. This is all the way a man hath to deal with God about such an evil; for such things are to be thought and spoken, such circumstances to be insisted on, and such pleas to be used, as are not meet to be communicated to or with others. And, for the most part, it will be found that constant, earnest, faithful, private prayer, and any strong corruption, will be like Moses and Amalek. When Moses' hands were down Amalek prevailed, but when they were lifted up Israel had the upper hand. And if a man engage into especial prayer in opposition unto any sin or corruption, whatever he thinks of his own resolutions, whatever confidence he hath in his purposes, as he begins to fail or faint in the constancy or fervency of that duty, so his sin gets strength in him, and will not fail to attempt him successfully on the next occasion; nor will the utmost effect of any man's wisdom, or care, or ability, work out his deliverance in this case, without a conscientious attendance unto and discharge of this duty.

Sundry other things of an alike nature unto these might be insisted on, but that I must not too far digress from my principal design. This I thought meet to interpose for the direction of such as may be kept off from a successful endeavour to "perfect holiness in the fear of God."

Footnotes:

13. See the author's Exposition of the Epistle to the Hebrews. -- Ed.

Chapter XIII – Directions to avoid the power of a prevailing apostasy

Unto the warnings given in the precedent chapter some directions may be added, perhaps not unuseful unto them who would be preserved from the occasions, causes, and danger, of the apostasy thus far inquired into; for although, as hath been declared, a watchful attendance unto all gospel duties, and a vigorous exercise of all gospel graces in general, are required unto our preservation, yet there are some things which have an especial respect unto the present state of the causes and circumstances of the evil insisted on, which ought in an especial manner to be remembered. And that things of this nature are by many despised is no argument why we should not be diligent in our attendance unto them; for if they are such things as the Scripture prescribeth in the like cases, the contempt of them proceeds only from that pride and security which are no small part of the apostasy complained of.

Our first direction of this kind is, that we should all labour for a true, real sense of the concernment of the glory of God in this matter, and what is our duty with respect thereunto. Where this is not, men are under the power of that security which is the broad way and wide gate leading unto apostasy; yea, where this is not the first and principal thing wherewith we are affected in any evil that falls out in the world, our hearts are not upright in what we profess.

When God threatened to disinherit the Israelites and destroy the whole congregation as one man, in the wilderness, because of their provoking rebellion, that wherewith Moses, in all the circumstances of his relation unto them and interest in them, was affected withal, was the concernment of the glory and name of God therein, Num. xiv. 11-19. And it was so with Joshua in the sin and punishment of the same people. "What wilt thou do," saith he, "unto thy great name?" chap. vii. 8, 9; words which have been made a public derision in the days wherein we live.

We cannot but have thoughts about these things, for they are the common subject of many men's discourse: but if our thoughts about them are confined unto a narrow compass, and, so that it be well with us and some few others in whom we are peculiarly concerned, the evil that is come on the world in other places is lightly set by; if we are sensible of no interest of the glory of God, of the honour of Christ and the gospel therein, or are regardless of them, -- we are scarce likely to be delivered from that fatal issue whereunto all these things are in an open tendency.

Is it nothing unto us that so many nations in the world, where the profession of the gospel and an avowed subjection of soul and conscience unto Jesus Christ did flourish for some ages, are now utterly overrun with Mohammedanism, paganism, and atheism? Do we suppose these things are fallen out by chance, or come to pass by a fatal revolution of affairs, such as all things in this world are obnoxious unto? Did ever any nation or people under heaven lose the gospel as unto its profession, who did not first reject it as unto its power, purity, and obedience? And is not the glory of God, is not the honour of Christ, peculiarly concerned herein?

Is it nothing unto us that innumerable souls, who yet continue to make an outward profession of the name of Christ, have so degenerated from the mystery, holiness, and worship of the gospel, as to provoke the holy God to give them up for so many generations unto the most woful bondage and slavery that ever any of the children of men were cast under from the foundation of the world, without the least hopes or appearance of relief? And is it not to be bewailed that, such is the power of that apostasy which brought all this evil upon them, as that they have not to this day accepted of the punishment of their sins, nor been bettered by all that they have undergone! And doth not that holy name whereby we are called suffer in these things? Is it not on their account evil spoken of? for do not the miseries, the long-continued, woful calamities and oppressions of innumerable multitudes of great nations, outwardly professing the Christian religion, become a snare to the world and a temptation against the truth of the gospel and the power of Jesus Christ The Jews themselves are not left unto more distresses, nor are more destitute of any pledges of divine protection, nor are more unreformed under their miseries, than many who are called Christians, upon the account of their apostasy from the gospel. It is true, great distresses and sore persecutions may befall the church in its best state and condition, but then God doth so dispose of all things as that their trials shall evidently tend both unto his own glory and their spiritual advantage who are exercised with them; and in the issue the gospel itself shall never be a loser by the suffering of its sincere professors. But in those horrible judgments which have befallen many parts of the apostatized Christian world, nothing offereth itself unto our minds but what is matter of lamentation and temptation.

Is it nothing to us that the greatest number of those who are called Christians, and enjoy prosperity in the world, do live in open idolatry, to the unspeakable scandal of Christian religion and imminent danger unto themselves of eternal ruin? -- nothing that so many do openly renounce the humble, meek spirit of Christ and the gospel, endeavouring to persecute, ruin, and destroy other Christians, perhaps better than themselves, because they cannot captivate their souls and consciences in obedience unto their impositions? -- nothing to see and hear of all those dreadful effects of this apostasy in all manner of outrageous sins that the world is filled withal?

Certainly, if we are not greatly affected with these things, if our souls mourn not in secret about them, if we are not solicitous about the small remainders of the interest of truth and holiness in the world, we are in no small danger ourselves of being, one time or other, carried away with the deluge.

If we are sensible of the concernment of the glory of God in these things, it may not be amiss to consider what is our duty with respect thereunto.

1. And the first thing required of us is, that we mourn in secret for that sad issue which the profession of Christianity is come unto in the world. God puts an especial mark on them who mourn for the prevalency of sin and the apostasy of the church in any season, Ezek. ix. 4; neither will he have regard unto any others when he comes to execute judgments on ungodly apostates. Men may suffer with them with whom they will not sin; for where we are unconcerned for the sins of men we shall not be so in their sufferings. It is therefore those alone who, out of a sense of the dishonour of God, and compassion towards the souls of perishing sinners, do sigh and cry over these abominations, that shall be either preserved from those public calamities wherein they may issue, or be comfortably supported under them.

And there is nothing of a more ominous presage that things are yet waxing worse, than that general regardlessness about them that is among the best of us. Whose "eyes run clown with waters because men keep not the law?" Who doth sufficiently bewail the decays of faith, truth, and holiness, that are in the earth? Most men, like Gallio, either "care for none of these things," or at best design to save their own houses in the general conflagration. Many measure all things by their own advantage, and can see nothing amiss in the profession of religion but only in the complaints that any things are so. And although the degeneracy of Christianity, in the present professors of it, be grown a common theme in the mouths of most, yet very few are affected with it in a due manner in their hearts.

2. It is in this state of things required of us to pray continually, pleading those promises which are recorded in the word of God for the restoration of the pristine glory, power, and purity of Christian religion. This was the way and means whereby the church was recovered of old, and the same duty is still enjoined unto us, Isa. lxii. 6, 7; and hereunto are all our present hopes reduced. There is nothing too hard for God. If he will work herein, none shall let him. Things are not gone beyond his cure. He can send peace, and truth, and righteousness from above, and cause them to prevail on the earth. Were all things left absolutely unto the wills of men, in that depraved state whereunto they are arrived in the world, nothing but an increase of overspreading abominations might be expected. Sovereign and effectual grace can yet give relief, and nothing else can so do. Truly in vain is salvation hoped for from the hills and the multitude of mountains; truly in the Lord our God is the salvation of Israel; -- but for all these will God be sought unto. And constancy in this duty for others, out of a deep sense of the concernment of the glory of God and zeal for the honour of the gospel, is the most effectual means of our own deliverance and preservation.

3. Constancy in our testimony against the prevalency of this apostasy is required of us. And hereof there are two parts:-- (1.) An open, avowed profession of and contending for the faith and troth of the gospel. The public contempt and scorn that is by a prevalent vogue cast on some important evangelical truths is ready to discourage many from the owning and profession of them. Men, for the most part, have so many things to take into consideration before they will undertake the defence of the truth that they can find no season for it, whilst noisome errors are vented every day with confidence and diligence. It is therefore now, if ever, a time for all those in whose hearts are the ways of God to "contend earnestly for the faith once delivered unto the saints." And if either sloth, or self-love, or carnal fears, or earthly, ambitious designs, do betray any into a neglect of their duty in this matter, it will at one time or other give them disquietment and trouble. But, (2.) Exemplary holiness, righteousness, and fruitfulness in good works, belong unto this testimony against the prevalent apostasy which is required of us. As this is our constant duty at all times, so the progress of the fatal evil complained of renders the doubling of our diligence herein at present necessary, and puts a lustre on it.

Secondly, Those who would be preserved in such a season must keep a due and careful watch over their own hearts with respect unto their duty and danger: for although temptations do abound, and those attended with all sorts of circumstances increasing their efficacy, and the outward means and causes of this evil are multiplied, yet the beginnings of all men's spiritual declensions are in their own hearts and spirits; for the different effects that these things have upon the minds and lives of men is principally from themselves. As they are careful, diligent, and

192

watchful over themselves in a way of duty on the one hand, or slothful, careless, negligent on the other, so are they preserved or prevailed against. The advice, therefore, I intend is that given by the Holy Ghost in this case: Prov. iv. 23, "Keep thy heart with all diligence, for out of it are the issues of life;" or, as it is emphatically expressed in the original, "Above all keeping, keep thy heart." The greatest exercise of men in the world is about keeping what they have, what they esteem their own; wherewith the desire of adding unto it is of the same nature. What belongeth hereunto, what care, what watchfulness, what diligence, what exercise of their utmost wisdom and industry, all men know, unless it be such as by the power of their lusts are given up unto prodigality and profuseness. But the care and diligence in keeping of our hearts (the Holy Ghost being judge) ought to exceed whatever of that kind is employed about other things; and it is too evident that there is much want of this wisdom amongst us in the world. Of all things, the least diligence is used by many in keeping of their hearts. So they can safeguard their other concerns, the heart may be left to take its own course: yea, the heart is never so much neglected usually, nor more lost, than in the use it is put unto in keeping other things; for whilst it is employed to keep our lives, to keep the world and the things of it, it is lost itself in worldliness, covetousness, carnal wisdom, negligence of holy duties, and barrenness in the fruits of righteousness. That this is no good bargain, that nothing is got hereby, yea, that all will be lost by it at last, heart and world, and every thing wherein we are concerned, the Holy Ghost plainly intimates in this direction, wherein we are commanded above all things to keep our hearts. And we are not only laid under this command, but a cogent reason is added to enforce our obedience: "For out of it are the issues of life." Hereon do all events depend. The heart being kept, the whole course of our life here will be according unto the mind of God, and the end of it will be the enjoyment of him hereafter. This being neglected, life will be lost, beth here as unto obedience, and hereafter as unto glory. This, therefore, is that which in the first place is to be applied unto the present case. Would any not be overtaken with the power and prevalency of any of the causes of apostasy mentioned before, let them look well unto their own hearts, seeing that from thence are the issues of life.

By the "heart" the Scripture understandeth all the faculties of our souls, as they are an entire rational principle of all moral and spiritual operations; and so do we also. The preservation of them in their due order, acting in all things according unto their distinct powers, and the duty of the whole soul with respect unto God, is that which is intended by this keeping of the heart. And hereunto, with reference unto the present duty, sundry things do belong in an especial manner; as, --

1. That the heart be kept awake and attentive unto its own deceitfulness. The wise man tells us that "he that trusteth in his own heart is a fool," Prov. xxviii. 26. The beginning of all security, -- which is an assured entrance into all evil, -- lies in men's leaving their hearts unto themselves and trusting in them. He is no wise man (the Holy Ghost being judge) who, after so many instructions and warnings given us in the Scripture of the deceitfulness of our hearts, or the deceitfulness of that sin which is bound up in them (which is all one), will carelessly trust it with his eternal concernments. The apostle Peter did so once, upon a strong confidence that his heart would not fail him; but we know what was the issue of it. It is apt to be so with most men in this matter. They think, and do really judge, that if all men should fall off and forsake the gospel, either wholly or as unto the degrees in obedience which they have attained, yet they would not so do; but all things are filled with visible examples of their disappointment. There are no apostates but

once thought they would not be so; for we speak only of them who had light into and conviction of their duty, and who had therefore necessarily resolutions to continue therein. Wherefore, a constant, watchful jealousy over our own hearts, as to their deceitfulness, their readiness to be imposed on, and secret pretences to countenance themselves in compliance with temptations, is the foundation of all other duties necessary unto our preservation.

Even this also is by some despised. They know of no deceitfulness in their own hearts, nor think there is any such thing in the hearts of others. They cannot but acknowledge that there is mutual deceit enough amongst mankind in the world; but that there should be deceit and treachery in men's hearts with respect unto themselves, their own actions, duties, and ways, with respect unto God and their own eternal condition, that they cannot apprehend: for what or whom should a man trust unto, if he may not safely repose his confidence in his own heart that it will be always true unto its spiritual and eternal interest? Happy men, were such apprehensions as these to be the rule of their present duty or future judgment! But is it not possible there may be in the hearts of men a blind self-love, so far predominant as practically to impose false apprehensions and notions of things upon the mind and affections with respect unto sin and duty? Is there no disorder in the faculties of our souls, nor confusion in their operations thereon? Are there no remainders of sin inseparable from them in this life, accompanied with all manner of spiritual deceitfulness? no corrupt reasonings for the procrastination of the most important duties? no inclinations unto undue precedences and presumptions? no vanity or uncertainty in the mind? Or can these things, with the like innumerable, be supposed without any deceit in them or accompanying of them? What one said of old to the Druids, --

"Solis nosse Deos et coeli Numina vobis
Aut solis nescire datum," --

may be applied unto the men of this persuasion: either they alone know the state of the heart of man with respect unto God, evangelical obedience, and their own eternal interest, or they alone are ignorant thereof. Until, therefore, we have more satisfaction in this novel pretended discovery, we dare not cease the pressing of men to be diligently attentive unto the deceits of their own hearts. If this be neglected, we shall labour in vain, whatever else we do. Blessed is he who thus feareth always! This will make men carefully and conscientiously avoid all occasions of all things, whether in their inward frames or outward practice, that may on any account have a tendency unto a declension from the gospel. A bold, hazardous, careless frame of spirit, venturing on all companies and temptations, complying with vanities and profane communications, offering itself with a fearless confidence unto ways of seduction, through "the cunning sleights of men that lie in wait to deceive," is that which hath ruined innumerable professors. Self-distrust, humility, fear of offending, with the like soul-preserving graces, will be kept up unto exercise only where men are awake unto the consideration of the deceitfulness of their own hearts.

2. We must keep our heart awake and attentive unto its help and relief; and this lies only in Christ Jesus, the captain of our salvation. After all Peter's confidence, it was the interposition of Christ alone that preserved him from utter ruin: "I have prayed for thee that thy faith fail not." And if any can once prevail so far as to deter men from looking for all spiritual help and relief from Christ, for daily supplies of

grace and strength from him alone; from a continual application unto him for directing, assisting, preserving, establishing grace (which they variously attempt), -- there is no need to fear but they will easily follow them into whatever else either they, or Satan, or the world shall have a mind to draw them. But in all our discourses we proceed on other principles. We look on Jesus Christ as the spring and fountain of all grace, as him who alone is able to preserve us in faith and obedience, and doth communicate supplies of effectual grace unto believers for that purpose. Unto him, therefore, are we to make our applications continually, by faith and prayer, for our preservation, as we are directed, Heb. iv. 15, 16. It is he alone who can "keep us from the hour of temptation, which is come upon all the world, to try them that dwell upon the earth," Rev. iii. 10. Whosoever, therefore, would be kept from the power of the temptations unto apostasy which every way encompass us, and threaten to bear down all before them, let them keep their hearts continually attentive unto their only help and relief. Those who have not taken in a sense of their danger will see little reason to concern themselves in these directions. But as for such as are affected with the visible ruin of multitudes and their own apparent hazard, from prevailing causes and innumerable occasions thereof, -- whose eyes are in any measure opened to see the general inclination that is in the world unto a relinquishment of all the principal concerns of the gospel, and by what various ways that inclination is furthered, followed, and pursued, -- they will not think it unneedful to be minded of a help and refuge whereunto they may betake themselves and be preserved.

3. Let the heart be kept attentive unto its own frames, its progress or decay in holiness. How secret, and even ofttimes imperceptible, the beginnings of spiritual declension are in many, with the reasons and causes thereof, hath been declared in our exposition of Heb. iv. 12, 13, whither the reader is referred. I shall here only offer, that he who, in such a season as that which is passing over us, cloth not often call himself unto an account how things stand with him as to the inner man, -- what is the state of his spiritual life, whether his faith and love do thrive or decay, whether God or the world gets ground in his affections, -- will be exposed unto more dangers than it may be he is readily able to deliver himself from. These things are all of them useful, yea, needful unto the course of our obedience at all times. That which is here intended is, their exercise and discharge with respect unto the evil and danger under consideration. When we have done the utmost of our duty, we shall have cause to rejoice in the grace of God if we are preserved and delivered. But if we be found slothful, negligent, and secure, what hopes can we have that we shall withstand the evil that doth on every side beset us? There is not any way of fraud or force wherein we either are not or may not be assaulted. The secret ways whereby this apostasy puts forth its efficacy are so various as not to be enumerated. The current, furthered by the winds of all sorts of temptations, lies strongly against us. New accessions are made unto it every day. New pretences against the truths and holiness of the gospel are sought out and made use of. By some they are secretly undermined, by others openly despised; and the hand of Satan is in all these thing. If we should now neglect a watchful care over our own hearts, and a diligent attendance unto all means of their preservation in soundness of doctrine and holiness of life, what assurance can we have that we shall finally escape?

Having premised these directions in general, those which ensue must have a particular respect unto some of the especial ways and means whereby this declension hath been carried on and promoted, peculiarly such as the present age and season are most obnoxious unto. And because this discourse is drawn forth to a length beyond my first design, I shall name a few things only, to intimate of what sort those directions are which might be more largely insisted on; and two only shall be named. Wherefore, --

Thirdly, Take heed of resting in or trusting unto the outward privileges of the church, and a participation of the dispensation of the ordinances of the gospel therein. It is known what various apprehensions as to the especial ways of outward solemn worship and the state of the church there are among all sorts of men. But whereas all men do approve of and adhere unto one church-state or other, one way of worship or other, I intend no one more than another in particular, but would speak unto all with respect unto that way which themselves do approve and practice. And it was before declared how greatly the world was deluded by a pretence of them. And we may not think to excuse the necessity of watchfulness in this matter, because all the good things of the church and all the ordinances of the gospel were then abused, corrupted, and defiled, whereas we now all of us, in our own apprehensions, enjoy their administration in purity, according unto the institution of Christ; for they are all of them no less liable to be abused in this kind when duly administered than when most corrupted: yea, in some cases they are more apt so to be, seeing there is a greater appearance of reason why we should place our confidence in them.

It is indeed an especial mercy for any to be intrusted with the privileges of the church and institutions of the gospel; yea, it is the greatest outward dignity and pre-eminence that any can be advanced unto in this world, however by the most it be lightly set by Theodosius, one of the greatest emperors that ever were in the world, affirmed that he esteemed his being a member of the church a greater dignity than his imperial crown. And although the ruin of the Jews arose principally from their carnal confidence in their spiritual or church privileges, yet the apostle doth acknowledge that they had great pre-eminence and advantage, and might have had great profit thereby, Rom. iii. 1, 2, ix. 4, 5. And theirs must be granted more excellent in every kind who enjoy that administration of holy things in comparison wherewith that committed unto the Jews had neither beauty nor glory, 2 Cor. iii. 10. By whomsoever, therefore, these things are despised or neglected, under whatever pretences they countenance themselves, they are utter strangers unto gospel holiness; for what holiness can there be where men live in an open disobedience unto the commands of Christ, and in a neglect of the use of those means which he hath appointed to beget and preserve it in our souls? Nothing, therefore, must be spoken to take off from the excellency, dignity, and necessity, of the privileges and ordinances of the church, when we would call off men from placing that confidence in them which may tend unto their disadvantage. And if persons can find no medium between rejecting all the ordinances of the gospel and trusting unto the outward performance or celebration of them, they have nothing but their own darkness, pride, and unbelief, to ascribe the ruin of their souls unto.

Again; there is not any thing in the whole course of our obedience wherein the continual exercise of faith and spiritual wisdom, with diligence and watchfulness, is more indispensably required than it is unto the due use and improvement of gospel privileges and ordinances; for there is no other part of our duty whereon our giving glory to God and the eternal concern of our own souls do more eminently depend. And he is a spiritually thriving Christian who knows how duly to improve gospel institutions of worship, and doth so accordingly; for they are the only ordinary outward means whereby the Lord Christ communicates of his grace unto us, and whereby we immediately return love, praise, thanks, and obedience unto him; in which spiritual intercourse the actings of our spiritual life principally do consist, and whereon, by consequence, its growth doth depend. It is therefore certain that our growth or decay in holiness, our steadfastness in or apostasy from profession, are greatly influenced by the use or abuse of these privileges.

That, therefore, which, in compliance with my present design, I intend, is only a warning that we do not rest in these things, the name, title, privilege, and outward observance of them, seeing so many have thereby been deluded into security and apostasy. Some there are (and of them not a few) all whose religion consists in going to church, and abiding there during the celebration of that sort of worship which they approve of. Herewith they satisfy their consciences as unto all that they have to do with God, especially if they are admitted unto a participation of the sacraments in the appointed seasons. And many others, it is to be feared, content themselves with a bare hearing of the word, and do treat their consciences into a quietness and security thereby. It were otherwise impossible that, among so great multitudes as crowd after the preaching of the word, so few should be brought over unto sincere and universal obedience. But I intend those in particular who make a profession of giving themselves up unto gospel obedience, and are thereon made partakers of all gospel privileges according to the rule. Let them take heed that they do not too much rest in nor too much trust unto these outward things, for so they may do sundry ways unto their disadvantage.

1. Men may herein deceive themselves by spiritual gifts, which may be reckoned in the first place among the privileges of the church. Some rest in the gifts of others, and the satisfaction they receive thereby; for by the use and exercise of them men's affections may be greatly moved, as also temporary faith and evanid joy be greatly excited. These things, it is to be feared, some live upon, without farther care after a spring of living water in themselves. Others may rest in their own gifts, their light, knowledge, ability to pray or speak of the things of God. But it is the design of the apostle, in the context before insisted on, to declare that the most eminent spiritual gifts, with all their effects, either in the souls or lives of them who are made partakers of them, or in the church for edification, will not secure any persons from total apostasy. So also some shall be utterly rejected at the last day, who were able to plead their prophesying and casting out of devils in the name of Christ, and that in his name they had done "many wonderful works," Matt. vii. 22, 23. And therefore, when his disciples (who were true but as yet weak believers) were greatly affected, and it may be lifted up, with the success they had had in casting out of devils in his name, he recalls them from any confidence therein, as unto their eternal concernment, unto a trust in God's free electing grace, with the fruits thereof, Luke x. 20; and the reason hereof is, because these gifts have no inseparable relation unto any of the especial and peculiar causes of salvation. That which seemeth to be of any difficulty is, that they are an especial fruit of the mediation of Christ, purchased by his death, given into his power upon his resurrection, and first communicated on his ascension. But all that followeth from hence is, that they are good and holy in themselves, and designed unto good and holy ends or uses, -- namely, the confirmation of the gospel and edification of the church. But it doth not thence follow that they are saving unto them that do receive them, unless they are accompanied with especial grace towards them and holy obedience in them; from both which they are separable. It is therefore greatly incumbent on all those who have received of these spiritual gifts to take care they be enlivened and acted by especial grace; for if they are not careful, they will give

them a pretence and apprehension of what they have not, and set a greater lustre upon what they have than it doth deserve; -- for in their actings, because the objects of them are spiritual and heavenly things, the same with that of especial grace, men are apt to suppose that grace is exercised when it may be far from them; and as to the profession that men make, these gifts will set it off with such beauty as shall render it very acceptable unto others and very well-pleasing unto themselves. Both these tend evidently unto the ruin of the souls of men, if not wisely managed and improved. Wherefore, by the way, to help us unto a right judgment in this matter, we may observe one certain difference between the operations of spiritual gifts which are solitarily so on the one hand, and saving grace on the other. Gifts have their especial works, which they are confined unto, according as their especial nature is. In them they act vigorously; out of them they influence not the soul at all. But the work of saving grace is universal, equally respecting all times, occasions, seasons, and duties; and although it may be acted more eminently at one time than another, in one instance of duty than another, yet it enliveneth and disposeth the heart alike unto all obedience. But of the difference that is between spiritual gifts and saving grace, as also concerning their whole nature and use, I shall, God assisting, treat at large in another discourse. [14] At present I intend only this caution, that men countenance not themselves by them, nor resolve a peace (or rather security) into their exercise, under real spiritual decays of grace and obedience.

2. Too high an estimation of any peculiar way of worship is apt to entice the minds of some into a hurtful confidence in these things. Having an apprehension that they alone have attained unto the right way of gospel worship and the administration of its ordinances, and that, perhaps, on such accounts as wherein they are eminently deceived, they begin first greatly to value themselves, and then to despise all others, and, if they can, to persecute them. This insensibly works them into a trust in that which they esteem so excellent, and that unto an open neglect of things of a greater weight and moment. Thus is it not unusual to see persons who are under the power of some singular opinion and practice in religion to make one thing almost their whole business, the measure of other things and persons, the rule of communion and of all sincere love; -- to value and esteem themselves and others according unto their embracing or not embracing of that opinion. There is here something of that which God complains of in the prophet, Isa. lxv. 5. And it were to be wished that such principles and practices were not visibly accompanied with a decay of love, humility, meekness, self-diffidence, condescension, and zeal in other things, seeing where it is so, let men's outward profession be what it will, the plague of apostasy is begun. Wherefore, although we ought greatly to prize and to endeavour after the true order of the church of Christ, the purity of worship, and regular administration of ordinances, yet let us take heed that we prize not ourselves too much on what we have attained; for if we do so, we shall be very apt to countenance ourselves in other neglects thereby, which will certainly bring us into a spiritual sickness and declension. And, one way or other, there is an undue confidence placed in these outward privileges, when either any or all of the things ensuing are found among us:--

(1.) A neglect of private duties. This ruinous event never falls out among professors, but it proceeds either from an over-fulness of the world and its occasions, or the prevalency of some predominant lust, or a sinful resting in or trusting unto the duties of public worship. When all these concur (unless God effectually awaken the soul), it is in a perishing condition. In particular, when men are satisfied, as unto religious worship, with that which is public or in communion with others, so as to countenance themselves in a neglect of the duties of their private retirements, they are in a high road unto apostasy.

(2.) The indulgence of any private lust, unto the satisfaction of the flesh. This great defect in the power of godliness is frequently countenanced by strictness in the form thereof. And a great effect it is of the deceitfulness of sin when it can delude the minds of men to justify themselves in any one sin, with the names, titles, reputation, and privileges of the church, or the ordinances whereof they are made partakers; and the secret efficacy of this deceit is not easy to be detected.

(3.) It is so, also, when a loose and careless frame in our walking is indulged unto on the same account. It is hard, indeed, to know directly whence this is come to pass, that so many professors of the gospel should give up themselves unto a negligent and careless walk, but that it is so come to pass is certain. There is no truth more acknowledged than that a strict and close walk with God, an attendance thereunto on all occasions with diligence and circumspection, with a continual conscientious fear of sin, is indispensably required unto acceptable, evangelical obedience or holiness; yet so it is, that many professors walk with that looseness and carelessness, that venturous boldness, with respect unto the occasions of sinning, that liberty or rather licentiousness of conversation, as are utterly inconsistent therewithal. As there are many causes hereof, so I fear this may be one among them, that they too much satisfy themselves with their interest in the church and its privileges, and with their observance of public worship and the ordinances thereof, according to their respective stations and capacities.

Wherefore, the sum of this direction is, that if we would be preserved from the prevalency of the present apostasy, we must have a strict regard unto our principles and practice with respect unto the privileges of the church and ordinances of gospel worship. If we neglect or despise them, we cast off the yoke of Christ, and have no ground to look for his acceptance of us or concernment in us. It is but folly for them to pretend a hope in his mercy who defy his authority. And if, on the other hand, we so rest in them as to countenance ourselves in any of the evils mentioned, we shall succeed into their room who, under the name and pretence of the church and its privileges, fell into an open apostasy from Christ and the gospel; for the same causes will produce the same effect in us as they did in them. There is a middle way between these extremes, which whoso are guided into will find rest and peace unto their souls; and this is no other but an humble, careful, conscientious improvement of them all unto their proper ends. And it may not be amiss to name some of those things whereby we may know whether our hearts are upright and rightly disposed in the use of gospel ordinances. And we may judge of ourselves herein:--

1. If our hearts are bettered by them, or humbled for it if they are not. Their end, with respect unto us, is to excite and put forth all grace into exercise. When, therefore, we find faith and love, delight in God, longing after an increase of grace and holiness, with a detestation of sin, fruitfulness in good works and all duties of obedience, joy in spiritual things, self-abasement, and admiration of grace, stirred up in us by them, our hearts need not condemn us as to want of sincerity in these duties, though we are sensible of many weaknesses and imperfections. And whereas, through the power of corruptions and temptations, through the weakness of the flesh and prevalency of unbelief, we come sometimes short of a sensible experience of this effect on our souls by and under them, there may yet remain a relieving evidence of some sincerity in what we do; and this is, if, rejecting all other pretences and prejudices, we charge ourselves alone with our

unprofitableness, and be humbled in a sense thereof. Want hereof hath been the reason why some have rejected the ordinances of the gospel as dead and useless, and others have grown formal, careless, and barren, under the enjoyment of them. When all veils and coverings shall be taken away and destroyed, these things will appear to be the fruits of pride and of the deceitfulness of sin.

2. It is so when, in the dispensation of the ordinances, spiritual things are realized and made nigh unto us. When in the preaching of the word we find Jesus Christ "evidently set forth, crucified before our eyes," Gal. iii. 1; when the form of the things delivered is brought upon our minds, Rom. vi. 17; when we do, as it were, feel and handle the word of life, and the things hoped for have some kind of subsistence given them in our souls, as Heb. xi. 1, -- then are we exercised in a due manner in this part of our obedience. To this purpose our apostle discourseth, Rom. x. 6-9. The word as preached and other ordinances do not direct us unto things afar off, but bring the Lord Christ with all the benefits of his mediation into our hearts. But if we content ourselves with empty light, with unaffecting notions of spiritual things, if we rest satisfied with the outward performance of our own duty and that of other men, we have just cause to fear that our hearts are not right in the sight of God in this matter.

3. When we find that a conscientious attendance on all the ordinances of instituted worship doth quicken our diligence and watchfulness unto all other duties of obedience that are required of us, we are conversant in them in a due manner. When under a pretence of them, and a mistaken satisfaction in them, men countenance themselves in the neglect of other duties, how way is made for farther apostasy from holiness hath been declared. Wherefore there can be no greater evidence of our due attendance unto them than when we axe excited, quickened, enlarged, and confirmed by them unto and in all the ways of universal obedience. Those, therefore, who most conscientiously make use of church privileges and gospel ordinances are they whose hearts are most engaged unto all other duties by them.

Lastly, It is an evidence of the same importance when we have that experience of Christ and his grace in the administration of gospel ordinances according unto his will, as that we are strengthened thereby to suffer for him and them when we are called thereunto. The time will come when neither mere light and conviction of truth nor the gifts of the ministry will secure men unto their profession. But he who hath tasted how gracious Christ is in the ways of his appointment will not easily be removed from his resolution of following him whithersoever he goeth.

Fourthly, Take heed of the infection of national vices. What I intend hereby hath been before declared. And this caution is most necessary when they are most prevalent among any people; for commonness will take off a sense of their guilt, and countenance will insensibly take away shame. Besides, when some go out unto an open excess, others are apt to justify themselves in vain practices and sinful miscarriages, because they rise not up unto the same height of provocation with them. This makes lesser vanities, in habits, attires, pleasures, misspense of time in talking-houses, [15] excess in eating and drinking, corrupt communication, and careless boldness in common converses, whereby persons tread in the steps, and sometimes on the very heels, of the predominant sins of the place and age, so to abound among us. Some openly show what they have a mind to be at, if they durst, and that it is more reputation and the power of convictions than the love of gospel holiness that restrain them from running forth into the same excess of riot with others. Israel of old "dwelt alone, and was not reckoned among the nations," Num.

xxiii. 9; and "the remnant of Jacob is to be so in the midst," in the bowels "of many people," as to be a blessing unto them, Mic. v. 7, not to be corrupted by them. If professors will so immerse themselves into the body of the people as insensibly to learn their manners, they will be carried down the stream with them into perdition; and the danger hereof is beyond what most men conceive. Grace was but sparingly administered unto the community of the people under the old testament, and therefore, after the giving of the law, God would not trust them to live among other people, nor other people to live among them, as knowing how unable they were to withstand the temptations of conformity unto them. Hereon he appointed that all the nations should be utterly extirpated where they were to inhabit, that they should not learn their customs, Lev. xviii. 30. The neglect of this wisdom of God, the transgression of his will herein, by mixing themselves with other nations and learning their manners, was that which proved their ruin. Under the gospel there is a more plentiful effusion of the Spirit. God now intrusts all that are called unto the obedience of it to live in the midst of all nations under heaven; yet he so cloth it as to warn them of their danger thereby, and to require them to stand upon their guard herein continually. This is that part of true religion which the apostle James calls the "keeping of ourselves unspotted from the world," chap. i. 27. Most men think it enough that no more can be required of them nor expected from them than that they wallow not in the mire and pollutions of it. If their practice be free from actual open sins, they care not what spots of a worldly conversation are upon them; but they know not what will be the end thereof.

It may be it will be said, that unless we do conform ourselves in some things unto the customs that are prevalent among us, as in habit, and fashion, and way of converse, we shall be despised in the world, and neither we nor ours be of any regard.

I answer, -- 1. That I am not contending about small things, nor prescribing modes of attire or manner of deportment unto any. There is none who doth more despise the placing of religion in clothes, in gestures, in the refusal of civil and just respects, than I do; nor have I any severity in my thoughts against a distinction in these things among persons, according to their degrees and conditions in the world, though apparently there be an excess in all sorts herein. But that which I intend is, a compliance with the world in those things which border on and make some kind of representation of the predominant vices of the place and age wherein we live; and if you think you shall be despised if you come behind the rest of your rank and quality in the world in these things, still you will be so unless you come up unto them in all abominations, 1 Pet. iv. 3, 4; -- and whether it be fit to relinquish God, and Christ, and the gospel, all holiness and morality, to have the friendship of the world, judge ye. And, -- 2. Be sure to outgo them in fixed honesty, kindness, benignity, usefulness, meekness, moderation of spirit, charity, bowels of compassion, readiness to help and relieve all men according unto your power, and you will quickly find, even in this world, how little you are concerned in that contempt of the vilest part of mankind whereof you seem to be afraid.

Fifthly, Carefully avoid all those miscarriages of professors which alienate the minds of men from the gospel, and countenance them in the contempt of the profession of it. Some of them we have mentioned before, and many of the like nature might be added unto them. As the scandalous, profligate lives of those in general who are called Christians give that offence unto Jews, Mohammedans, and Gentiles, all the world over, that hardens them unto a contempt and detestation of Christianity, and bath brought the whole matter of religion in the world unto force and the sword, so the miscarriages of the strictest sort of professors do greatly countenance others in their dislike of and enmity against the power of godliness which they profess; and so far as we continue in them, we have a share in the guilt of the present defection. Not to insist on particulars, the things of this nature that are charged on them may be reduced unto three heads:-- 1. Want of love and unity among themselves; 2. Want of usefulness and kindness towards all; 3. Spiritual pride and censoriousness, or rash judging of other men.

These are the things which are commonly charged on some professors; and although, it may be, they are but few who are guilty of all or any of these things, at least not as they are charged and reproached by others, yet they may all learn what in an especial manner to avoid, that they give no advantage unto those who seek for it and would be glad of it. It is our duty, by a watchful, holy conversation in all things, to "put to silence the ignorance of foolish men," and so universally to approve our sincerity unto God and men, that whereas we are, or may be at any time, "evil spoken of, as evil-doers, they may be ashamed, beholding our good conversation in Christ, and glorify God in the day of visitation." This is the law that we have brought ourselves under, not to fret and fume, and in our minds seek for revenge, when we are traduced and evil spoken of, but by a "patient continuance in well-doing," to overcome all the evil that the malice of hell or the world can cast upon us; and if we like not this law and rule, we had best relinquish our profession, for it is indispensably required of all the disciples of Jesus Christ, And he whose heart is confirmed by grace to do well whilst he is evil spoken of will find such present satisfaction, in a sense of his acceptation with Christ, as to make him say, "This yoke is easy, and this burden is light," Especially ought we carefully to avoid the things mentioned and appearances of them, whereby public offence is taken, and advantage made by evil men to countenance themselves in their sins. You are but few unto whom these things are communicated, and so may judge that all your care in and about them will be of little significancy to put any stop unto the general declension from gospel holiness; but it is hoped that all others are warned in the same manner, yea, and more effectually than you are. However, every vessel must stand on its own bottom; "the just shall live by his" own "faith;" "every one of us shall give account of himself to God;" and no more is required of you but your own personal duty.

It is true, you cannot put an end unto those differences and divisions, that want of love and agreement, that is among professors; but you may take care that the guilt of none of these things may be justly charged on you. Love unto the saints without dissimulation; readiness to bear in meekness with different apprehensions and palpable misapprehensions, not intrenching on the foundation; freedom from imposing your sentiments on those who cannot receive them, and from judging rashly on supposed failures; readiness for universal communion in all religious duties with all that "love the Lord Jesus Christ in sincerity," -- as they are our duties, as they are some of the principal ways whereby we may truly represent the Lord Christ and the doctrine of the gospel unto others, so they will disarm Satan and the world of a great engine whereby they work no small mischief unto the whole interest of religion.

Again: were all professors meek, quiet, peaceable, in their societies and among their neighbours; sober, temperate, humble in their personal conversation in the world; useful, kind, benign, condescending towards all; cheerful in trials and afflictions, always "rejoicing in the Lord," -- men not given up to a reprobate sense ([men] who are [so, are] not to be regarded) would at length be so far from taking offence at them as to judge that they should not know what to do without them, and be won to endeavour a conformity unto them. In like manner, were those rules more diligently attended unto which are prescribed unto all believers as unto their conversation in this world, it would be of no small advantage unto religion. See Phil. iv. 8; 1 Pet. ii. 12; 2 Cor. xiii. 7; Rom. xiii. 12, 13; 1 Thess. iv. 11, 12; Heb. xiii. 18. Did honesty, sincerity, uprightness in all the occasions of life, in the whole converse of professors in the world, shine more brightly and give more evidences of themselves than at present among many they seem to do, it would undoubtedly turn unto the unspeakable advantage of religion.

And, lastly, for that judging or condemning of others wherewith they are so provoked, there is but one way whereby it may be done so as to give no just offence, and this is in our lives. The practice of holiness judgeth all unholy persons in their own breasts; and if they are provoked thereby, there is nothing in it but a new aggravation of their own sin and impiety.

Footnotes:

14. In his Discourse on Spiritual Gifts, vol. iv., which was not published till 1693, ten years after the death of the author. -- Ed.

15. The author seems to allude to the coffee-houses, which, established in the time of the commonwealth, soon became a distinctive feature of London life. When no public meetings were allowed, and no public journals existed, the only method by which the news of the day could be learned was by a visit to a coffee-house; in which, besides the information reciprocated in private talk, there were leading orators who harangued the crowd on the current topics of public interest. So powerful was the expression of public opinion through the imperfect channel of these coffee-houses, that the government at one time attempted to suppress them; but the system had become so popular and so interwoven with the habits of the Londoners, that no enactment against it could be enforced. Much time, doubtless, would be wasted in these "talking-houses," and it is against this sin that the remarks of Owen are directed. -- Ed.

www.ingramcontent.com/pod-product-compliance
Lightning Source LLC
Chambersburg PA
CBHW060338100426
42812CB00003B/1042